INDEX and ABSTRACTS of Wills

Sonoma County
California

1850-1900

*Sonoma County
Genealogical Society, Inc.*

HERITAGE BOOKS
2007

HERITAGE BOOKS
AN IMPRINT OF HERITAGE BOOKS, INC.

Books, CDs, and more—Worldwide

For our listing of thousands of titles see our website
at
www.HeritageBooks.com

Published 2007 by
HERITAGE BOOKS, INC.
Publishing Division
65 East Main Street
Westminster, Maryland 21157-5026

Copyright © 2007 Sonoma County Genealogical Society, Inc.

Other books by the author:
CD: *Sonoma County [California] Records, Volume 1*
Early School Attendance Records of Sonoma County, California, Beginning 1858
Index to Naturalization Records in Sonoma County, California, Volume 1: 1841-1906
Index to The Sonoma Searcher*: Volume 16, No. 1 to Volume 28, No. 3*
(Including Index to The Sonoma Searcher*: Volume 1, No. 1 to Volume 15, No. 4, SCGS, August 1993)*
Index to Vital Data in Local Newspapers of Sonoma County, California, Volume 1: 1855-1875
Index to Vital Data in Local Newspapers of Sonoma County, California, Volume 2: 1876-1880
Index to Vital Data in Local Newspapers of Sonoma County, California, Volume 3: 1881-1885
Index to Vital Data in Local Newspapers of Sonoma County, California, Volume 4: 1886-1890
Index to Vital Data in Local Newspapers of Sonoma County, California, Volume 5: 1891-1899
Index to Vital Data in Local Newspapers of Sonoma County, California, Volume 6: 1900-1903
Indigent Records in Sonoma County, California 1878 to 1926, Volume 1: The Indigents
Indigent Records in Sonoma County, California 1878 to 1926, Volume 2: Taxpayers Who Certified Indigent Need
Militia Lists of Sonoma County, California, 1846 to 1900
Naturalization Records in Sonoma County, California, Volume II: 1906-1930
Santa Rosa Rural Cemetery, 1853-1997
Sonoma County, California Cemetery Records, 1846-1921, Third Edition
Sonoma County, California Death Records, 1873-1905, Second Edition
The 1930 School Census of Sonoma County, California

All rights reserved. No part of this book may be reproduced or transmitted in any form or by any means, electronic or mechanical, including photocopying, recording or by any information storage and retrieval system without written permission from the author, except for the inclusion of brief quotations in a review.

International Standard Book Number: 978-0-7884-4492-0

INDEX AND ABSTRACT OF WILLS

SONOMA COUNTY, CALIFORNIA 1850 - 1900

Compiled by

Joyce L. Collins

Harriet R. Foster

Florence McColly

June M. Smith

Edited by

Audrey Herman

Sonoma County Genealogical Society

Published by

Sonoma County Historical Records Commission

under the aupices of

Sonoma County Board of Supervisors

PREFACE

The original copies of these wills are in the Sonoma County Archives, located at the Sonoma County Library, 3rd & E Sts., Santa Rosa, California, 95404.

Microfilm copies have been retained by the Office of the County Clerk, 600 Administration Drive, Santa Rosa, California, 95401.

Wills are filed in numerical sequence. Refer to #0000 when requesting document.

Names are listed in the index only if surname differs from that of the testator.

When age of deceased is given it is at the time of signing the will. Unless otherwise noted, address of all those mentioned in the will and witnesses is same as testator. Ages of children in parentheses are at time of probate.

ABBOTT, MINERVA   Written: 25 Aug. 1883   #1388
                         Dated: Dec. 1883

Spouse: Thomas
Children: Oliver McDonnoll, French McPherson, Stonewall
               McPherson, Buell McPherson, Erly McPherson,
               Mary E. McPherson, Annie McPherson
Grandson: James Sylvester, son of daughter Dulancy
Executor: Brother, F.C. St. Clair
Witnesses: M.C. Bailey, R.F. Bailey

ABELBECK, F. D.   Written: 8 Feb. 1873   # 594
                         Dated: 13 Feb. 1873
                         Filed: 10 Mar. 1873

               All possessions to friend J.M. Roney, his wife
               Mary A. Roney and their infant daughter Alice
               Mary

Executor: J.M. Roney
Witnesses: J.T. Hardin, M. Johnson

ACKERMAN, B. HENRY   Written: 25 Jan. 1866   # 460
                         Dated: 30 Sep. 1870
                         Filed: 10 Oct. 1870

Nephew: Louis Dan Ackerman (minor), son of deceased
               sister, Mary Ackerman
Executor: Thomas Schlusser
Witnesses: William D. Blip, Henry H. Harmen, Joshua H.
               Lewis

ACKERMANN, MARY   Written: 13 May 1865   # 288
                         Dated: 13 May 1865   Bk. A, Pg. 134
                         Filed: 20 Jul. 1865

Brother: B. Henry Ackermann
Son: Louis Dan Ackermann (minor)
Executor: B. Henry Ackermann
Witnesses: William D. Blip, Isaac M. Marshall, B. Henry
               Ackermann

ADAMS, EVA G.   Written: 3 Aug. 1896   #2708
          Age 38   Dated: 24 Dec. 1896   Bk. G, Pg. 11
                         Filed: 19 Apr. 1897

Spouse: John M. Adams
Children: Edith Frances Adams, Herbert Bradford Adams,
               Clifford Flint Adams
Executor: John M. Adams
Witnesses: Mrs. Emma Warren, Francis A. Getchell, Caroline
               L. Flint

ADLER, LEWIS   Written: 25 Apr. 1896   #2641
Sonoma   Age 76   Died: 20 May 1896   Bk. F, Pg. 521
                            Rec.:   16 Jun. 1896

    Wife: Martha
    Child: Un-named
    Executor: Wife
    Witnesses: Robert A. Poppe, Edward Carr

ALBEE AUREL   Written: 3 Jan. 1883   #1291
Cloverdale   Age 60   Died: 9 Jan. 1883   Bk. C, Pg. 341
                            Filed: 28 Jan. 1883

    Wife: Hannah T.
    Daughter: Mary E.
    Executor: Wife
    Witnesses: Millard F. Patterson, Levi L. Shelford

    Description of real property in Cloverdale, Ca.; also real
    property in Adair Co., Iowa

ALEXANDER, CHARLES   Dated: 3 Jun. 1876   #2769
                            Died: 20 Sep. 1897
                            Filed: 20 Sep. 1897

    Wife: Achsak Alexander
    Sons: Laurance Alexander, Julius Alexander
    Daughters: Mrs. Amelia H. May, Mrs. Josaphine Spoon (?),
                Mrs. Alice H. Crawford
    Executors: Wife, Achsak; son, Laurance
    Witness: L.A. Norton

ALEXANDER, CYRUS   Written: 27 Dec. 1870   # 589
                            Died: 26 Dec. 1872
                            Filed: 24 Feb. 1873

    Wife: Rufina
    Daughters: Margaret, wife of William Mulligan; Caroline
    Sons: Joseph, Thomas, George Cyrus
    Executor: Wife
    Witnesses: L.A. Norton, Mrs. L.A. Norton

ALLEN, B. B.   Written: 15 Jan. 1885   #1890
                            Died: 3 Oct. 1889   Bk. E, Pg. 166
                            Rec.:   21 Oct. 1889

    Wife: Ann W.
    Son: George L.
    Daughter: Katie Leah
    Executor: Son
    Witnesses: J.H.P. Morris, T.M. Rickert

```
ALLEN, WILLIAM T.          Written:   4 Nov. 1890              #2140
Healdsburg      Age 72     Died:     28 Nov. 1891
                           Rec.:     25 Jan. 1892

   Daughter:     Elizabeth M. Hendricks (35)
   Son:          George R. (30)
   Executors:    Son; son-in-law, Jas. M. Hendricks
   Witnesses:    William Smith, J.G. Coffman


ALMEIDA, GEORGE SILVEIRA   Written:  17 Sep. 1901              #3377
AKA ARMEDA, GEORGE S.      Codicil:  30 Sep. 1901    Bk. H, Pg. 67
AKA ARMEDA, JROGE S.       Died:      8 Oct. 1901
AKA ALMEDA, GEORGE S.      Filed:    28 Oct. 1901

   Sisters:      Isabel Armeda of the Azores; Juoquina Armeda of
                 Sausalito, Ca.; Rosie Dabla of Sausalita, Ca.;
                 Lauriana Armeda of Azores; Marie Armeda of Lisbon,
                 Portugal
   Godchildren:  Frank Avella of Ocean View, Sonoma Co., Ca.; Rosie
                 Dabla of Sausalito, Ca.
   Bequests to:  Rev. J.F. Cleary, Anton Cardoza
   Executor:     Anton Cardoza
   Witnesses:    F.A. Meyer, William B. Haskell
   Codicil:      A. Laurence, J.C. Teixeira of Sausalito, Ca.


ANDREWS, AMASA B.          Written:  15 Apr. 1884              #1952
San Francisco              Died:     30 Oct. 1888    Bk. E, Pg. 237
                           Rec.:     28 Apr. 1890

   Wife:         Margaret W.
   Executor:     Wife
   Witnesses:    Marcus P. Wiggin of Alameda, William G. Wells of
                 San Francisco


APPLETON, ELIZA            Written:   3 Mar. 1871              #1724
                           Died:     27 Feb. 1888 (prior to)
                           Filed:     8 Mar. 1888

   Brother:      E. Price Greenleaf
   Grand-
   Daughter:     Of late husband, William G., Elisabeth Greenleaf
                 Pattee; Elisabeth Greenleaf Appleton
   Bequests to:  Wm. Greenleaf Appleton Pattee; Dr. Wm. M. Ogden;
                 Thomas Brooks; Julia McCarthy; Mrs. Mary E.
                 Dawes, wife of George
   Children:     Of late husband: Elisabeth H. Appleton, William
                 E. Appleton, Carline H. Carnes, Sarah H.
                 Appleton, Mary E. Pattee, Horatio Appleton
   Executors:    Charles P. Curtis, Richard C. Greenleaf
   Witnesses:    Robert Codman, Thomas Gray, Henry A. Johnson
   Codicils:     Two
```

ARBUCKLE, JAMES H.	Written:	15 Apr. 1902	#3478
Petaluma Age 55	Died:	7 Jun. 1902	Bk. H, Pg. 130
	Filed:	30 Jun. 1902	

Wife: Deceased
Bequests to: William Conway; Mrs. Conway, mother of Wm.; Mrs. Platt Gilbert; Henry J. Horwege; Lilian Horwege (61); Dr. A. Anderson; Mrs. Henry J. Horwege
Executor: Henry J. Horwege
Witnesses: Thomas C. Denny, William B. Haskell both of Petaluma

ARCHER, WINSTON	Dated:	11 Apr. 1866	# 369
	Died:	12 Apr. 1866	Bk. A, Pg. 137
	Filed:	13 Mar. 1868	

Wife: Rebecca Archer
Children: Elizabeth Jackson, John Henry, Mary A. (Polly Ann Phillips), Jas. William, Andrew J., Caleb J., Martha J. (Vivian), Taylor Archer (minor)
Executors: John H., Jas. Wm. Archer
Witnesses: Zadock Jackson, Thomas L. Carothers

ARMSTRONG, ARTHUR E.	Written:	8 Jul. 1899	#3086
Petaluma Age 50	Died:	28 Oct. 1899	Bk. G, Pg. 357
	Rec.:	4 Dec. 1899	

Wife: None mentioned
Children: Edward J., Mrs. Cal Todd, Arthur B., Lewis Al, Albert, Frank E. (?), Carl N., Ruby A., Roy V., Hazel
Executor: Edward J.
Witnesses: George M. Brush, N. King

ARMSTRONG, KATE	Written:	19 Aug. 1895	#2922
Cloverdale	Died:	5 Sep. 1898	Bk. G, Pg. 215
	Filed:	26 Sep. 1898	

Sister: Lizzie Armstrong
Brother: Walter Armstrong
Executor: Lizzie Armstrong
Witnesses: Lewis Holloway, Reuben E. Baer

ARTUS, ALEXANDER	Written:	7 Apr. 1902	#3454
Healdsburg Age 37	Died:	8 Apr. 1902	Bk. H, Pg. 119
	Filed:	28 Apr. 1902	

Sister: Alexandrine Ducon of Mielan (?), Dept. Gers., France
Bequest to: Mrs. A. Simon of Healdsburg, Ca.
Executors: A. Simon, Dr. J.R. Swisher
Witnesses: Chas. Rodoni, J.T. Coffman both of Healdsburg

```
ASTON, GEORGE PETER         Written:  22 Jan. 1891            #3491
                            Died:      9 Apr. 1898   Bk. H, Pg. 135
                            Filed:    25 Aug. 1902
```

- Wife: Emily C. Aston of South Los Guilicos, Sonoma Co., Ca.
- Business Partner: Louis S. Stone of Aston & Stone
- Executor: Emily C. Aston
- Witness: J.F. Mulgrew

```
ATKINS, NANCY JANE          Written:  28 Oct. 1891            #2170
Santa Rosa                  Died:     16 Jan. 1892   Bk. E, Pg. 553
```

- Sons: Lilburn W. March of Santa Rosa, James T. March, Andrew H. March
- Grandson: William J. March
- Executor: Robert Bruce Allen
- Witnesses: John Brown, D.R. Gale

```
ATWATER, HENRY H.           Written:  26 Mar. 1896            #2774
Petaluma        Age 59      Died:     10 Aug. 1897   Bk. G, Pg.  60
                            Filed:     7 Sep. 1897
```

- Wife: Addie A. Atwater
- Son: Frank H. Atwater
- Executor: Wife
- Holographic

```
AUGSBERG, LOUISE MARIE      Written:  26 Sep. 1862            #1601
JOSEPHINE                   Died:     27 Mar. 1885
(Late Miss Henrichsen)
Copenhagen
```

- No Issue: See will of husband, Peter, below
- Witnesses: N.C. Lindhard (master mason), C.F. Jacobsen (master shoemaker)

```
AUGSBERG, PETER GEORGE      Written:  14 Dec. 1883            #1601
Copenhagen                  Died:     11 Sep. 1885   Bk. D, Pg. 634
Master Cooper               Rec.:     29 Oct. 1888
```

- Brothers: Carl Mortensen in America, Niels Christina (blacksmith)
- Sisters: Ane, wife of Lifler or Lifner (weaver); Marie, wife of Lund (brickmason)
- Foster Daughter: Anna Thorazelle, wife of Peter Chr. Erland
- Witnesses: C.F. Jacobsen, L.V. Hansen

```
BACKMAN, JOHN              Written:   8 Nov. 1881              #2397
Berkeley, Ca.   Age 55     Died:     12 Mar. 1894     Bk. F, Pg. 224
                           Sonoma County
                           Rec.:     16 Apr. 1894

    Wife:       Anna Maria
    Son:        Herman
    Executor:   Son
    Witnesses:  Hugo Fugel, Leopold Neller both of Oakland, Ca.


BADGER, FRANCIS ANN        Written:   6 Jul. 1886              #1575
Santa Rosa Tnsp.           Died:      6 Aug. 1886     Bk. D, Pg. 298
           Age 22          Rec.:     11 Oct. 1886

    Children:   Beshie(?), Pearl (7), Percy(?)(10), Calla (4)
    Executor:   John Hughes, father
    Witnesses:  A.B. Warn, Chas. A. Kennedy


BAILEY, JOHN HENRY         Dated:    22 May 1886               #3118
                           Died:     20 Jan. 1900    Bk. G, Pg. 400
                           Filed:     5 Mar. 1900

    Wife:       Mary Ann
    Children:   Un-named
    Executor:   Wife


BAILEY, SAMUEL N.          Dated:    22 Jul. 1897              #3015
           Age 68          Died:      1 May 1899     Bk. G, Pg. 287
                           Filed:    22 May 1899

    Wife:       Sarah A. Bailey
    Executor:   Wife
    Witnesses:  A.D. Laughlin, M.J. Streining

BAILLIE, GEORGE H.         Written:  21 Sep. 1858              # 146
                           Processed: 1 Sep. 1859    Bk. A. Pg.  54

    Wife:       Hannah M. of Illyria, Lorain Co., Ohio
    Executor:   O.L. Crandall, a relative
    Witnesses:  William D. Blip, Parker E. Weeks
```

BAKER, MARY BRUNDAGE	Written:	7 Nov. 1892		#2298
Healdsburg	Died:	13 Jan. 1893	Bk. F, Pg. 95	
	Filed:	27 Mar. 1893		

- Husband: Benjamin F. Baker
- Daughters: Matie B. Baker, Kate E. Gowell
- Sister: Kate E. Younglove
- Grand-Children: Edyth Lucy Gowell, Frank Baker Gowell
- Bequests to: 1st Congregational Church of Oakland, Ca.; Ladies Foreign Missionary Society; Ladies Home Missionary Society
- Executor: Matie B. Baker
- Witnesses: John Joseph Jones, J.C. Hickok

BANNON, JOHN	Written:	29 Nov. 1890		#2146
	Died:	17 Dec. 1891	Bk. E, Pg. 517	
	Rec.:	18 Jan. 1892		

- Wife: Mary
- Sons: John, Peter
- Daughter: Mary Ann Kenney
- Executor: Daughter
- Witnesses: J.H. Knowles of Petaluma, G.C. Sears of Sonoma

BARBARIAN GRATIE IV		Written:	15 Apr. 1889	#2296
(BAKER)		Died:	15 Feb. 1893	Bk. F, Pg. 78
Sonoma	Age 50	Rec.:	6 Mar. 1893	

- Neices: Rosalie; Julie; Hortense; daughters of brother, Louis, living in Reiz, Dept. of Basses-Alpes, France; Augustina, daughter of brother, Jean Baptiste, of Napa Co.
- Brother: Jean Baptiste
- Executor: Jean Baptiste
- Witnesses: Lorenzo Modini, Solomon Schocken

BARBARIN, JEAN BAPTISTE		Dated:	13 Jun. 1898	#2894
Sonoma	Age 63	Died:	22 Jun. 1898	
		Filed:	24 Jun. 1898	

- Daughter: Augustina Barbarin
- Executor: Lorenzo Modini, friend
- Witnesses: Robert A. Poppe, Agostino Pinelli

BARLOW, S. Q. Two Rock Valley	Written: Died: Filed:	12 Jan. 1894 20 Aug. 1895 23 Sep. 1895	#2526 Bk. F, Pg. 415

- Wife: Louisa E. Barlow
- Daughters: Mary Grace Barlow, Florence Barlow
- Son: Thomas E. Barlow
- Executor: Louisa E. Barlow

BARNES, AARON Age 80	Dated: Died: Filed:	11 Aug. 1896 28 Mar. 1897 19 Apr. 1897	#2734

- Sons: William P. Barnes, Henry A. Barnes, Benjamin F. Barnes, Aaron Barnes, Jr. (deceased)
- Executors: Sons
- Witnesses: George A. Strout, James W. Oates

BARNES, AARON, JR.	Written: Died: Filed:	8 Nov. 1888 16 Nov. 1888 3 Dec. 1888	#1789 Bk. E, Pg. 11

- Daughters: Dora Harlan (3), Ethie Ellen (5)
- Executor: Wife
- Witnesses: Jas. H. McGee, Arthur Hughes

BARNUES, JEHU Penn's Grove Age 68	Written: Died: Filed:	15 Jun. 1897 18 Jun. 1897 30 Jun. 1897	#2761

- Daughters: Mary Ellen Craig of Occidental, Rettie DeCoe of Santa Rosa, Mattie V. Wilkinson of Penn's Grove
- Son: Henry Barnes
- Son-in-law: Thomas Wilkinson
- Wife: Sarah Ann (died 8 Apr. 1897)
- Executors: Henry Barnes; Thomas DeCoe, son-in-law
- Witnesses: Wm. B. Haskell, Thos. C. Denny

BARNES, RUTH (FULKERSON) Widow	Written: Codicil: Died: Filed:	16 Apr. 1883 9 Jul. 1883 21 Jul. 1887 15 Aug. 1887	#1662 Bk. D, Pg. 481

- Children: Richard O. Barnes, Thompson Mize, Albert Mize, Amanda Moore, Mary Murdock, Mariah Hawkins
- Grand-Children: Maud Hawkins, Mamie Hawkins, Mark Hawkins
- Executors: L.A. Murdock, son-in-law; L.J. Hawkins, son-in-law
- Witnesses: Wm. E. McConnell, S.B. Wright, Thos. Rutledge

BARRY, RICHARD	Written:	11 Aug. 1870	# 521
	Died:	31 Dec. 1871	Bk. A, Pg. 254-
	Filed:	4 Mar. 1872	259

- Wife: Julia Barry
- Sons: Thomas, William (minor)
- Daughters: Nellie Agnes, Mary Elizabeth, Julia, Susannah Barry (minors)
- Executors: A.P. Whitney, John Skiffington
- Witnesses: D.D. Carder, Isaac Bernhard

BARTLETT, CALEB	Written:	15 Jul. 1879	#1021

- Wife: Mary Jane
- Sons: Harris, James Willard, Eldridge, John
- Daughters: Ellen, Alice, Lydia Anne
- Executors: Wife; son, Harris
- Witnesses: Frank W. Shattuck, J.P. Rodehaver

BARTON, CHAS. HENRY	Written:	12 Feb. 1885	#1459
Age 54	Died:	16 Feb. 1885	Bk. D, Pg. 30
	Rec.:	23 Mar. 1885	

- Wife: Sarah A.
- Son: James E.Y.
- Executor: Wife
- Witnesses: Francis A. Barton, F.G. Nagle

BARUH, HERMAN	Written:	4 Aug. 1883	#1841
Petaluma	Died:	13 Aug. 1883	Bk. C, Pg. 422
	Rec.:	11 Sep. 1883	

- Wife: Sarah
- Sons: Moses, Joseph
- Executor: Wife
- Witnesses: Jacob Phillips, J.P. Rodgers

BAYLIS, HONORA	Dated:	18 Oct. 1880	#1121
	Filed:	8 Nov. 1880	Bk. C, Pg. 112

- Sister: Mrs. Mary Murray
- StepMother: Standish O'Grady of Glourie, Co. Kerry, Ireland
- StepSister: Annie O'Grady of same place

    Minnie, Willie & Lizzie Thoroughgood; Theodore Baylis; Thomas, Francis, Theodore Connelly; Richard, Theodore & Leo Dowdal
    Sisters of Charity of Petaluma, Rev. J.F. Harrington of St. Francis, S.F.
    Rev. I. Cleary, Pastor of Petaluma; Orphan Asylum at San Rafael
- Executor: Rev. John F. Harrington
- Witnesses: Patrick Sweeney, Wm. J. Slatterns

BEESON, CAROLINE W. Healdsburg	Written: Died: Rec.:	28 Mar. 1889 12 Feb. 1890 30 Jun. 1890	#1980 Bk. E, Pg. 290

Husband: W.S. Beeson
Children: Guy W. Wolcott, Luella Wolcott, Frank Wolcott (property from grandfather, Horace Wolcott, held in trust)
Holographic

BEESON, MARY Petaluma	Written: Died: Filed:	18 Dec. 1899 30 Jan. 1900 4 Nov. 1901	#3378 Bk. H, Pg. 73

Daughters: Mary Leichau, Mrs. Anne Bowbeer
Holographic

BEESON, ROBERT Petaluma	Written: Filed:	17 Jul. 1878 16 Aug. 1880	#3378 Bk. C, Pg. 101

Wife: Mary Beeson
Children: Mrs. Sarah Overton, Mary Beeson (now Mrs. Mary Lechon), Anne Beeson
Executors: F.F. Maynard; Theodore Skillman (deleted by codicil); Mrs. Mary Beeson, wife
Witnesses: G.R. Codding, Frank W. Shattuck, William Tucker, H.A. Hardin

BEHLER, CHARLES Age 70	Written: Died: Rec.:	1 Feb. 1893 11 Nov. 1893 2 Jan. 1894	#2369 Bk. F, Pg. 192

Wife: Anna
Sons: Charles (17), Bernard, Wilhelm (16)
Daughters: Maria; Lena Gorum, wife of James
Executor: Wife
Witnesses: F. Breitenbach, Geo. Breithenbach both Sonoma City

BELL, J. S.	Dated: Died: Filed:	9 Apr. 1896 9 Jul. 1899 5 Jun. 1899	#3020

Son: Geo. S. Bell
Daughters: Mary Josephine Chadbourne, Ida May Stone
Holographic

BENNETT, DANIEL   Written: 24 Jul. 1883   #1379
                         Died: 3 Jan. 1883   Bk. C, Pg. 483
                         Rec.:   21 Nov. 1884

    Wife: Eliza
    Daughters: Sarah Eliza Briggs, wife of Henry H.; Mary Ann
                  Banta, wife of John
    Son: Jacob D.A.
    Executor: Wife
    Witnesses: Thos. R. Tutt of Eureka, Ca.; H.E. Caroet

BENNETT, FANNIE   Written: 1 May 1902   #3465
Santa Rosa   Age 50   Died: 5 May 1902   Bk. H, Pg. 123
Widow   Rec.:   26 May 1902

    Son: Seeley J. Bennett
    Daughter: Lora
    Mother: Susanna Faviner (?)
    Brother: George L. Faviner (?)
    Executor: Son
    Witnesses: Ada R. Fowler, R.F. Crawford both of Santa Rosa
    Real property in Fresno, Co., Ca.

BERMEL, J. G.   Written: 7 Mar. 1884   #1423
Healdsburg   Age 53   Died: 17 Sep. 1884   Bk. C, Pg. 605
                         Rec.:   6 Oct. 1884

    Wife: Celine (returned to France 1877)
    Children: Amelia Thompson, wife of Geo. M.; Pauline;
                  Ernestine
    Executor: Daughter, Ernestine
    Witnesses: J.W. Rose, A.E. Cochran

BERRY, HARRISON   Written: 9 Oct. 1902   #3539
              Age 73   Died: 28 Nov. 1902   Bk. G, Pg. 536
                         Rec.:   22 Dec. 1902

    Wife: Elizabeth (deceased 1887)
    Children: Theodore W. of N. Yakima, Wash.; John T.; Mary
                  E. Fay of Carson Vly, Nev.; Nancy (or Nina) McBain
                  of West Point, Ca.; Walter of Alpine Co., Ca.;
                  Iolena Coman near Seattle, Wash.
    Executor: A.B. Hill
    Witnesses: P.H. Atkinson, H.L. Atkinson

BEW, GEORGE   Written: 26 Sep. 1889   #2278
                         Died: 2 Dec. 1892   Bk. F, Pg. 46
                         Filed: 9 Jan. 1893

    Wife: Caroline
    Witnesses: George C. Jones, Lovinah B. Jones

```
BICE, MARY ANNIE M.      Written:  19 Nov. 1888              #1935
Healdsburg    Age 34     Died:     24 Feb. 1890    Bk. E, Pg. 210
                         Rec.:     31 Mar. 1890

    Son:            Frank S. (10)
    Brothers:       John N. McClish, James McClish
    Bequests to:    Charles A. Bice, Isaac K. Bice, Venia Grover
                    Ethel Sargent, Nellie McClish, Florence McClish,
                    Mrs. Lizzie Sargent, May Bice
    Executor:       Brother, John N. of Healdsburg
    Witnesses:      J.W. Rose, Milton Martin


BIDWELL, FRANKLIN        Written:  25 May 1883               #1593
Healdsburg               Died:     10 Nov. 1886    Bk. D, Pg. 333
                         Rec.:     20 Dec. 1886

    Wife:           Sophia (deceased)
    Daughter:       Sarah J. Crisp (adopted)
    Bequest to:     Caroline Brown (infant)
    Wife's
    Relatives:      Alzera Walter, John McMinn, Morgan Mathews,
                    Joseph McMinn
    Sister:         Polly Brooks
    Brothers:       Christopher, Elisha, William, John
    Executors:      Henry Brooks, E.H. Barnes
    Witnesses:      J.L. Bates, Isaac Gum


BIHLER, WILLIAM          Written:  29 Apr. 1896              #2650
                         Died:      5 Jul. 1896    No Bk.
                         Rec.:     10 Aug. 1896

    Sister:         Gennagel Bihler
    Children:       of deceased sister, Eliz. Kimmerling, Barbara
                    Stengel
    Nephew:         Christian Stengel
    Bequest to:     Mrs. Pauline Durie
    Executor:       Christian Stengel
    Witnesses       Geo. Eggleton, Geo. B. Keene


BINGHAM, ALPHEOUS W.     Filed:    24 Jan. 1881              #1136
                         Dated:    29 Sep. 1880

    Wife:           Ann Bingham
    Daughter:       Mrs. Emma Harriet Veale
    Executor:       Ann Bingham
    Witnesses:      J.T. Barnes, Frank W. Shattuck
```

```
BLACKBURN, CHARLES        Written: 10 Sep. 1869              #2805
Petaluma                  Died:    27 Nov. 1897   Bk. G, Pg.  77
                          Filed:   13 Dec. 1897

    Wife:        Jimima J. Blackburn
    Sons:        John S. Charles, Alen H., Frank L.
    Daughters:   Mary I., Hester C., Emma H., Lille M.
    Executor:    Wife
    Witnesses:   Frank W. Shattuck, D.D. Carder


BLAKE, HIRAM              Written: 29 Jul. 1891              #2141
Petaluma        Age 57    Died:       Dec. 1891   Bk. E, Pg. 489
                          Rec.:     4 Jan. 1892

    Daughter:    Minnie M. Quant (Mrs. W.E.)
    Sons:        Hiram H., George S. (minor, born 18 May 1881)
    Executors:   Minnie & Hiram
    Witnesses:   Morgan Jarvis, Stony Point; Lyman Green, Petaluma


BLEDSOE, SOPHIA           Written:  3 Jan. 1900              #3116
Santa Rosa     Age over   Died:     7 Feb. 1900   Bk. G, Pg. 394
               21         Rec.:    27 Feb. 1900

    Sister:      Mrs. Margaret Smith
    Bequest to:  A.H. Smith
    Executor:    Brother, Jeff. D. Bledsoe
    Witnesses:   Jas. W. Oates, Aubrey Barham


BLEDSOE, ZURITHY          Written: 13 Jun. 1876              #2133
                          Died:    26 Feb. 1886   Bk. E, Pg. 475
                          Rec.:    14 Dec. 1891

    Brother:     Anthony C. Bledsoe
    Bequest to:  James W. Byrns
    Executor:    Brother
    Witnesses:   A.J. Gordon, E.H. Barnes


BLISS, ALEXANDER          Written: 27 Feb. 1893              #2845
                          Died:    30 Apr. 1896   Bk. G. Pg. 131
                          Filed:    7 Mar. 1898

    Employees:   Nathaniel Ruffin, William Christmas
    Son:         William Julian Albert Bliss
    Daughter:    Elizabeth Bancroft Bliss
    Executor:    William Julian Albert Bliss
    Witnesses:   Wm. C. Hill, 1724 H St. N.W., Wash., D.C.;
                 Bernard H. Johnson, 1207 19½ St. N.W. Wash.,
                 D.C.; Jno. M. Maury, 1307 Corcoran St. N.W.,
                 Wash., D.C.
```

BLISS, WM. D.   Written: 21 Oct. 1886   #1588
Petaluma   Died: 1 Nov. 1886   Bk. D, Pg. 320
                      Rec.:   29 Nov. 1887

  Wife: Ellen Louise
  Brother: Col. Alexander Bliss of Washington, D.C.
  Executor: Wife
  Witnesses: Alex. B. Hill, Geo. P. McNear

BLUM, FREDERICK GUSTAVUS Written: 21 Nov. 1888   #2009
Freestone   Age 72 Probate: Denied
Member California   Filed: 8 Oct. 1890
Pioneers

  Grand-
  Daughter: Clara Buettner (?)
  Daughter: Maria Ignacia Valenzuela (adopted), now wife of
              Gustavus Burghard
  Bequests to: May Burghard, Minnie Burghard
  Brother: W.M. Blum of Leipsig, Germany
  Great Neice: May Brammer
  Executors: Brother-in-law, O.M. Lefebire of Bloomfield; L.
              Fare of Occidental

BOAK, SAMUALE A. (CAPT) Dated: 10 Jun. 1853   # 23
(BROOKE)   Filed: 27 Jun. 1853   Bk. A, Pg. 24

  Brother: Robert Boaks of S---, Ohio
  Executors: Wm. Waldo, Robert D. Foster
  Witnesses: Martin E. Cooper, John Hendley, John A. Brewster,
              Archibald Jennent

BOGGS, ANTHONY B.   Written: 22 Dec. 1870   # 606
                       Died: 5 Apr. 1873
                       Filed: 12 May 1873

  Wife: Mary
  Daughters: Lavica Jane, wife of Geo. Allen; Minerva, wife of
              David Odell; Susannah, wife of Simpson Odell
  Sons: James C., Joel (deceased)
  Executor: James C. Boggs
  Witnesses: John D. Price, E.W. Price

BONACICH, MARCO   Written: 29 Dec. 1899   #3113
Born Austria   Died: 20 Jan. 1900   Bk. G, Pg. 391
                       San Francisco
                       Rec.:   26 Feb. 1900

  Bequest to: Mary Silva
  Witnesses: Jos. W. Henry, Bernard J. Skelly

BOND, JOSHUA L.		Written:	1 Aug. 1871	# 625
		Died:	29 Jun. 1873	
		Filed:	4 Aug. 1873	

- Wife: M.M.
- Executor: Wife
- Witnesses: Frank W. Shattuck, John B. Christie

BOND, J. W.		Dated:	13 May 1900	#3159
Healdsburg	Age 60	Died:	22 May 1900	Bk. G, Pg. 435
		Filed:	18 Jun. 1900	

- Wife: Sarah C. Bond
- Children: Lee R. Bond (33); Charles A. Bond (29); Lizella E. Bond (28), wife of Ed Hollingshead; Lola E. Bond (17)
- Executor: Sarah C. Bond
- Witnesses: Ira A. Wheeler, S. McElhany

BOND, MARTHA M.	Written:	3 Sep. 1874	#2632
Petaluma	Codicil:	19 Dec. 1893	Bk. F, Pg. 512
	Died:	2 Apr. 1896	
	Rec.:	25 May 1896	

- Bequests to: Mrs. S.O. Shattuck; J.D. Bond of Lebanon, Tenn.; Mattie Bond of Lebanon, Tenn.; Dr. W.D. Kelly of Galveston, Tex.; Effie Kelly & Mary E. Kelly of Galveston, Tex.; O.V. Walker, Mary Lane, Willie Shattuck, Rena Shattuck, Frank Shattuck, Mattie Shattuck, Lee Shattuck all of Petaluma; Lora White, wife of W.A., of San Francisco; Mrs. B. Haskell; Mrs. L.B. Green, wife of Morgan, of Simmons, Tex.
- Codicil
- Bequests to: Lester Towne, J.H. Bond, Mrs. Newhall, Mrs. Palache
- Executors: Dill W. Seaton, O.V. Walker
- Witnesses: Wm. E. Cox, A.T. Johnson

BONES, WILLIAM	Written:	1 Sep. 1882	#2387
Age 67	Died:	14 Nov. 1893	Bk. F, Pg. 232
	Rec.:	2 Apr. 1894	

- Sons: William Henry, John F., James E. of Ariz.
- Daughters: Betsy Ann Lovel of San Diego Co., Ca.; Sarah M. Fletcher; Mary Jane Fletcher
- Sons: Joseph B. of Ariz.; Charles M.
- Executor: Son, William
- Witnesses: Matt Burnett, W.H. Mead both of Santa Rosa

BONNER, JOHN		Written: 18 Sep. 1876	#1246
	Age 69	Filed: 17 Jul. 1882	Bk. C, Pg. 236
	in 1876	Dated: 26 Jun. 1882	

- Son: Charles D. Bonner
- Daughter: Annie C. Bonner
- Step-Daughter: Mary D. Irving Bonner
- Executor: Daughter, Jeannie C. Bonner
- Witnesses: John C. Jamison, Eliza Stoddart of Alameda Co.

BOWLES, JOSEPH M.	Written: 14 Mar. 1892	#3498
Petaluma	Codicil: 13 Oct. 1896	Bk. H, Pg. 140
	Died: 11 Aug. 1902	
	Filed: 27 Jul. 1903	

- Wife: Octavia P. Bowles
- Daughters: Louisa C. Scott, wife of J.C. Scott, of Petaluma; Annie E. Bolza, wife of William Bolza, of Oakland
- Sons: Scott Bowles of Tulare City; Jesse M. Bowles of Sisson; Bourbon Bowles of Tulare City
- Executors: Octavia P. Bowles, Scott Bowles, John C. Scott
- Witnesses: D.B. Fairbanks, Geo. C. Young
- Codicil: D.B. Fairbanks

BOWMAN, JOHN H.		Written: 26 Oct. 1882	#1271
Cloverdale	Age 56	Died: 26 Oct. 1882	
		Probate: 20 Nov. 1882	

- Wife: Frances Josephine
- Children: John Percy, Robert Brading, Hattie Prescott
- Executor: Henry Kier
- Witnesses: Jno. B. Harmon, Millard F. Patterson

BOYD, JAMES	Written: 25 Feb. 1880	#1087
San Francisco	Died: 12 Jun. 1880	Bk. C, Pg. 96
	Filed: 12 Jul. 1880	

- Wife: Mary
- Executor: Wife
- Witnesses: John Doh
  Holographic

(16)

```
BOYDEN, ALONZO           Dated:   15 Jan. 1898              #2830
 Formerly of Waterville, Filed:    7 Feb. 1898
New Haven, Conn.         Died:    20 Jan. 1898

   Wife:       Elizabeth Laura Boyden
   Nieces:     Hattie Baker, Minnie DeMott
   Nephews:    Byron D. Welton, Harry Leithrop
   Executor:   Elizabeth Boyden
   Witnesses:  Jno. T. Campbell, William B. Griggs, W.R. Mead


BRACKETT, JOSHUA S.     Written:  22 Dec. 1886              #1712
Petaluma       Age 68   Died:      2 Feb. 1888   Bk. D, Pg. 575
                        Filed:    12 Mar. 1888

   Bequest to: Sarah Ann Philpott, Lunn, Mass.
   Sons:       Frank Orleans Brackett (22) of San Diego Co., CA;
               Joshua Barney Brackett (20) of San Diego Co., CA
   Daughter:   Fannie Eliza Brackett (17) of Petaluma
   Executor:   Son, F.O. Brackett
   Witnesses:  Geo. W. Lamoreaux, Petaluma, CA; Frank W.
               Shattuck, Petaluma, CA

Left property in Sonoma, Marin, San Diego, and Humboldt
counties.


BRADFORD, JOSEPH        Written:  11 Dec. 1878              #1066
                        Died:      2 Feb. 1880   Bk. C, Pg.  87
                        Filed:    16 Feb. 1880

   Wife:       Nancy
   Executor:   Wife
   Witnesses:  John Price, D.D. Phillips


BRADSHAW, FRANCES B.    Written:  18 Aug. 1893              #2466
Santa Rosa              Died:     14 Oct. 1894   Bk. F, Pg. 309
                        Rec.:     29 Oct. 1894

   Daughters:  Catherine Kerr, Mariah Combs
   Children:   of deceased daughter; Hettie B. Hoyt, Jessie
               Hoyt, Bertie Hoyt
   Executor:   Wm. E. McConnell
   Witnesses:  W. Finlaw, J.W. Ragsdale


BRAY, MARY              Written:  18 Nov. 1891              #2234
             Age 58     Died:      7 Jul. 1892   Bk. F, Pg.  21
                        Rec.:      1 Aug. 1892

   Friends:    Mrs. Maxwell, Mrs. Winter
   Executors:  Above friends
   Witness:    Holographic
```

```
BREITTAUCH, (?) WILLIAM      Written:   4 Jan. 1892              #2161
                Age 66       Died:      5 Jan. 1892    Bk. E, Pg. 521
                             Rec.:     25 Jan. 1892
```

Wife: Deceased
Bequests to: Fred Zophy (?); Mary Filitz; children of Mrs.
              Mary West of Santa Rosa
Executor: Robt. A. Forsythe
Witnesses: John Brown, Wm. H. Harris both of Santa Rosa

```
BRICKWELL, JOHN              Written:  15 Apr. 1891              #2319
Willow River, Pine Co.,      Died:     17 Nov. 1892    Bk. F, Pg. 108
Minn.                        Rec.:     22 May  1893
```

Wife: Sarah
Children: Of deceased daughter Sarah Wisdom: Samuel B.,
            Annabel (both minors)
Executors: John Wisdom of Willow River, Minn.; Joseph
            Brickwell of Lewiston, Wisc.
Witnesses: John Wisdom, Frank Ehr both of Willow River
Codicil: Dated 16 Nov. 1892, change in amounts only to heirs

```
BRIGGS, PHEBE ADELINE        Written:   1 Jan. 1875              #1295
                Age 40       Died:     20 Feb. 1883    Bk. C, Pg. 348
                             Filed:    29 Jun. 1883
```

Sisters: Jane Briggs, Ada Laughlin, Frances E. Laughlin
Brothers: Hiram Briggs, Frank Briggs, Jerome Briggs
Aunt: Minerva Briggs
Nephews: Murry Ward Briggs, Paul Creighton Briggs (both
            minors)
Executor: Hiram Briggs

```
BRINK, ALZADA MATILDA        Written:  20 Mar. 1884              #1699
Petaluma        Age 62       Died:      6 Dec. 1887    Bk. D, Pg. 546
                             Filed:    27 Dec. 1887
```

Sons: Wm. Frank, Henry Orr
Grand-
Daughter: Emma Grace Rogers
Executors: Henry O. Brink
Witnesses: Joseph Gibbs, Amanda Gibbs

```
BRINK, J. E. (EDWARD)        Written:  15 Jun. 1867              # 347
                             Died:     17 Jun. 1867 (on or about)
```

Wife: Alzada Matilda
Children: Ella (12), Wm. (14), Henry O. (9)
Executor: Wm. Hill
Witnesses: J.P. Rodehaver, O.H. Lovett

BRITTON, MARTIN A.	Written:	23 Aug. 1882	#1424
Spring Vly. Twsp.	Died:	18 Jun. 1884	Bk. C, Pg. 610
Colusa Co., CA	Rec.:	20 Oct. 1884	

- Wife: Zerilda C.
- Daughter: Louisa Ennice (Baker, at time father died)
- Son: Norman Asa
- Executor: Wife
- Witnesses: L.H. Baker, Charles Denmark

BROWN, FRANCES E.	Written:	24 Nov. 1884	#2365
	Died:	21 Oct. 1893	Bk. F, Pg. 165
	Rec.:	26 Dec. 1893	

- Children: Ella F. Kellogg, Anna N. Kellogg, Clara Kellogg, Emma B. Kellogg
- Executors: Ella F., and "my brother"

BROWN, HENRY K.	Written:	14 Aug. 1875	#2034
Healdsburg	Died:	20 Nov. 1890	
	Rec.:	5 Jan. 1891	

- Wife: Eliza J.
- Children: Nellie B., Henry B.
- Executor: Wife
- Witnesses: H.M. Willson, J.W. Clack

BROWN, RICHARD	Dated:	3 Sep. 1900	#3213
	Died:	30 Aug. 1900*	Bk. G, Pg. 461
	Filed:	15 Oct. 1900	

- Daughter: Dora Brown, other children not named
- Wife: Not named
- Witnesses: Ira A. Wheeler, M.D.; Mrs. E.A. Wheeler

* Mr. Brown was fatally injured on 30 Aug. His spoken wishes were reduced to writing on 3 Sep. 1900.

BROWN, SAMUEL	Written:	5 Dec. 1902	#3546
Petaluma	Died:	17 Dec. 1902	
	Rec.:	5 Jan 1903	

- Wife: Harriett
- Children: Mary Mabel, Samuel
- Nephew: Robt. S. Brown, Guardian of children
- Executor: Robt. S. Brown
- Witnesses: Frank K. Lippitt, L.E. Rankin

BROWN, SAMUEL C.   Dated: 29 Dec. 1863   # 239
            Age 40-45 Written: 29 Dec. 1863   Bk. A, Pg. 105
                      Died: 2 Jan. 1864
                      Filed: 18 Jan. 1864

    Wife: Mary L. Brown
    Executor: Lewis Lamberton
    Witnesses: David J. Lee, M. Thurston, I.G. Wickersham

BRUGGY, MARY   Written: 2 Oct. 1886   #1580
Near Windsor   Died: 8 Oct. 1886   Bk. D, Pg. 291
                        Rec.:   1 Nov. 1886

    Children: Wm. P. Bruggy, Jeremiah, Margaret Griffin, Kitty
                 Roberts, Geo. H.W.
    Nephew: Joseph Griffin
    Nieces: Lola Griffin, Maggie Griffin
    Executor: Friend, Michael McCullough
    Witnesses: Harry Pool, J.T. Baker

BRUNER, JACOB   Written: 8 Jan. 1855   # 30
                        Filed: 26 Dec. 1854

    Brothers: Christina, Peter of Switz., Peter (deceased)
    Sister-in-
    Law: Wife of Christian
    Sisters: Margt., Eliz.
    Others: Georgianna and Eliza Donner
    Witnesses: Israel Brockman, John E. McNair

BRUNING, HENRY WILLIAM   Written: 20 Mar. 1890   #1942
Glen Ellen   Age about Died: 23 Mar. 1890   Bk. E, Pg. 231
                 62   Rec.:   28 Apr. 1890

    Wife: Carolina
    Children: Christopher Henry, Minnie
    Executor: Son
    Witnesses: H.W. Bruning, S.M. Shinn

BRUNK, HESSEKIAH   Written: 20 Oct. 1871   # 520
San Bernardino Co.   Died: 29 Oct. 1871   Bk. A, Pg. 250
                Age 31 Filed: 2 Apr. 1872

    Wife: Dorothy (?) Ann
    Children: Of wife: John Buchanan Stevens, Louisa Jane
                 Stevens Posthumous, Jesse Lodoc (?) Brunk, Albert
                 Trovers (?) Brunk
    Trustees: Santa Rosa Lodge IOOF
    Witnesses: Zadock Jackson, Henry M. Willis

BRUNNER, CHRISTIAN   Filed: 27 Oct. 1857   # 33
            Age 55   Dated: 27 Oct. 1857   Bk. A, Pg. 34

   Wife: Maria
   Brothers: Peter, children of Lewis (deceased)
   Sisters: Children of Margaret (deceased, children of Elisa
                (deceased)
   Executors: William Cassenbaum, Israel Brockman, Haral S. Kamp
   Witnesses: John Hendley, William Ross

BURCHARD, LOUISA ANN   Dated: 21 Sep. 1895   #3346
Mendocino Co. Age 66   Died: 21 May 1901   Bk. G, Pg. 508
                        Filed: 26 Aug. 1901

   Husband: John L. Burchard
   Children: Dr. L.S. Burchard, Mary M. Twombly, D.W. Burchard
   Grand-
   Daughters: Martha Mildred Burchard; Mary J. Burchard;
                daughters of D.W. Burchard
   Executors: Dr. L.S. Burchard, D.W. Burchard
   Witnesses: J.L. White, W.P. Thomas

BURKE, ELLEN   Written: 7 Jan. 1882   #1245
San Francisco   Died: Jun. 1882   Bk. C, Pg. 231

                Formerly wife of Hugh Smith
   Husband: Laurence of Donohue's Landing
   Children: Patrick Smith of Robinstown Co., W. Meath;
                Charles; Oliver; Mary Smith
   Grandson: Hugh, son of Charles Smith
   Executors: Chas. Foster, Bridget Phelan both of San Francisco
   Witnesses: Mattie Sullivan, Geo. J. Seitz

BURNETT, CHARLES K.   Written: 5 Feb. 1896   #2618
Jackson, Madison Co.,   Boerne, Tex.   Bk. F, Pg. 487
Tenn.   Age 27   Died: 4 Mar. 1896
                           Rec: 23 Mar. 1896

   Aunt: Maggie M. Crawford, wife of R.F., of Santa Rosa,
                Ca.
   Executor: Aunt
   Witnesses: W.M. Sauders of Denison, Tex.; Frank P. Deig of
                Mt. Vernon, Ind.
                Holographic

BURNS, ELIZABETH		Written: 7 Oct. 1886		#1891
		Died: 2 Oct. 1889	Bk. E, Pg. 174	
		Rec.: 11 Nov. 1889		

Husband: Peter, Sr.
Son: Peter, Jr.
Daughters: Elizabeth F. Grissom, Anna J. Howell, Maria Burns
Executors: Thos. W. Howell, Peter Burns, Jr., Maria Burns
Witnesses: John T. Campbell, W.P. Thompson both of Santa Rosa

BURNS, JAMES   Written: 16 Dec. 1886   #1599
Analy Tnsp.   Age 71   Died: 19 Dec. 1886   Bk. D, Pg. 347
                            Rec.:   10 Jan. 1887

Wife: Sarah
Brother: Thomas of Co. Lestrine (?), Ire.
Sisters: Ann of Providence, RI; Kate Loyd of CA
Niece: Kate Oliver of Sonoma Co.
Bequest to: Fanny Munday
Nephews: Eugene Burns, Lewis A. Burns
Executor: Wife
Witnesses: James Niblock, John Cavanagh

BURNS, JAMES   Written: 14 Aug. 1892   #3325
Sonoma   Died: 10 Jun. 1901   Bk. G, Pg. 493
                            Rec.:   8 Jul. 1901

Wife: Un-named
Children: George, Edward, William, John, Mary Ellen, Katie,
            Lizzie, Emma, Joseph
Executor: Son, Edward
Witnesses: Robt. A. Poppe, Henry Ernest Boyes

BURRIGHT, WARREN   Written: 2 Sep. 1884   #1869
                Age 74   Died: 4 Apr. 1889   Bk. E, Pg. 137
                            Filed: 8 Jul. 1889

Wife: Anna
Children: Wilson of Mendocino Co,; Hulda Jane Hatch; Amanda
            Tilton; Loretta Burright of Illinois; Henrietta
            Reed of Mo.
Step-
Daughter: Lizzie Lance, wife of J.A. of Mendocino Co.
Executors: Son, Wilson; Lizzie Lance
Witnesses: D.B. Morgan, D.F. Spurr of Cloverdale

BURTON, CAROLINE   Written: 9 Jul. 1882   #1573
Petaluma   Died: 19 Jul. 1886 Bk. D, Pg. 278
                            Rec.:   11 Oct. 1886

Son: Francis A.
Executor: Son
Witnesses: C.S. Farquar, Geo. C. Clark

BUSHNELL, AMASA	Written:	1 Aug. 1902	#3529
Analy Tnsp.	Died:	8 Nov. 1902	Bk. G, Pg. 521
	Rec.:	8 Dec. 1902	

- Children: John D., Sarah Pitkin, Linda Templeman, of deceased son Frank; Winifred, Alpha Harry, Edward
- Executor: F.G. Nagle
- Witnesses: M.G. Hall, P.E. Gilman

BUTCHER, SQUIRE	Written:	17 Sep. 1900	#3318
	Died:	25 May 1901	Bk. H, Pg. 56
	Rec.:	12 Jun. 1901	

- Wife: Deceased
- Son: Chas. Walter
- Executor: Wm. Willson
- Witnesses: Wm. E. McConnell, Jno. T. Campbell

CAIN, JAMES A	Written:	12 Mar. 1898	#2869
Freeston, Sonoma Co.	Died:	12 Mar. 1898	Bk. G, Pg. 164-165
	Filed:	9 May 1898	

- Wife: Catherine
- Children: Joseph, Mary, Frances
- Executor: Daniel O'Sullivan, brother-in-law
- Witnesses: George O'Grady, Daniel O'Sullivan

CALDWELL, F. M.	Written:	16 Nov. 1887	#1694½
Age 54	Died:	26 Nov. 1887	Bk. D, Pg. 558
	Filed:	19 Dec. 1887	

- Wife: Mary Lincoln (24)
- Sons: George W. (19) of Auburn, CA; Francis M. (15) of Auburn, CA; Charles E. (21) residence unknown; Burt (9); Wm. E. (not in will)(13) of Santa Rosa
- Executor: Wife
- Witnesses: James H. McGee, J.A. Barham

CALDWELL, JOSEPH ROBERT	Written:	13 Apr. 1887	#1679
Sonoma Co.	Died:	5 Sep. 1887 Placer Co., CA	Bk. D, Pg. 508
	Filed:	3 Oct. 1887	

- Mother: Amanda Jane Caldwell (nee' Ingram)
- Father: F.M. Caldwell
- Brothers: Chas. E. Caldwell (22), Geo. W. Caldwell (14), Frances M. Caldwell, Jr. (14), Wm. Caldwell (12), Bertie Caldwell (10)
- Executor: Amanda Jane Caldwell
- Witnesses: R.H. McGinley, 103 Calif. Ave., San Francisco, CA; Alfred C. Goldner, 103 Calif. Ave., San Francisco, CA

```
CALLAWAY, DAVID          Written:  1 Feb. 1896              #3387
Sonoma         Age 70    Died:    10 Mar. 1900      Bk. H, Pg.  80
                         in Sacramento Co.
                         Filed:   25 Nov. 1901
```

Widower, no surviving children

Brother: Silas M. Callaway, Sacramento Co., CA
Executor: Robert A. Poppe, Sonoma, Sonoma Co., CA
Witnesses: Joseph B. Small, Sonoma City, CA; Louis H. Green,
            Sonoma City, CA

```
CARLSON, CHARLES EPHRIAM Dated:   25 Feb. 1899              #3147
              Age 45    Died:    30 Jan. 1900      Bk. G, Pg. 437
                        Filed:   23 Jul. 1900
```

Sisters: Augusta Nathalia Johnson (deceased); Martini
            Bernhardina Carlson, AKA Betty Carlson, #17
            Albogaten St., Annadal, Guttenborg, Sweden
Executor: W.K. Johnson (husband of deceased sister)
Witnesses: Marvin T. Vaughn, J.R. Lyppo

```
CARRIGER, NICHOLAS       Written: 27 Nov. 1878              #1482
Santa Rosa    Age 62     Died:    30 Jun. 1885      Bk. D, Pg.  78
                         Rec.:    20 Jul. 1885
```

Wife: Mary Ann
Children: Eliz. J. Shetter (42), Levisa Lewis (40), David W.
            (37), A. Boggs (35), Louisa L. Powell (33),
            William W. (28), Emma D. (25), Solomon H. (23),
            Evaine N. Tufts (29)(deceased)
Executors: Wife, David, Solomon
Witnesses: F.T. Clark, A.D. Laughlin, Barclay Henley

```
CARILLO, GUADALUPE       Written: 23 Apr. 1874              # 688
                         No death or file dates    Bk. A
                         on documents
```

Husband: Joaquin
Children: Henry G. (20); Mary Josephine Holmes (19) wife of
            Albert; Eliz. A. (17); J. Frank (16); Frederick A.
            (13); Amelia C. (11); Mary Frances (9); Louisa A.
            (4); Catherine A. (3); Albert Ronaldo (10 mos.)
Executor: Albert Holmes, son-in-law
Witnesses: H.J. Smith, B.B. Berry

```
CARROLL, JAMES           Written: 16 Sep. 1865              # 400
Born Ireland             Died:    11 Oct. 1868
                         Filed:   23 Nov. 1868
```

Brother: Patrick of Sonoma Co.
Executor: Patrick Carroll
Witnesses: William D. Blip, William Lynch

CARSON, DOROTHY   Written: 31 Dec. 1881   #1212
          Age 49   Died: 1 Mar. 1882   Bk. C, Pg. 196
                       Filed: 24 Apr. 1882

    Daughter: Maria Kent
    Sons: Richard Facey, James F. Dolan, Charles,
                 Thomas M. Carson
    Daughters: Katie A. Dolan, Annie L. Dolan
    Executor: Richard Facey, also guardian of minor children
    Witnesses: C.S. Gibson, Johan Jonzon

CARTER, HANSFORD F.   Written: 15 May 1861   # 193
                           Probate: 20 Jul. 1861   Bk. A, Pg. 80

    Mother: Nancy Evans, wife of Henry, leaves land in Polk
                 Co., Ore.
    Brother: Andrew Carter
    Witnesses: O.(?)R. Mims, G.N. Sanborn

CARTER, JOSIAH W.   Written: 13 Dec. 1888   #1972
Santa Rosa   Age 51   Died: 3 May 1890   Bk. E, Pg. 284
                           Rec.:   16 Jun. 1890

    Wife: Sarah F.
    Daughter: Julia Erman(?)(minor)
    Executors: James Rogers, James A. Hardin
    Witnesses: W.R. Thompson, W. Coughran

CARTER, MARY E.   Written: 26 May 1879   #1023
                           Filed: 25 Aug. 1879   Bk. C, Pg. 50

    Sole Heirs: Children, Nancy Virginia; Margaret Luvinia;
                 Andrew Jackson (minor)
    Executor: Wm. E. Cooke of Santa Rosa
    Witnesses: Thos. J. Jones, A.C. Dickenson, Clarissa J.
                 Jones

CARTER, MATILDA A.   Written: 6 May 1896   #2667
                           Brooklyn, NY
                           Died: 23 Aug. 1896
                           Albany, NY

    Husband: Geo. B. Carter
    Son: Elmer Carter
    Executor: Elmer Carter

CARVER, H. E.   Written: 3 May 1888   #1753
             Age 38   Died: 29 May 1888   Bk. D, Pg. 603
                             Filed: 23 Jun. 1888

    Children: Dora C. Carver, Rolla E. Carver
    Executor: J.F. Mulgrew
    Witnesses: Chas. E. Runyon, J.P. Woodworth

CARY, BARTLEY   Written: 20 Feb. 1884   #1840
Petaluma   Age 55   Died: 15 Jan. 1889   Bk. E, Pg. 99
                             Filed: 8 Feb. 1889

    Wife: Maria
    Sons: Eddie F., Freddie C.
    Executor: Wife
    Witnesses: John Power, J.L. Dinwiddie

CARY, PERMILIA   Written: 23 Mar. 1894   #2399
Petaluma   Died: 28 Mar. 1894 Bk. F, Pg. 218
                             Rec.:   16 Apr. 1894

    Bequest to: D.B. Fairbanks
    Brother: J.C. Carey
    Executor: D.B. Fairbanks
    Witnesses: Wm. B. Haskell; Mrs. M. Dandel of San Francisco;
                A. Anderson

CASE, A. B.   Written: 29 Sep. 1896   #3544
Petaluma   Died: 6 Dec. 1902 Bk. G, Pg. 539
                             Rec.:   29 Dec. 1902

    Wife: Harriet
    Daughter: Carrie
    Executor: Wife
                Holographic

CASERES, CERO F.   Written: 19 Jul. 1894   #2448
Bodega Tnsp. Age 54   Died: 25 Jul. 1894 Bk. F, Pg. 299
Saloon Keeper   Rec.:   17 Aug. 1894

    Bequest to: S.W. Stump, Mrs. Susan C. Stump
    Executors: Daniel Dumilin, O.H. Hoag
    Witnesses: Bruce T. Cockrill, M.D.; Jno. Murray

CHAMPLIN, CHARLES C.   Written: 19 Feb. 1891   #2244
Sonoma   Age 78   Died: 7 Aug. 1892 Bk. F, Pg. 26
                             Filed: 12 Sep. 1892

    Wife: Sarah N.
    Children: Asa W., Mrs. Emma Linda Agnew, Mrs. Mary S. Shafer
    Executor: Wife, son
    Witnesses: Murray Whallon, J.C. Scott both of Petaluma

```
CHAPMAN, THOMAS M         Written:  27 May 1880                #1226
                          Died:     20 Feb. 1882   Bk. C, Pg. 207
                          Filed:    19 Mar. 1882
```

Wife: Mary C.
Children: Edwin A., Harry, Elliot, Phoebe, Mary L.
Executors: Wife & Edwin A.
Witnesses: Platt B. Gilbert, Frank W. Shattuck

```
CHARLES, MARTIN LUTHER    Written:  23 Jun. 1901                #1843
Sonoma                    Died:     1 Jan. 1902    Bk. 14, Pg. 103
                          Rec.:     17 Feb. 1902
```

Gives all he posseses to School District

Executor: Robt. A. Poppe
Witnesses: Jos. B. Small, A.M. Thomson

```
CHENEY, EDMUND H.         Written:  3 Mar. 1889                 #1843
Bodega                    Died:     14 Mar. 1889   Bk. E, Pg. 93
                          Rec.:     8 Apr. 1889
```

Wife: Sarah
Children: Edmund H., Thomas H., Jas. A. White (step-son)
            Rebecca L., Sarah E. Addie M. Billett
Witnesses: Sam'l. W. Stump, L.G. Goodman

```
CHURCH, FRANK HAIL        Dated:    16 Apr. 1900                #3152
           Age 39         Died:     17 Apr. 1900   Bk. G, Pg. 420
                          Filed:    7 May 1900
```

Wife: Carrie Church
Child: Edith Church
Brother: Herman Church, Guardian of the estate of
            Edith Church
Executor: Father, --- Church (initials)
Witnesses: J.P. Rodgers, Carrie Church

```
CHURCH, SAMUEL H.         Dated:    23 Jul. 1900                #3199
           Age 71         Died:     23 Jul. 1900   Bk. G, Pg. 456
                          Filed:    17 Sep. 1900
```

Wife: Cynthia Church
Children: Howard, Walter, Herman, Delbert, Raymond,
            Olive Rea, Belle Armstrong, Clara Kryer(Sp.?),
            Laura Stice, Glenda Ormsby
Grand-
Daughter: Edith Church
Executor: C.G. Church, wife
Witnesses: George Ivancovich, J.P. Rogers

CLARK, ANDREW   Written: 12 Oct. 1871   # 522
                         Died: 13 Jan. 1872   Bk. A, Pg. 260-
                         Filed: 4 Mar. 1872   263

   No relatives in this country

   Bequest to: Eddie Reniff (S of A C A), Mary
   Executor: Mrs. Mary Reniff
   Witnesses: James Heynes, Frank W. Shattuck

CLARK, CHARLES   Written: 3 Jul. 1879   #1407
San Francisco Age 50   Variance: 13 Jul. 1881   Bk. C, Pg. 565
 Master Mariner   Died: 25 Sep. 1883
                         at sea
                         Rec.:   4 Aug. 1884

   Wife: Harriet M.
   Son: Charles Edward
   Executor: Wife
   Witnesses: Cyril V. Grey, J.G. Sevensaler

CLARK, CHARLES   Written: 12 Apr. 1887   #1714
               Age 68   Died: 17 Jan. 1888

   Wife: Mary Margaret
   Next of Kin: Eleanor L. Lindsay of Windsor, CA; Martha Ann
                Mannon of Ukiah, CA; Margaret Elvira Brotherton
                of Los Angeles; Uretta J. Windsor of Spokane
                Falls, Wash. Terr.; Robert Masalon Clark of
                Berlin, Colusa Col, CA
   Executors: Wife & Jas. M. Mannon
   Witnesses: Henry Clay Brooks, Jacob Speck Clark

CLARK, DAVID   Written: 23 Jan. 1900   #3320
Santa Rosa   Age 85   Died: 13 May 1901   Bk. G, Pg. 495
                         Rec.:   15 Jul. 1901

   Children: Eliz. Ann Bergers (?), Mary Ellen Carithers, Thos.
                Ewing Clark, Nancy Armida Taylor, Sam'l Berry
                Clark, David Curtis Clark
   Grand
   Children: Henry M. Forsyth, Martha C. Forsyth, Arthur
                Bradshaw
   Executors: Son-in-law, John S. Taylor; Son, David
   Witnesses: M.J. Striening, Frank B. Cornue

```
CLARK, FRED S.              Written:  10 Oct. 1898              #2935
Preston, Sonoma Co.         Died:     22 Oct. 1898      Bk. G. Pg. 228-
         Age 54             Filed:    14 Nov. 1898                 230

    Mother:        Mrs. C.B. Clark
    Brother:       Samuel P.B. Clark
    Sister:        Laura Ella Young 537 Broadway, Everett, Mass.
    Sister-in-
    Law:           Minnie A. Clark
    Cousins:       Mrs. Alice Blinn (?), Mrs. Jennie Ham, Mrs.
                   Grace Blinn, Mrs. Annie C. Whitcomb
    Bequest to:    Mrs. Bickford, Mrs. Emily Preston
    Executor:      W. Appleton, Preston, CA
    Witnesses:     G.W. Hoyle, Cloverdale, CA; Henry Hubbard,
                   Preston, CA


CLARK, JAMES                Written:  20 Jan. 1873              # 643
Petaluma                    Died:      4 Sep. 1873
                            Filed:    20 Oct. 1873

    San Francisco Catholic Orphan's Asylum; Protestant
    Orphan's Asylum

    Executor:      I.J. Wickersham
    Witnesses:     John Kenney, Jesse C. Wickersham


CLARK, JAMES LEONARD        Written:  21 Nov. 1897              #2802
Santa Rosa    Age 74        Died:     27 Nov. 1897      Bk. G, Pg.  80
                            Filed:    27 Dec. 1897

    Bequest to:    Harriet Gill, Ferndale, Humboldt Co., CA
    Nieces:        Earla Terrell, Edna Terrell
    Executor:      R.M. Swain (?)
    Witnesses:     H.S. Shamp, Santa Rosa; B.H. Palmer, Windsor


CLARK, JAMES P.             Written:   9 Jun. 1886              #1554
Santa Rosa                  Died:      9 Jun. 1886      Bk. D, Pg. 222
                            Rec.:     28 Jun. 1886

    Children:      Lillie, Fredrick, Estelle, Gertrude
    Executor:      Friend, Jas. H. McGee
    Witnesses:     W.R. Smith, Charley E. Eberhard


CLEMMENSEN, CARL J          Written:  15 Aug. 1885              #1496
Petaluma                    Died:     29 Aug. 1885      Bk. D, Pg.  96
                            Rec.:     13 Oct. 1885

    Wife:          Paulina
    Children:      Frieda, Charles
    Executor:      Wife
    Witnesses:     E.L. Lippitt, C. Kubec
```

CLEMONS, ABIGAIL W.		Written:	4 Jun. 1887	#1673
Fulton	Age 71	Died:	27 Aug. 1887	Bk. D, Pg. 495-501
		Filed:	28 Oct. 1887	

- Son: Edward George Kidd
- Daughters: Abigail W. Cozzens, Mary A. Drennan
- Grand-Daughters: Alice Almina Kidd, Katy Ella Rambo
- Executor: F.G. Nagle
- Witnesses: Henry W. Hudson, Walter S. Davis

CLEVELAND, EZRA	Written:	9 Feb. 1888	#2514
Petaluma	Died:	18 Feb. 1895	Bk. F, Pg. 344
	Rec.:	18 Mar. 1895	

- Daughter: Ellen
- Son: Hamilton of Los Angeles Co.
- Daughter: Mary Tustin (widow) of Columbus
- Executors: William Hill, or his son, Allie Hill
- Witnesses: F.A. Meyer, Wm. B. Haskell

CLEWE, JOHANN FRIEDRICH	Written:	18 Mar. 1896	#3506
ERDMANN	Codicil:	14 May 1902	Bk. H, Pg. ---
Sonoma	Died:	14 May 1902	
	Rec.:	29 Sep. 1902	

- Wife: Maria
- Children: Un-named
- Bequest to: Adelheid Riensch
- Executor: Wife
- Witnesses: G.S. Harris
- Holographic
- Codicil Witnesses: G.D. Rich, Wm. Clewe

CLYMAN, MARY	Written:	1 Nov. 1869	# 457
	Died:	7 Dec. 1869	
	Filed:	10 Oct. 1870	

- Husband: Lancaster
- Children: Sophronia Strout, Luvisia Jane Clyman, Mary Eliza. Clyman, Frances Melvina Clyman, Alice Clarissa Clyman, James Ira Clyman, Rhoda Bella Clyman
- Executor: Lancaster Clyman
- Witnesses: Jacob Strout, Miles H. Chenoweth

```
COBB, CHARLES              Written: 17 Apr. 1874              #683
                           Died:    27 Apr. 1874
                           Filed:    1 Jun. 1874

    Mother:     Eunice
    Sisters:    Juliet, Fanny, Caroline Ann Harlow (child
                of sister Mary Packer)
    Brothers:   Ezra, Henry
                (All but Henry of New London, Conn.)
    Executor:   I.G. Wickersham
    Witnesses:  C.T. Hatch, Martin Armstrong


COCKE, WILLIAM E.          Written: 25 Sep. 1882              #1312
                           Codicil: 27 Mar. 1883   Bk. C, Pg. 405
                           Died:    14 Apr. 1883
                           Filed:   19 Sep. 1883

    Daughters:  Louisa Francis Wooldridge, wife of John M
                Wooldridge; Mrs. Rebekah W. Farmer, wife of
                G.T. Farmer; Mrs. Mary Ellen Forsyth, wife
                of Robert Forsyth
    Nephews:    Wm. B. Forsyth (minor), Edward Lee Forsyth
                (minor)
    Nieces:     Sarah F. Forsyth (minor)
    Grand-
    Daughter:   Mary M. Forsyth (minor)
    Executors:  E.T. Farmer, W. E. McConnell
    Witnesses:  W.E. Orear, A.H. Smith
    Codicil
    Witnesses:  T.J. Ludwig, A.H. Smith


COCKRILL, DIDAMIA          Written: 24 Dec. 1881              #1592
Bloomfield                 Died:    24 Oct. 1886   Bk. D, Pg. 326
                           Rec.:     6 Oct. 1886

    Sons:       T.G., R.L., Bruce, all of San Francisco
    Daughters:  Eda J. Cannon, Elizabeth Haog of Santa Rosa,
                Helen Lake
    Grandsons:  E.J. & Wm. W. Fowler, Fred H. & Geo. E. Miller
    Admns:      Wm. W. Fowler, Eda J. Cannon
    Witnesses:  C.C. Farnsworth, L.L. Cannon


COCKRILL, HARRISON         Written: 23 Jan. 1857              # 38
Santa Rosa                 Filed:   18 Feb. 1857   Bk. A, Pg. 44

    Wife:       Ruhama
    Child:      Un-named
    Executor:   Wife
    Witnesses:  Un-readable
```

CODDING, G. R.   Written: 10 May 1884   #1410
Petaluma   Died: 29 Jun. 1884   Bk. C, Pg. 576
                              Rec.:   11 Aug. 1884

    Wife: Millie M.
    Children: Geo. C., Wm. T., C.R., T.M., Anna L., Ella S.
    Executor: Wife
    Witnesses: E.S. Lippett, Thos. A. Gilbert

COE, F. H.   Written: 15 Apr. 1873   # 630
                              Died: 1 Jun. 1873
                              Filed: 29 Sep. 1873

    Wife: Not mentioned
    Son: Frank H. (deceased) buried in Laurel Cemetery,
                 San Francisco
    Daughter: Caroline
    Executor: S.M. McCullough
    Witnesses: Jeremiah Beam, E.W. Maslin

COFER, ELLIOTT   Written: 26 Aug. 1862   # 218
                              Probate: 8 Oct. 1862   Bk. A, Pg. 83

                 Nothing to "other sons and daughters", un-named
    Sons: George W., Elliott M.
    Executor: Henry Hall
    Witnesses: F.D. Colton, Richard O'Brien, H. Peter

COLLINS, LA FAYETTE   Dated: 25 Feb. 1867   # 338
              Age 71   Died: 25 Feb. 1867   Bk. A, Pg. 179
                       Filed: 8 Apr. 1867

    Sons: Waldo H. of New York City; Germain of Petaluma; D.
                 Hayden of Petaluma; Henry E.
    Brothers: Thomas Munk, F.W. of Rochester, NY
    Executor: Columbus Tustin, Germain A. Collins
    Witnesses: J.B. Southard, G.R. Codding

COLLINS, MATHEW   Written: 10 Feb. 1883   #1302
Sonoma   Age 57   Died: 12 Mar. 1883   Bk. C, Pg. 355
                              Rec.:   2 Jul. 1883

    Sister: Julia Collins of Greenville, Conn.
    Brother: John Collins of Ireland
    Bequests to: Mrs. Ellen Eagan of New York; Patrick Haley of
                 Greenville, Conn.; Mrs. Margaret Watson, Jesse
                 St., San Francisco; Mrs. Ellen Doyle, Clementina
                 St., San Francisco; Fred Keller; Mary Keller, next
                 of kin
    Executor: Fred Keller
    Witnesses: L.B. Lawrence, F. Britenbach

```
COLWELL, CAROLINE        Written:   15 Nov. 1890              #2046
ELIZABETH                Rec.:      16 Feb. 1891    Bk. E, Pg. 350
Santa Rosa      Age 60

    Husband:     Edwin Brown
    Daughter:    Alice
    Executor:    Husband
    Witnesses:   Charlotte Sumner Smythe, Anabel McGaughey Stuart


COLWELL, EDWIN B.        Written:    6 Jun. 1891              #2287
Santa Rosa               Died:       8 Jan. 1892    Bk. F, Pg.  67
                         San Mateo Co.
                         Rec.:      18 Feb. 1893

    Wife:        Caroline E. (deceased)
    Daughter:    Alice
    Sons:        Harry C., Charles E.
    Executor:    Daughter
    Witnesses:   H.W. Massey, Florence May Massey


COMSTOCK, PHILENA C.     Written:   18 Oct. 1884              #1444
Seattle, Wash. Terr.     Died:       2 Nov. 1884    Bk. D, Pg.   1
                         Rec.:      22 Dec. 1884

    Daughters:   Helen A. Raymond of Healdsburg, CA; Cornelia
                 E. Jenner of Seattle
    Executor:    Daughter Helen Raymond for Calif. property;
                 (relationship ?) Chas. K. Jenner for Wash.
                 property
    Witnesses:   Lyman P. Andrews, Ellen J. Worthington both
                 of Seattle


CONNIFF, BRIDGET C.      Written:    6 Feb. 1893              #2727
           Age over      Died:       4 Mar. 1897    Bk. G, Pg.   8
           45            Filed:     22 Mar. 1897

    Daughter:    Sarah F. Conniff (youngest) of Stockton, CA
    Executor:    Sarah F. Conniff
    Witnesses:   F.A. Meyer, L.E. Rankin
```

```
CONRAD, SIMON              Written:   6 Jul. 1872              # 609
                           Codicil:  21 Feb. 1873
                           Died:     19 Apr. 1873
                           Filed:    26 May  1873

    Sons:         Wm. N. Conrad, Thomas C. Conrad (Guardian),
                  Benjamin F. Tuttle
    Executor:     Benjamin F. Tuttle
    Codicil
    Executor:     Hiram T. Fairbanks
    Witnesses:    W.K. Davis, Frank W. Shattuck
    Codicil
    Witness:      W. Davis


CONZELMANN, GOTTLIEB       Written:   8 Dec. 1883              #1414
St. Louis, Mo.             Died:     23 Apr. 1884
                           Filed:     8 Aug. 1884

    Wife:         Deceased
    Brother:      Jacob F. of Washington Co., Mo.
    Niece:        Caroline P. Klingel
    Daughter:     Emilie Jorgine wife of Chas. V. Riby
    Son:          Wm. Eliot, Theophilus (wife Emma)
    Sister-in-
    Law:          Mary Hoen of Santa Rosa, CA (wife of Berthold Hoen)
    Niece:        Kate Klingel (deceased)(her inheritance given to
                  Washington University as memorial)
    Executor:     Son, William Eliot or Theophilus
    Witnesses:    Edward S. Rowse, Arthur L. Thompson


COOK, DAVID P.             Written:  12 Nov. 1870              # 464
                           Died:     17 Nov. 1870
                           Filed:    21 Nov. 1870

    Children:     J.W. Cook, P.J. Reynolds, H.G. (?) Menefee
    Witnesses:    M. Mason, G.W. Lowery, John Shuster, J.P. Anderson


COOK, GILBERT              Written:  29 Aug. 1885              #1606
               Age 79      Died:     21 Dec. 1886      Bk. D, Pg. 357
                           Rec.:     14 Feb. 1887

    Wife:         Catherine
    Children:     Isaac Fountain (55); Wm. Newton (53) of Georgetown,
                  CA; Abner Fisher (50); Eliz. Ann - - - (?) (48);
    Grand-
    Children:     Katie Cook (23) of Georgetown, CA; Benj. Gilbert
                  (20)
    Executors:    Isaac & Wm. Scoville
    Witnesses:    H. Moore, F.B. Ward
```

```
COOLEY, CHARLES H.          Written: 11 Dec. 1896              #3043
Cloverdale     Age 74       Died:    27 Jun. 1899    Bk. G, Pg. 317
                            Filed:   28 Aug. 1899
```

Wife:	Deceased
Daughter:	Mariette F. Sink
Sons:	M.V.H. Cooley, John B. Cooley, E.A. Cooley
Grand-Daughter:	Carrie McCray of Cloverdale, Ca.
Nieces:	Maud Walker of Stanislau Co., Ca.; Lizzie Walker (Mrs. John) of Cloverdale, Ca.
Nephew:	Chas. H. Westover of Cloverdale, Ca.
Grandson:	Chas. H. Cooley
Daughter-in-Law:	Flora Cooley
Executors:	Sons; J.B. and E.A.
Witnesses:	S.W. Knowles, George B. Baer both of Cloverdale
Appraisers:	Wm. T. Brush, Conrad Haehl, Thos. B. Wilson

```
COOPER, JAMES               Dated:    8 Jun. 1853              #  36
                            Died:     5 Sep. ----   Bk. A, Pg. ---
                            Filed:   11 Oct. 1858
```

Wife:	Sarah and yet unborn offspring
Sons:	Thomas, John
Daughter:	Barbara
Guardians:	John Rose, William Burns
Witnesses:	William Burns, William Benson

```
COOPER, JOHN A.             Written:  8 Aug. 1868              # 491
Santa Rosa                  Died:    23 Mar. 1871
                            Rec.:     2 Jul. 1871
```

Wife:	Rhoda Cooper
Children:	Lewis B. Cooper, Martha Chamberlain, wife of David Chamberlain; William M. Cooper; John D. Cooper; Sidney R. Cooper; Harriet Tupper, wife of George A. Tupper; Julia R. Cooper; Mary L. Douglass, wife of William Douglass
Executors:	Rhoda Cooper, William M. Cooper, David Chamberlain
Witnesses:	James H. McGee, L.D. Latimer

```
COOPER, RHODA               Dated:   26 Jan. 1892              #2998
               Age 82       Died:    21 Mar. 1899    Bk. G, Pgl 274
                            Mendocino Co.
                            Filed:   10 Apr. 1899
```

Children:	John D. Cooper, Harriet R. Tupper, Martha A. Chamberlain, Lewis S. Cooper all of Santa Rosa; Mary L. Douglas, Julia R. Richardson both of San Francisco
Grand-Children:	Three children of Sidney R. Cooper (deceased)
Executor:	Mary L. Douglass
Witnesses:	D.R. Gale, Thomas Hopper

```
COOPER, WM. MC KINDRA      Written:   28 May  1879              #1394
Santa Rosa                 Died:      31 Mar. 1884    Bk. C, Pg. 546
                           Rec.:       3 Jan. 1885
```

- Mother: Rhoda
- Brothers: Lewis S., John D., Sidney R.
- Sisters: Harriet R. Tupper wife of Geo. A., Martha A. Chamberlain wife of David, both of Santa Rosa; Julia R. Richardson wife of Wm. A., Mary L. Douglass wife of Wm. A., both of Tulare
- Executors: Sidney R. & David Chamberlain
- Witnesses: James H. McGee, S.E. Davidson

```
COREY, MELINDA             Written:   12 Jan. 1881              #1148
Widow of C.R.              Died:       1 Apr. 1881    Bk. C, Pg. 131
Bloomfield                 Filed:     23 May  1881
```

- Sons: Noah (oldest), Hiram, Reuben
- Daughters: Melinda Reynolds (oldest), Adelaide Case, Minerva Hoag, Augusta Hall, Pauline Bently (deceased), Sarah Littlefield (deceased)
- Grand-Daughters: Bertha Reynolds, Ida Tyler, Amelia George
- Bequests to: Rose, Cynthia Stocking, Irene Corey, Geo. Case, J.C. Hoag, Wm. Hall
- Littlefield Children: Emma, Eddie, Rosa, Warren
- Stocking Children: Frank, Flora, Anna, Minnie, George, Charlie, Ernest
- Bentley Children: Reuben, Horatio, Rodney, Willie
- Corey Children: Nora, Josiah, Florence
- Hoag Children: Charlie, Linda --Eldie, Eddie
- Case Children: Georgie, Addie, Walter, Letta
- Hall Children: Willie, Hattie, Lester, Lena
- Reynolds Children: Charlie, Bennie
- Executor: Wm. P. Hall
- Witnesses: M.F. Milnes, Chas. G. Milnes, C.A. Stowell

```
COUNCILMAN, ALMEDA JULIA   Written:    2 Aug. 1895              #2557
Fresno Co.     Age 56      Died:       4 Aug. 1895    Bk. F, Pg. 431
                           Rec.:      11 Nov. 1895
```

- Son: Frederick A. Dinsmore
- Sister: Mrs. Hattie May Corey
- Executor: Wm. F. Corey of Cotati, CA
- Witnesses: John Robertson, Robert E. Shore

COURTNEY, PATRICK	Written:	30 Oct. 1891	#2196
Age 62	Died:	5 Mar. 1892	Bk. E, Pg. 583
	Rec.:	21 Mar. 1892	

- Sisters: Ellen Escalle, Catherine Holleran
- Bequest to: John T. Campbell
- Executor: John T. Campbell
- Witnesses: R.M. Swain, Martin Muller both of Santa Rosa

COWLES, NATHAN C.	Dated:	20 Feb. 1863	# 225
Age 27	Died:	20 Feb. 1863	Bk. A, Pg. 87
	Filed:	6 Apr. 1863	

- Brother: John I. Cowles of Kansas, Loyld A. Cowles
- Sister: Emily Vestal of Sonoma
- Nephew: Thomas Vestal
- Brother-in Law: Lewis Vestal
- Executors: Lewis Vestal, Caleb Railsback
- Witnesses: J.H. Ranard (?), Henry Gibbs

COX, JOHN T.	Dated:	30 Apr. 1860	# 171
	Written at Stockton		Bk. A, Pg. 87
	Filed:	1 Aug. 1860	

- Wife: Mary
- Children: Married children not named; James C. Cox, Thomas C. Cox, Louisa E. Cox (all minors)
- Executor: Mary, wife
- Witnesses: C. Campbell, J.C. Westbay

CRANE, ROBERT	Dated:	7 May 1893	#3230
Age 60	Codicil:	16 Oct. 1895	Bk. G, Pg. 475
	Died:	31 Oct. 1900	
	Filed:	19 Nov. 1900	

- Wife: Susan C. Crane
- Children: Mary J. Lowrey, George Silas Crane, Charles Burton Crane, Martha K. Ward, James W. Crane, Hettie Forest Crum (Sp.?), Thomas Jackson Crane, Robert Lee Crane, Estilla Hope Crane, Wade Hampton Crane (minor)
- Codicil: Robert H. Ward, Charles D. Ward, Ellen F. Ward, and Estilla M. Ward, children of Martha K. Ward (deceased)
- Executor: Susan C. Crane
- Witnesses: H.G. Hahman, A.D. Hoskins
- Codicil Witnesses: John S. Taylor, A.B. Ware

```
CRISP, JOHN W.            Dated:    25 Jan. 1860              # 161
                          Died:     Not given        Bk. A, Pg.  62
                          Rec.:     5 Mar. 1860
```

  Children: Margaret, Sarah, John, William Crisp
  Executors: James H. Laughlin, Philamon Warner
  Witnesses: Daniel Gile, Wm. W. Wallace, Theophilus Pool

```
CROCKETT, JEREMIAH T.     Written:  30 Apr. 1860              # 167
                          Probate:  11 Jun. 1860    Bk. A, Pg. ---
```

  Daughter: Abbey Luella Crockett of Maine
  Executors: Parker E. Weeks, Robt. Douglas both of Petaluma
  Witnesses: Elija Sprague, Wm. W. Main

```
CULLIGAN, JAMES           Written:  17 Jul. 1872              # 563
                          Died:     25 Jul. 1872    Bk. A, Pg.  15
```

  Wife: Bridget
  Mother: Mary Culligan
  Cousin: John Culligan of San Francisco
  Children: Michael, Mary
  Executors: Wife, Wm. McDermott, John Merritt
  Witnesses: John Merritt, Wm. McDermott, John Cavan

```
CUMMINGS MICHAEL          Written:  16 Jul. 1895             #3504
Santa Rosa                Died:     26 Aug. 1902    Bk. H, Pg. 144
                          Rec.:     22 Sep. 1902
```

  Wife: Catherine
  Children: Un-named
  Executor: Wife
  Witnesses: Thos. Rutledge, L.A. Pressley

```
CUNNINGHAM, ROBERT        Written:  19 Aug. 1869              # 421
                          Died:     22 Aug. 1869
                          Rec.:     23 Aug. 1869
```

  Wife: Isabella Cunningham
  Daughter: Mary Jane McClellan
  Grand-
  Daughter: Ella Isabella McClellan
  Executor: Benjamin Clark
  Witnesses: J. Oliver Ogle, Charles Clark

CURTISS, JAMES HALL   Dated: 2 Jan. 1895   #2978
                           Died: 27 Jan. 1899   Bk. G, Pg. 248
                           Filed: 20 Feb. 1899

    Wife: Sarah Jane Curtiss
    Sons: Thomas Edwon Curtiss, George Charles Curtiss,
                 Jame C.(?) Greene (step-son)
    Orphan: Mary E. Rich
    Executors: Sarah Jane Curtiss, Thomas Edson Curtiss,
                 George Charles Curtiss
    Witnesses: None

CUTTER, JOSEPH SMITH   Written: 22 Oct. 1871   # 510
                           Died: 5 Nov. 1871   Bk. A, Pg. 243-
                           Filed: 4 Dec. 1871   246

    Bequests to: G. Warner; John Calder; Mrs. J.A. Frazier, wife
                 of Fred of Petaluma; G.W. Eidleman
    Aunt: Mrs. Hannah Smith of Ipswich, Mass.
    Brother: Charles Henry Cutter of Ipswich, Mass.
    Executor: I.G. Wickersham
    Witnesses: Frank Shattuck, Lewis G. Nay

DABNER, JOHN   Written: 17 Feb. 1882   #1216
                           Died: 18 Feb. 1882   Bk. C, Pg. 191
                           Filed: 20 Mar. 1882

    Wife: Mary
    Sons: William, Anton, Frank, Manuel, John
    Daughter: Louisa F. Focha
    Executor: Wife
    Witnesses: Frank W. Shattuck, A.B. Lopez, Mariano Vallejo

DABNER, MARY   Dated: 9 Nov. 1893   #2890
           Age 64   Died: 28 May 1898   Bk. G, Pg. 195-
                           Filed: 13 Jun. 1898   197

    Children: John Dabner, Louisa Foucha (?), William Dabner,
                 Anton Dabner, Frank Dabner, Manuel Dabner
    Executors: William Dabner, John King
    Witnesses: Peter Ehlinger, W.W. Scudder

DABNEY, MARTHA C.   Written: 28 Jun. 1888   #1767
                           Died: 21 Jul. 1888   Bk. D, Pg. 622
                           San Francisco
                           Filed: 20 Aug. 1888

    Sisters: Mrs. W.W. Porter of Santa Rosa, Miss Nannie
                 Dabney of Jackson, Miss., Mrs. T. Marshall
                 Miller of Jackson, Miss.

```
DAKIN, ZEPHENIAH          Written:  2 Nov. 1889              #1918
Petaluma       Age about  Died:    31 Dec. 1889    Bk. E, Pg. 199
               70         Rec.:    27 Jan. 1890
```

- Sister: Lousie (Louise?) Hill of England and children of sister Lousie
- Executor: J.L. Dinwiddie of Petaluma
- Witnesses: A.B. Hill, H.P. Brainerd both of Petaluma

```
DANA, ALFRED W.           Written: 15 Feb. 1883              #2333
Santa Rosa                Died:     7 Mar. 1893    Bk. F, Pg. 132
                          Rec.:    17 Jul. 1893
```

- Wife: Mary
- Children: Un-named
- Executor: Wife

```
DANCER, W. H.             Written: 12 Mar. 1894              #2396
Santa Rosa                Died:    16 Mar. 1894    Bk. F, Pg. 236
                          Rec.:     2 Apr. 1894
```

- Daughters: Mrs. G. L. Brainerd, Mrs. Sarah Holliday both of San Francisco
- Executor: Geo. A. Tupper
- Witnesses: G.A. Tupper, W.F. Cowan

```
DANIELS, HENRY            Written:  9 May 1889               #1855
Santa Rosa     Age 59     Died:    12 May 1889     Bk. E, Pg. 123
                          Rec.:    27 May 1889
```

- Bequest to: A.L. Fisher
- Executor: A.L. Fisher
- Witnesses: Frank Steele, Col. W. Finlaw

```
DARWIN, ANDREW M.         Written:  8 Jun. 1878              #1948
                          Codicil: 10 Jul. 1888    Bk. E, Pg. 226
                          Died:    28 Mar. 1890
                          Rec.:    21 Apr. 1890
```

- Adopted Daughter: Georgie E.
- Bequest to: James D. Collins
- Executor: Wife, with assistance of John A. Patterson of Tulare Co., CA and (relative) J.D. Collins of Fresno Co., CA
- Witnesses: E.C. Ferguson, J. Burchalter
- Codicil Witnesses: Frank B. Cornue, John S. Taylor

DAVIDSON, ANNA M.		Written:	29 Jun. 1886	#1568
Petaluma		Died:	24 Jul. 1886	Bk. D, Pg. 262
		Rec.:	20 Sep. 1886	

                    No mention in will of husband, Robert, of Canada
Children: Of brother, James McGarvey (deceased), of Canada;
                    of sister, Eliza Sterling (deceased), of Redwing, Minn.
Brothers: John McGarvey of Canada, Henry McGarvey of Ogdensburg, NY
Sisters: Martha Brown of Redwing, Minn.; Belle Sterling of Redwing, Minn.
Sister-in-Law: Mrs. Alexander Anderson of Toronto, Canada
Executor: John Shearer
Witnesses: Frank Shattuck, W.R. Veale

DAVIDSON, JACOB E.		Written:	12 Feb. 1870	#1445
		Died:	25 Nov. 1884	Bk. C, Pg. 629
		Rec.:	29 Dec. 1884	

Wife: Un-named
Children: Smith E., Augustus W., Anna T. Shelton, Jane E. Crane, Walter A., Alexander T., Christopher C., Susan C. Crane, Mary L. Williamson, Amanda K., Norvil R., Isabella I.
Executor: Son, Alexander
Witnesses: Murray Whallon, A.W. Middleton, third name unreadable

DAVIS, GARY V.		Written:	15 Jul. 1892	#2600
	Age 58	Died:	8 Jan. 1896	Bk. F, Pg. 449
		Filed:	27 Jan. 1896	

Wife: Louisa M. Davis
Executor: Louisa M. Davis
Witnesses: H. Kier, D.R. Gale

DAVIS, JOSIAS		Written:	15 Jun. 1888	#1941
Santa Rosa	Age 68	Died:	10 Mar. 1890	Bk. E, Pg. 224
		Rec.:	15 Apr. 1890	

Wife: Martha Ann
Sons: Walter S., Preston R., Charles N.
Executor: Wife
Witnesses: F.G. Nagle, F.R. Williams

DAVISON, JOHN   Written: 25 Mar. 1892   #2210
                                 Died: 1 May 1892   Bk. E, Pg. 620
                                 San Francisco
                                 Rec.:   31 May 1892

  Bequest to
  Friends: Martha Jones, J.F. Parker
  Executor: Martha Jones
  Witnesses: A.D. Laughlin, Jno. G. Pressley both of Santa Rosa

DAVISSON, JESSE   Written: 28 Nov. 1854   # 40
(DAVIDSON)   Filed: 9 May 1857 Bk. Wills, Pg. 4-
                                                                                                      5

  Daughter: Elizabeth Burris
  Sons: Daniel (eldest), Thomas (second)
  Executor: Daniel Davisson
  Witnesses: Frank W. & D.O. Shattuck

DAWSON, LOUISA   Written: 6 Jul. 1891   #2211
                                 Died: 26 Apr. 1892   Bk. E, Pg. 617
                                 Rec.:   23 May 1892

  Daughter: Margaret
  Executor: Mrs. L.W. Burris
  Witnesses: Wm. E. McConnell, M.J. Striening

DAY, ELIAS   Written: 12 Mar. 1872   # 658
                                 Died: 4 Oct. 1873
                                 Filed: 15 Dec. 1873

  Bequests to: Eliza M. McElroy, Louisa Renfrow, Loreta
              Lewis
  Sons: Stephen, Elias Edwin Day, Damras Shrimplin
  Executors: Stephen Day, Wm. McElroy
  Witnesses: Sam H. Rupe, J.T. Seawell

DAY, JOSEPH W.   Written: 26 Sep. 1898   #2966
Santa Rosa   Age 64   Died: 3 Jan. 1899   Bk. G, Pg. 243-
                                 Filed: 6 Feb. 1899   245

  Wife: Mary E.
  Sons: Louis Franklin Day, Henry Wayne Day, Dana W.
              Day
  Daughters: Sarah C. Russ, Mary Alice White
  Executor: Wife
  Witnesses: Frank P. Doyle, A.B. Ware both of Santa Rosa

```
DAY, LOUIS T.              Written:   9 Mar. 1895              #2525
San Francisco              Died:     11 Mar. 1895    Bk. F, Pg. 357
                           Rec.:     22 Apr. 1895

    Wife:        Belle
    Executor:    Wife
    Witnesses:   Ben W. Day, Libbie Sponogle


DECARLY, J. B.             Dated:     8 May  1896              #3136
Duncans Mills  Age 44      Died:      6 Mar. 1900    Bk. G, Pg. 406
                           Filed:    16 Apr. 1900

    Wife:        Modesta DeCarly
    Children:    Names and numbers not mentioned
    Executor:    Modesta DeCarly
    Witnesses:   C.E. Field, T.B. Moore of Duncan's Mill


DEITRICH, GOTTLIEB         Written:  26 Sep. 1886              #3483
Sebastopol     Age 57      Died:     15 Jul. 1902    Bk. H, Pg. 133
                           Filed:    28 Jul. 1902

    Wife:        Albertine
    Step-
    Children:    Jeanne Elonore Hoffstetter, Jeanne Hoffstetter
    Executor:    Wife
    Witnesses:   Issac Parker, C. Wightman both of Sebastopol;
                 Alexander Wiley


DELAHANTY, JAMES           Written:   7 Jun. 1893              #2341
Bodega Tnsp.               Died:     17 Jul. 1893    Bk. F, Pg. 138
                           Rec.:     21 Aug. 1893

    Brother:     Patrick Delahanty
    Grandniece:  May Delahanty
    Nephew:      G. Patrick Delahanty of Bodega Tnsp.
    Witnesses:   Despard Taylor, W.J. Cunninghame


DEMARTIN, JOSEPHINE        Written:  14 Feb. 1889              #1839
Petaluma                   Died:      4 Mar. 1889    Bk. E, Pg. 114
Widow                      San Francisco
                           Rec.:      1 May  1889

    Children:    Of un-named deceased daughter; Julieta Tomasini
                 (7½), Lila Tomasini (5½), Valdo Tomasini (2½)
    Halfbrother: Manuel H. Girardin of San Francisco
    Executor:    Manual H. Girardin
    Witnesses:   W.L. Luther, Harold Leach
```

DEMARTINI, JOSEPH   Written: 16 Mar. 1901   #3503
                         Died: 24 Aug. 1902   Bk. H, Pg. 142
                         Filed: 2 Sep. 1902

  Wife: Johanna DeMartini
  Daughters: Rosa DeMartini, Lucy Guinassa, Mary Demartini,
              Jenny Biagi
  Sons: Paul DeMartini, John DeMartini, Frank J. DeMartini
  Witnesses: L. Quartaroli, Geo. H.H. Cornelius both of Sonoma

DENMAN, EZEKIAL   Written: 13 Sep. 1892   #2460
Petaluma   Died: 16 Dec. 1894   Bk. F, Pg. 336
Co-owner of Argus   Rec.:   14 Jan. 1895

  Wife: Isabel
  Sister: Fannie Cassidy
  Children: Frank H., Nellie L., Ida B. McNear, John R.,
              Catherine D., Carrie E. Allen of Rockville, Ind.
  Executors: Sons, Frank and John; Geo. P. McNear
  Witnesses: H.B. Higbee, D.B. Fairbanks

DERBY, A. B.   Written: 22 Dec. 1875   #2692
Petaluma   Died: 8 Dec. 1896   Bk. F, Pg. 583
                         Filed: 4 Jan. 1897

  Wife: Mrs. A.B. Derby
  Executor: Mrs. A.B. Derby
  Witnesses: N.P. Brainerd, John E. Guinn of Petaluma

DETURK, ISAAC   Written: 18 May 1893   #2621
                         Died: 16 Mar. 1896   Bk. F, Pg. 491
                         Filed: 6 Apr. 1896

  Nephew: Wm. S. DeTurk of Petaluma
  Brothers: Abraham DeTurk of Sumner Co., Kans.; Louis P.
              DeTurk of Morgan Co., Ind.
  Sisters: Sarah Hammond of Morgan Co., Ind.; Mariah
              Shireman of Morgan Co., Ind.; Hannah Orner of
              Nuckolls Co., Neb.
  Executor: Wm. H. Lumsden
  Witnesses: L.W. Burris, M.J. Striening, Wm. E. McConnell

DIANDO, G. R.   Written: 24 Jul. 1889   #1892
Santa Rosa   Age 39   Died: 25 Jul. 1889   Bk. E, Pg. 159
                         Rec.:   21 Oct. 1889

  Brother: Domenico
  Executors: A.J. Mills, P. Bertolani
  Witnesses: Francisco Guidotti, Florindo Guidotti

DINNING, JULIA A. Healdsburg	Written: Died: Rec.:	21 Jun. 1892 4 Jul. 1892 19 Sep. 1892	#2241 Bk. F, Pg. 75

- Daughters: Susan Frances Capell, Mrs. Lucy Knight (deceased), Mrs. Ellen James (deceased)
- Grand-Children: John Paul James, Joseph Knight, Emma Knight
- Executor: Daughter, Frances
- Witnesses: E.M. Norton, Louisa F. Norton

DODGE, SUSAN D.	Written: Died: Filed: Rec.:	19 Jul. 1882 25 Aug. 1882 18 Sep. 1882 25 Apr. 1883	#1260 Bk. C, Pg. 286

- Sons: Henery Lavalley (Lovalla) (50), Daniel T. Lavalley (Lovalla)
- Daughters: Caroline Hendricks, Sarah A. Robinson (perhaps Bosworth), Theresa Spergen, Jane Thompson (deceased)
- Executor: L.A. Norton of Healdsburg, CA
- Witnesses: William D. Owen, Edward Leemoine

DONALDSON, JOHN	Written: Died: Filed:	13 May 1875 3 Jun. 1875 29 Jun. 1875	# 749 Bk. B, Pg. 166

- Wife: Maria
- Executor: Maria Donaldson
- Witensses: A.L. Farrar, G.W. Brush, Charles Doescher

DONNER, GEORGE	Written: Died: Filed:	17 Jan. 1874 10 Feb. 1874 10 Mar. 1874	# 673

- Wife: Margaret J.
- Child: Un-named
- Executors: John Walker, S. Green McMahon
- Witnesses: Albert Armstrong, Jas. Martin

DOPKINS, SAMUEL	Dated: Died: Filed:	3 Dec. 1858 Not given 13 Jan. 1859	# 157

- Wife: Christiana Dopkins
- Executor: Not named
- Witnesses: Frank W. Shattuck, George Pearce

```
DOUGHERTY, ELLEN          Written:  15 Aug. 1882              #1546
Petaluma                  Died:      7 Apr. 1886    Bk. D, Pg. 208
                          Rec.:     10 Jun. 1886

    Daughters:   Mary Keenan, Annie Small
    Son:         P.E.
    Executor:    Brother, Peter Donohue (deceased by 1886 and his
                 son J.M. appointed by court)
    Witnesses:   Patrick A. Foley, E.S. Lippitt


DOUGLAS, JOHN             Written:  11 Jul. 1885              #1908
Borough of Leicester,     Died:     18 Mar. 1889    Bk. E, Pg. 268
England                   Cloverdale
                          Filed:    18 Apr. 1890

    Sisters:     Margaret, Isabella, Agnes, Barbara, Jane all of
                 Isle of Arran
    Brothers:    James, Archibald, Gilbert
    Executors:   Bryce Douglas of Leicester, James McCall
    Witnesses:   W. Maurice Williams, Chas. Beaumont


DOUGLAS, ROBERT           Written:  22 Apr. 1886              #1804
            Age 66        Died:     30 Nov. 1888    Bk. E, Pg.  32
                          Filed:    24 Dec. 1888

    Wife:        Hannah
    Daughter:    Emma Irene Roberts
    Executor:    Alex. Wiley of Analy Tnsp.
    Witnesses:   B.B. Allen, John Walker both of Sebastopol


DOZIER, A. W.             Written:   1 Aug. 1874              # 716
Santa Clara               Died:     31 Oct. 1874    Bk. B, Pg. 120
                          Filed:     7 Dec. 1874

    Brother:     Melville Dozier
    Others:      E.C. Dozier, Alvin Dozier, Roland ---
                 (relationships undetermined)
    Executor:    Melville Dozier
    Witnesses:   None


DRAPER, BARBARA ANN       Written:  21 Jan. 1870              # 395

    Daughters:   Lucinda Jones, Emeline Shumaker
    Son:         James Satterfield
    Grandsons:   Reuben Edmunds, Joseph Edmunds
    Grand-
    Daughter:    Mary Edmunds
    Husband:     David Peters (Intended)
    Witnesses:   Z. Middleton, Wm. L. Anderson
```

```
DRAPER, ELIZABETH            Written:   15 Jun. 1893              #2545½
Healdsburg      Age 60       Codicil:   11 Mar. 1895
                             ---         8 Jul. 1895

    Husband:       J.H.
    Nephew:        Joseph Ryan of Clio, La.
    Codicil Adds
    Niece:         Margaret Armstrong of Newport, RI
    Executor:      C.W. Weaver
    Witnesses:     John Wallace Wilson, J.T. Coffman


DRAPER, REUBEN               Dated:      9 Sep. 1867              # 395
                             Died:      14 Aug. 1868
                             Filed:     10 Oct. 1868

    Wife:          Barbara Ann Draper
    Admn.:         Barbara Ann Draper
    Witnesses:     T.M. Ames, J.P.; Emeline Shoemake; Nancy Ann
                   Satterfield


DRESS, DIEDREICH C.          Written:    3 Oct. 1873              #1865
Petaluma        Age 48       Died:      10 May  1889         Bk. E, Pg. 134
                             Filed:      8 Jul. 1889

    Wife:          Maria A.C. (Lohrmann)
    Executor:      Wife
    Witnesses:     A. Morstadt, I.G. Mayer


DRESEL, EMIL                 Dated:     11 Aug. 1865              # 419
San Francisco   Age 46       Died:      27 Jun. 1869
                             Filed:     30 Aug. 1869

    Friend &
    Partner:       Jacob Gundlach
    Brother:       Julius Dresel of San Antonio, Tx.
    Executor:      Jacob Gundlach
    Witnesses:     John A. Reichert, A.V. Nohl both of San Francisco


DRESEL, JULIUS               Written:   19 Feb. 1891              #2149
                             Died:       7 Dec. 1891         Bk. E, Pg. 509
                             Weisbaden, Germany
                             Rec.:      18 Jan. 1892

    Children:      Carl, Helene, Gustav
    Executor:      Son, Carl
    Witnesses:     Geo. Engler, Jesse Burris
                   In partnership with Theo Blanckenburg in firm of
                   Dresel & Co.
```

```
DRISCOLL, JANE E          Written:  7 Nov. 1884              #2546
                          Died:    28 Jun. 1895   Bk. F, Pg. 389
                          Rec.:    29 Jul. 1895
```

- Husband: Lemuel R. (deceased)
- Sister: Maria L. Wilson of Fall River, Mass.
- Brother: Henry C. Wilkie, Teniton (?) Four Corners, RI
- Executor: Wm. C. Cr--lon
- Witnesses: M.V. Corley, D.B. Morgan both of Cloverdale

```
DRISCOLL, LEMUEL R.       Written: 28 Dec. 1882              #1322
Cloverdale    Age about  Died:    10 Apr. 1883   Bk. C, Pg. 389
              50         Rec.:    12 Jul. 1883
```

- Wife: Jane E.
- Executor: Wife
- Witnesses: D.B. Morgan, second witness unreadable

```
DROSBACK, ANDREW          Written: 18 Sep. 1893              #2352
                          Died:    24 Sep. 1893   Bk. F, Pg. 173
                          Rec.:    30 Oct. 1893
```

- Wife: Frederika
- Sons: Not named
- Executor: Wife
- Witnesses: Simon Graham, Thomas Crawford

```
DRUMMOND, JOHN HAMILTON   Written: 28 Aug. 1889              #1914
Glen Ellen                Died:    20 Dec. 1889   Bk. E, Pg. 190
                          Rec.:    13 Jan. 1900
```

- Wife: Frances (Bioletti)
- Daughters: Elizabeth, Roberta, Kathleen
- Guardians: Of any minor children: Parents, David & Elizabeth (Kelsey)
- Brother: Patrick Hamilton Drummond
- Sister: Eliza P. Gunn
- Executors: Mrs. K.F. Warfield of Glen Ellen; Henry Perry, Atty. of San Francisco; Eliz. K. Drummond, David Drummond, Patrick H. Drummond, Eliza P. Gunn all of Dublin, Ireland
- Witnesses: Edward P. Ryan, John J. Morgan both of San Francisco

DUCKER, SARAH		Dated:	15 May 1897	#3146
		Died:	31 Mar. 1900	Bk. G, Pg. 416
		Filed:	23 Apr. 1900	

Daughters: Susan J. Brown of Washington Co., Oregon; Mary Amanda Starvolt (deceased)
Children: Maria Benjamin, Andrew Ducker, Benjamin Ducker, John Ducker
Children: Of deceased daughter Mary Amanda Starvolt: Alice Starvolt, Charles Starvolt
Children: Of John Ducker: Barta Ducker, Georgia Ducker
Children: Of Benjamin Ducker: Minnie Cook
Executor: Maria Benjamin
Witnesses: John T. Campbell, Rachel Brooks

DUNRING, FREDERICK		Dated:	12 Nov. 1877	#1884
Sonoma	Age 62	Revoked:	9 May 1888	Bk. E, Pg. 151
		Died:	20 Aug. 1889	
		Rec.:	13 Sep. 1889	

Wife: Dorothea
Son: Fred P.
Daughter: Agnes Julia
Witnesses: C.M. Harvey, Geo. W. Clark

DUNN, CALEB LATHROP	Written:	22 Apr. 1881	#1259
Sonoma	Died:	24 Apr. 1881	Bk. C, Pg. 276
	Filed:	11 Sep. 1882	

Wife: Julia Dunn of San Francisco
Brothers: Thomas M. of Sonoma City, Samuel A., James C.
Sisters: Mary Jane Pattison, wife of Wm.; Jeanette E., Margaret A.
Brother: John R.
Executors: James C. Dunn, Wm. Pattison
Witnesses: John A. Jenkins, George Meigh, H.R. Dorchester

DUNN, JOHN	Written:	12 Mar. 1874	# 691
	Died:	21 May 1874	
	Filed:	6 Jul. 1874	

Wife: Catherine G.
Children: Elizabeth, John Donald, Francis Richard
Executor: Wife
Witnesses: John Cavanaugh, Mrs. Lucretia A.A. Hatch

DUNN, THOMAS M.   Written: 12 Mar. 1883   #3030
         Age 62   Died: 18 May 1899   Bk. G, Pg. 297
                       Filed: 3 Jul. 1899

    Wife: Fannie Dunn
    Sons: E.M. Dunn, R.J. Dunn, Chas. Dunn, B.W. Dunn,
                 Lathrop Dunn, Harry Dunn, Willie Dunn
    Daughters: Josephine Dunn, Lillie Dunn, Fannie Dunn
    Executor: Wife, Fannie Dunn
    Witnesses: Wm. E. McConnell, Thos. Rutledge

DUTTON, EMILY   Written: 8 Jul. 1897   #2770
Santa Rosa   Died: 22 Jul. 1897   Bk. G, Pg. 57
                               Filed: 16 Aug. 1897

    Sons: Albert Warren Dutton, Frank Dutton, George
                 Washington Dutton
    Daughters: Lucilia Huntley, Emma Jane Denike, Ada Belle
                 McMinn, Lucina Dutton
    Bequest to: William Reed Dutton
    Executors: Geo. Washington Dutton, Lucina Dutton
    Witnesses: John T. Campbell, Charles Desilets

DYER, CLABORN   Written: 3 Jan 1878   #1029
                               Died: ---------
                               Filed: 25 Sep. 1879

    Brothers: Wm. A. Dyer of Savannah, Nelson Dyer
    Sisters: Louisa Dearin, Margaret Whitson
    Mother: Sarah Ditty
    Executor: Zachariah F. Gilmore
    Witnesses: W.E. Brown, M.D.; Hardin Asher; James Elliott

EDMINSTER, MARY L   Written: 15 Mar. 1892   #2207
Petaluma   Age Over Died: 9 Apr. 1892   Bk. E, Pg. 606
               50   Rec.:   9 May 1892

    Children: William S., James L., Jessie E. Brainerd
    Executor: Son-in-law, Henry P. Brainerd
    Witnesses: James D. Bailey, Wm. B. Haskell

EDWARDS, MARTHA ANN   Written: 14 Sep. 1898   #2948
Healdsburg   Age 51   Died: 14 Sep. 1898   Bk. G, Pg. 233
                         San Francisco
                         Filed: 19 Dec. 1898

    Daughter: Eva Jane Mills
    Son: Arthur Eden Edwards
    Executor: Emma G. Stockton
    Witnesses: Addie C. Bates, corner Post & Jefferson, Alameda, CA;
                 Rachel B. Stockton, Healdsburg, CA

```
EDWARDS, THOMAS           Written:   7 May 1872              # 559
                          Died:     26 Jun. 1872   Bk, B, Pg.   2

   Wife:        Elizabeth
   Children:    Edward; Thomas, Jr.; Elizabeth; James
   Executor:    Wife
   Witnesses:   Altemus McGuire, John Cavanaugh


EGGERS, H. F.             Dated:    17 May 1900              #3193
                          Died:     13 Aug. 1900   Bk. G, Pg. 445
                          Filed:    27 Aug. 1900

                "No relatives in this country"
                Frank Stegemonn
   Executor:    Frank Stegemonn
   Witnesses:   H.P. Brainerd, L.A. Wick


ELDRED, J. J. (JOHN)      Written:  22 May 1883              #1783
                          Filed:     5 Nov. 1888   Bk. D, Pg. 638

   Wife:        Nancy Emeline
   Witnesses:   Jennie Staley, D.A. Cazswell


ELMORE, MARY JANE         Written:  14 Nov. 1878             #2568
          Age 56          Died:     15 Mar. 1895   Bk. F, Pg. 423
                          Rec.:     14 Oct. 1895

   Daughter:    Annie Upham, wife of F.F., of Dixon, Ca.
   Sons:        John Edward Stephenson, Orvis Washington Elmore
   Executor:    Hiram T. Fairbanks of Petaluma
   Witnesses:   Wm. B. Haskell, M.H. Falkner both of Petaluma


ELMORE, SAMUEL O.         Written:  -- May 1870              # 602
                          Died:      2 Feb. 1873
                          Filed:     7 May 1873

   Wife:        Mary Jane
   Son:         Orvis
   Step-
   Children:    John Edward Stevenson, Anna Mary Upham
   Children:    By former wife, Abba C., Frederick, Adelaide
   Witnesses:   F.D. Colton, A.B. Derby, Fred. Hogg
```

(51)

EMERSON, WILLIAM J.	Written:	9 Apr. 1894	#2406
Analy Tnsp. Age 65	Died:	12 Apr. 1894	Bk. F, Pg. 243
	Rec.:	7 May 1894	

- Son: Charles Sidney (minor)
- Executors: Wm. Taylor of Green Valley, Chas. Johnson of Pleasanthill
- Witnesses: P.H. Atkinson, E.E. Mann both of Sebastopol

ENGELBERT, CHARLES W.	Written:	24 Apr. 1893	#2401
Sonoma Age 34	Died:	24 Mar. 1894	Bk. F, Pg. 221
	Santa Clara Co.		

- Wife: Eva C.
- Executor: Wife
- Witnesses: Carl Dresel, F. Grothaus

ENGELHART, FREDERICK	Written:	6 Jul. 1901	#3344
Petaluma	Died:	29 Jul. 1901	Bk. G, Pg. 505
	Rec.:	26 Aug. 1901	

- Children: Of brother John: August, Richard, Frederick, Mary, Lizzie
- Executor: Geo. Griess
- Witnesses: F.A. Meyer, A.L. Tibbitts

ENGLER, MATHIAS	Written:	8 Aug. 1874	#1014
Sonoma Tnsp.	Died:	26 Mar. 1879	Bk. C, Pg. 34
	Filed:	16 Jun. 1879	

- Wife: Hannah (present wife; previous wife deceased)
- Daughter: Emily Comelines, Rosa (over 3)(daughter by Hannah)
- Son: George
- Guardian: Of George, Jos. A. Williams
- Executor: Geo. H.H. Comelines
- Witnesses: Henry Winkler, Jr., Edw. Steiger

ENNIS, FRANK F.	Written:	19 Sep. 1891	#3045
Petaluma Age 56	Died:	4 Jul. 1899	Bk. G, Pg. 314
	Filed:	15 Aug. 1899	

- Wife: Sarah Jane Ennis
- Executor: Wife
- Witnesses: Wm. B. Haskell, John Fritsch, both of Petaluma

ETHRIDGE, DARIUS Cloverdale	Written: Died: Rec.:	8 Jun. 1888 3 Sep. 1894 24 Feb. 1896	#2602 Bk. F, Pg. 478

- Nieces: Mrs. Allie Collins of San Jose, Ca.; Emma Ethridge Barlow, Amy Fay Hendry, Athline Ethridge all of Michigan
- Holographic

EVANS, THOMAS Geyserville	Written: Died: Filed:	13 Nov. 1875 16 Nov. 1875 24 Jan. 1876	# 781 Bk. B, Pg. 223

- Wife: Mary Ellen
- Executor: Wife
- Witnesses: Z.Z. Wood, H. Wiedersheim, W.H. Adamson

FACE, SOLOMON	Written: Died: Filed:	18 Mar. 1874 13 Apr. 1874 11 May 1874	# 681

- Sister: Caroline Penington of Winchester, Randolph Co., Indiana
- Partner: Henry S. Miser
- Executors: Lewis R. Giles, Geo. Miller
- Witnesses: Donald Jewell, Mary Jewett

FAIO, ANTON BROWN AKA ANTOINE BROWN	Written: Died: Filed:	15 Jul. 1896 15 Jul. 1896 10 Aug. 1896	#2652 Bk. F, Pg. 530

- Wife: Frances Brown
- Daughters: Maria Brown Faio, Mariana Brown Faio, Amelia Brown Faio, Ida Brown Faio
- Executor: Frances Brown
- Witnesses: John King, F.A. Meyer

FALLON, MARY (CALAHAN)	Written: Died: Rec.:	26 May 1895 16 Jun. 1895 8 Jul. 1895	#2544 Bk. F. Pg. 380

- Husband: Martin
- Sister: Maggie Meehan (Sister Mary Magdalene)
- Daughter: Mary Josephine (minor)
- Executor: Husband
- Witnesses: Thos. Rutledge, Mrs. E.E. Reynolds both of Santa Rosa
- Holographic

FARMER, E. T.	Written:	8 Jan. 1885	#1504
Santa Rosa	Died:	20 Oct. 1885	Bk. D, Pg. 113
	Rec.:	9 Nov. 1885	

- Wife: Rebekah W.
- Children: Charles R., Henry Thos., Sarah Angeline Fox wife of C.M. of San Francisco, Lillie Bell, Francis Mary
- Executors: Columbus C. Farmer, Wm. E. McConnell
- Witnesses: Ben S. Wood, Frank B. Cornul (?)

FARRAR, JANE	Written:	10 Nov. 1884	#1888
	Died:	25 Sep. 1889	Bk. E, Pg. 163
	Filed:	21 Oct. 1889	

- Husband: Anderson S.
- Bequests: Irma Winfred Silsby, Harriet Silsby, daughters of Albion Waldow & Marcia Belle of Montesano, Washn. Terr.
- Executor: Husband
- Witnesses: H.C. Thompson, Wm. Brooks

FAULKNER, JAMES	Written:	4 Jul. 1882	#1268
Bodega	Codicil:	5 Jul. 1882	Bk. C, Pg. 35
	Died:	1 Oct. 1882	
	Filed:	11 Nov. 1882	

- Wife: Susanna
- Half-Brothers: Henry Spencer Jones, John Whitfield Jones
- Mother: Mary Rebecca Jones
- Brother: Richard Douglas Faulkner
- Executor: Wife
- Witnesses: Holographic, proof of handwiring: C.S. Smyth

FAWCETT, THOMAS	Written:	25 Aug. 1872	# 653
	Died:	13 Sep. 1873	
	Filed:	1 Dec. 1883	

- Wife: Mary Otis and our family
- Executor: Wife
- Witnesses: Jas. H. Ovendale, Douglas Church, Jas. Kennedy

```
FAY, HIRAM                    Written:  27 Apr. 1900              #3244
formerly of Aberdeen,         Died:     14 Dec. 1900    Bk. H, Pg. 16
Brown Co., So. Dakota         Napa Co.
                              Filed:    31 Dec. 1900
```

- Daughters: Lillie Ann Fay, Ida Fay both of Duluth, Minn.; Ora Fay; Adda Fay; Ido A. Fay; Lulu A. Fay
- Executor: None
- Witnesses: Dr. A.C. Griffith, R.F. Crawford both of Santa Rosa

```
FAY, WILLIAM JOSEPH           Dated:    23 Dec. 1870              # 471
                              Died:      8 Jan. 1871    Bk. A, Pg. 212
                              Filed:    20 Feb. 1871
```

- Mother: Bridget Teresa Fay
- Father: William Fay
- Brothers: Phillip Steven Fay, Jeremiah G. Fay, Edward P Fay, Thomas J. Fay
- Executor: Phillips Steven Fay
- Witness: Frank W. Shattuck

```
FEELY, BRIDGET                Written:   3 Oct. 1901              #3404
Santa Rosa     Age 64         Died:     21 Dec. 1901    Bk. H, Pg. 93
Widow                         Rec.:     13 Jan. 1902
```

- Sisters: Sarah Griffin, Catherine Coggins of Pawtucket, RI
- Nieces: Eliz. Stewart, Catherine Coggins, Catherine Dempsey all of Pawtucket, RI
- Grand-Niece: Annie Dempsey of Pawtucket, RI
- Bequest to: James Higgins, Thos. Higgins, Edward Higgins of Pawtucket, RI; Rev. J.M. Cassin of St. Rose Church, Santa Rosa; Sister Mary Alice of St. Vincent De Paul of San Francisco
- Sisters: Winnifred Kenney (deceased), Ellen ----(?) (deceased) both of Marysville, CA.
- Brother: Patrick Higgins (deceased) of Marysville, CA
- Brother-in Law: Michael Kenney (deceased) of Marysville, CA
- Niece: Catherine Hallinan, wife of Thos. of Currinebal, County Mayo, Ireland
- Executor: Sarah Griffin
- Witnesses: R.F. Crawford, E.H. Crawford

FERGUSON, JOHN F.		Written:	10 Dec. 1901	#3405
Cloverdale	Age 50	Died:	19 Dec. 1901	Bk. H, Pg. 98
		Rec.:	20 Jan. 1902	

- Mother: Emily Eliz.
- Sister: Mary
- Brothers: Robert, L.K., Joseph, James
- Executors: Henry Hubbard, John Barnes
- Witnesses: Jas. Avery, G.W. Hoyle

FERNALD, JOHNSON		Written:	4 Aug. 1887	#2086
Petaluma	Age 64	Died:	10 Jun. 1891	Bk. E, Pg. 403
		Rec.:	6 Jul. 1891	

- Wife: M. Lillian
- Son: Orlando
- Executor: Wife
- Witnesses: Geo. M. Saul, John P. Rodgers

FERNALD, MARY LILLIAN		Written:	10 Aug. 1893	#2377
Petaluma	Age 40	Died:	8 Jan. 1894	Bk. F, Pg. 207
		Rec.:	5 Feb. 1894	

- Son: Orlando Johnson Fernald
- Executor: Joseph Campbell
- Witnesses: Holographic

FERRETTI, LUIGI		Written:	16 Jun. 1889	#1880
Petaluma	Age 46	Died:	12 Jul. 1889	Bk. E, Pg. 150
		Rec.:	10 Sep. 1889	

- Wife: Maria
- Exeuctor: Wife
- Witnesses: Antonio Cereghino, J.P. Rodgers

FERRIS, JOHN MILTON		Written:	20 Aug. 1900	#3311
Guerneville		Died:	9 May 1901	Bk. H, Pg. 55
		Rec.:	3 Jun. 1901	

- Nephew: Chester Beach
- Executor: Eliz. Beach, sister
- Witness: Holographic

FICK, JOHN FREDERICK		Written:	20 Mar. 1888	#1743
	Age 46	Died:	28 Apr. 1888	Bk. D. Pg. 600
		Filed:	5 May 1888	

- Wife: Margretha Friedrike Fick
- Daughters: Annie Sophia Fick, Emma Mary Fick, Hermine Dorethe Fick
- Sons: John Frederick Fick, Henry William Fick
- Executors: Margrethe Friedrike Fick, John Schroder
- Witnesses: F.C. Nagle, M.H. Dignan

```
FIELD, THOMAS A.          Written:  28 Jul. 1874              # 713
                          Died:     ------------    Bk. B, Pg. 117
                          Filed:    13 Nov. 1874
```

- Wife: Emma Field
- Children: Racilla R. Flack, Ada E. Browning, Walter E. Field
- Executor: Walter E. Field
- Witnesses: J.W. Rase, E.K. Vaughn

```
FINE, ABRAHAM             Written:  26 Jun. 1888             #2276
                          Died:      6 Dec. 1892    Bk. F, Pg.  51
                          Rec.:     16 Jan. 1893
```

- Wife: Amanda
- Children: Narcissa T., Mrs. Mary M. Davis, Igdaliah (son)
- Step-Son(?): John S. Saunders
- Executor: Wife
- Witnesses: W.W. Wilson, Jos. H.P. Morris

```
FISHER, EDWARD            Written:  14 May  1855              # 267
                          Probate:  15 Feb. 1865 Bk. Wills Pg. 127
```

- Wife: Arabella
- Sons: Fenwick, Charles Edward, Samuel Hanson
- Daughters: Margt. Edward, Emilie Carson
- Executor: Wife
- Witnesses: Wm. Ross, P.M. Case

```
FISK, ANDREW JACKSON      Writted:   3 Aug. 1874              # 711
                          Died:      4 Aug. 1874    Bk. B, Pg. 112
                          Filed:     9 Nov. 1874
```

- Wife: Clara S. Fisk
- Executors: Clara S. Fisk, E.H. Vance
- Witnesses: Samuel Potter, E.H. Vance, J.C. Fisk

```
FITZGERALD, ENOS          Written:  27 Apr. 1887             #1636
Healdsburg    Age 31      Died:     29 Apr. 1887    Bk. D, Pg. 442
                          Rec.:     ------------
```

- Cousin: John M. Coons
- Sisters: Lucy (35), Alice (26) both of Creve Coeur, St. Louis Co., MO
- Brother: Marshall (30) of Creve Coeur, St. Louis Co., MO
- Executors: August Hardegen in Calif., John W. McElhinney of Claytom, MO in places other than Calif.
- Witnesses: J.W. Rose, Peter Fortier

FIX, JOSHUA   Written: 8 Feb. 1901   #3527
Sebastopol   Age 70   Died: 30 Oct. 1902   Bk. G, Pg. 524
                              Probate: 8 Dec. 1902

   Brother: Jesse K. of Hanford, CA
   Niece: Mary Ann Smith, daughter of Eliz. Tyler (deceased)
   Grand-
   Nieces: Serena Tyler, Viola Tyler both of San Francisco;
                Josephine Tyler of Nome, Alaska
   Nephew: Joseph Leander Tyler
   Bequests: Maria Pierce, Delila Jane Bush, Louisa Farris
   Executor: Geo. Baxter
   Witnesses: Wm. Douglas, Wm. T. Searles

FLOGDELL, DAVID WICKHAM   Dated: 22 Apr. 1856   # 43
              Age 30   Died: 23 Jun. 1856   Bk. A, Pg.   8
                           Filed: 14 May 1856

   Wife: Honora
   Executor: Wife
   Witnesses: John O Murray, Thomas Fulcher Baylis

FOLGER, HIRAM   Written: 1 Aug. 1881   #2145
                              Died: 25 Dec. 1891   Bk. E, Pg. 525
                              Rec.:   25 Jan. 1892

   Brother: Seth Folger
   Sister: Elizabeth Macy
   Niece: Lizzie R. Macy
   Executor: Brother
   Witnesses: Harry Macy, Wm. F. Geiman both of San Francisco

FORTIER, PETER   Written: 15 Apr. 1890   #1954
Healdsburg   Age 33   Died: 18 Apr. 1890   Bk. E, Pg. 240
                              Rec.:   12 May 1890

   Wife: Hattie
   Sons: Peter, Edward, Willie (Hattie's son)
   Executor: J.W. Rose
   Witnesses: W. R. Madeira, H.C. Murphy

FOWLER, STEPHEN L   Written: 21 May 1867   # 375
                Age 42   Filed: 7 Apr. 1868

   Wife: Phebe E.
   Parents: Stephen C. Rebecca
   Sons: Edgar James, William Warren
   Executors: Phebe E. Fowler, Jas. E. Fowler, John H. Fowler
   Witnesses: C.P. Soper, Wm. Withrow both of Valley Ford

```
FOX, OTTO                    Written:  5 Aug. 1893          #2940
New York, NY                 Died:     5 Nov. 1898    Bk. G, Pg. 303
                             Filed:    13 Mar. 1899
```

- **Wife:** Rose
- **Executor:** Wife, Jesse I. Eppinger
- **Witnesses:** Chas. O. Ehlert, 92 1st St. New York, NY; Albert Cyriax, 619 Jefferson Ave., Brooklyn, NY

```
FRAISIER, JULIA A.           Written:  18 Oct. 1872         # 590
                             Died:     21 Dec. 1872
                             Filed:    29 Jan. 1873
```

- **Husband:** John F.
- **Children:** Addie E., Wm. J.
- **Guardians:** Of Addie & Wm.: Julia's sisters, Mary A. & Margt. J. Denning of San Francisco
- **Executor:** James Burke
- **Witnesses:** Nathan M. Hedges, Frank W. Shattuck

```
FRAZEE, CHARLES D.           Written:  13 Jan. 1892         #2344
                             Died:     13 Aug. 1893   Bk. F, Pg. 151
                             Rec.:     11 Sep. 1893
```

- **Wife:** Isabella I.
- **Sons:** Edwin Charles, Henry DeWitt (minor)
- **Admn:** Wife; son, Charles
- **Witnesses:** J.A. Lovelady, James M. Godman

```
FREDERICHS, GERHARD          Written:  7 May 1890           #2634
Analy Tnsp.                  Died:     1 May 1896     Bk. F, Pg. 501
                             Rec.:     25 May 1896
```

- **Wife:** Francisco
- **Children:** Sophia A. Barnes, George A. Frederichs, Mary Frederichs, William Frederichs, Caroline Frederichs, Johanes Frederichs, Rosa Frederichs
- **Executor:** Wife, Frederick A. Janssen
- **Witnesses:** Fred. A. Janssen, John S. Saunders

```
FREEBORN, ELEANOR            Written:  24 Dec. 1880         #2536
San Francisco                Died:     28 Apr. 1895   Bk. F, Pg. 372
                             Rec.:     11 Jun. 1895
```

- **Brother:** Wm. Freeborn
- **Sister:** Mary Jane wife of Benjamin Goodwin
- **Children:** Of sister Mary Jane: James Livingston Goodwin, Wilhelmina Goodwin
- **Executor:** Brother, William
- **Witnesses:** Geo. H. Palmer, James Freeborn

FREELAND, ARNOLD CLARK   Written: 25 Apr. 1857   # 44
                            Filed: 9 May 1857   Bk. A, Pg. 56

  Wife: Nancy N.
  Son: Albert Clark (minor)
  Executor: Wife
  Witnesses: Wm. Freeland, Julio Carillo, Jackson Temple

FREELAND, WILLIAM   Written: 13 Mar. 1858   # 114
                            Filed: 4 May 1858

  Wife: Ellen
  Father: Abraham
  Mother: Phebee
  Executor: Ellen Freeland
  Witnesses: Joel Crane, Wm. R. Roberts
            Land in Macomb Co., Mich.

FRREMAN, JOHN M.   Written: 20 Sep. 1883   #1997
Petaluma   Died: 27 Jul. 1890   Bk. E, Pg. 302
                            Rec.:   25 Aug. 1890

  Wife: Eliza Jane
  Step-
  Daughter: Alizia B. Cashdollar
  Children: Merrick Lewellen, Warren Israel, Charles John
            (minor), Marilla Eliza, Laura Lydia
  Executors: Merrick & Warren Freeman
  Witnesses: Adam F. Gunn of Berkeley, Wm. B. Haskell of
            Petaluma

FRITSCH, JOHN   Written: 25 Nov. 1899   #3475
                            Codicil: 15 May 1902   Bk. H, Pg. 126
                            Died: 1 Jun. 1902
                            Filed: 23 Jun. 1902

  Wife: Emma A. (also a previous deceased wife)
  Sons: Walter S., John Raymond
  Daughters: Kate A. Perry, Nellie L. Hedges
  Mentions: Wm. Zartman
  Executors: Sons
  Trustees: Sons, Petaluma Savings Bank
  Witnesses: Wm. B. Haskell, Thos. C. Denny both of Petaluma
  Codicil: Wm. B. Haskell, Mrs. Emily Heath
            Mentions real property on Liberty Street and Marin
            Street in Petaluma, Ca.

```
FRUITS, MARTHA ANN        Written:   26 Nov. 1884        #2663
         Age 71           Died:       1 Sep. 1896    Bk. F, Pg. 540
                          Rec.:      23 Sep. 1896
```

Son:	John V. Gauldin of Arkansas
Niece:	Laura Hall, wife of J.H.
Daughter:	Martha A. Zelhart, wife of Wm.
Sons:	Benj. F. Gauldin, Willis W. both of Los Angeles
Executor:	Son, Willis
Witnesses:	Matt Burnett, Jno. Brown both of Santa Rosa

```
FULKERSON, RICHARD        Written:    6 May 1882         #1695
                          Codicil:   30 Jul. 1887    Bk. D, Pg. 539
                          Died:      24 Nov. 1887
                          Filed:     19 Dec. 1887
```

Sons:	John Fulkerson, Stephen T. Fulkerson
Daughters:	Mrs. Ruth Barnes, Mrs. Phoebe Harris, Mrs. Mary Henderson
Grandsons:	Richard Fulkerson, Richard O. Barnes
Grand-Daughters:	Phoebe F. Harris, Julia Mize, Amanda Mooer, Mary Murdock
GreatGrand-Children:	Maud Hawkins, Mamie Hawkins, Mark Hawkins
Executors:	Jacob Harris, son-in-law; or John Fulkerson; or Stephen T. Fulkerson, Ruth Barnes, Phoebe Harris and Mary Henderson
Witnesses:	T.S. Fulkerson, T.M. Harris, Wm. E. McConnell, T.W. Burris, O.H. Hoag

```
FULTON, DAVID             Written:   29 Oct. 1872        #1391
Fulton   Age 70           Died:       4 Feb. 1884    Bk. C, Pg. 525
                          Rec.:       2 Jan. 1885
```

Grand-Daughter:	Albertina Manahan
Daughters:	Children of Ibby Gray (deceased); children of Mary Manahan (deceased); children of Susan Blair
Sons:	Children of Tilman (deceased); Thomas
Executors:	Friends, James Fulton and Jas. W. Gray
Witnesses:	A. Thomas, C.C. Farmer

```
FULTON, RICHARD           Written:   20 Apr. 1868        # 380
                          Died:      23 Jul. 1868
                          Filed:     12 Aug. 1868
```

Daughter:	Elizabeth Frank(?), heirs of Jane Huffman
Sons:	Thomas, James
Grandson:	Richard Tower
Executor:	James Fulton
Witnesses:	Chester Poole, Richard Stephenson Johnson

FURBER, GEO. CAMPBELL   Written: 13 May 1874   # 701
Cloverdale   Died: 5 Jul. 1874   Bk. B, Pg. 99
Physician & Surgeon   Rec.:   31 Aug. 1874

                    Nothing to wife under any circumstances
    Son: Wm. S.
    Daughters: Sarah, Georgianna, Henrietta
    Bequests to: Jas. F. Hoadley
    Witnesses: D.B. Morgan, Theo. Harper, S.L. Hamond, John Dixon

GALE, DEMUS   Died: 5 Jan. 1899   #2968
              Age 68   Filed: 6 Feb. 1899   Bk. G, Pg. 246

    Wife: Cordelia
    Sons: Wallace, Milton
    Daughters: Sophia McGrew, Lucy A. Mayfield, Alice Johnson,
                    Mary Roberts
    Executors: Wife, sons
    Witnesses: L.D. Gale, J.P. Rodgers both of Petaluma, Ca.
                    Description of real property in Petaluma

GANLIA, GEORGE   Written: 20 Aug. 1869   # 628
                           Died: 7 Jul. 1873
                           Filed: 4 Aug. 1873

    Bequests to: Delia Sullivan, widow of James; Geo. Sullivan (son)
                    and three other children
    Father: Francisco Ganlia of Malta
    Mother: Un-named
    Sister: Rosina
    Niece: Carmina
    Executor: John Maria Lamond
    Witnesses: Wm. D. Blip, S.R. Dickey

GARDNER, JOEL   Died: 18 Jan. 1903   #3563
Rock Valley, Iowa   Filed: 18 Feb. 1903   Bk. G, Pg. 568

    Wife: Emma R. Gardner
    Daughter: Effie L. Gardner
    Son: Glen A. Gardner (adopted)
    Executor: Emma R. Gardner
    Witnesses: C.W. Carter, Clemmie P. Carter

GARDNER, JOHN WM.   Written: 25 May 1894   #22455
Sebastopol   Died: 27 Aub. 1894   Bk. F, Pg. 305
                           Rec.:   8 Oct. 1894

    Sons: John William, George Edward (wife, Octavia)
    Executor: Wm. Rogers of Green Valley
    Witnesses: Wm. Symmonds, Eva Symmonds

GASKELL, ABIGAL   Written: 25 Apr. 1871   # 539
                           Filed: 6 May 1872

    Husband: Courtland Gaskill
    Nieces: Cordelia Bush, Alice Electa Barnes
    Nephews: Edward C. Barnes, Oscar Barnes
    Brothers: James Barnes of Wisconsin and his children:
                Anna, Wm., Chas., Frank; Samuel Barnes of
                New Buffalo, Indiana
    Executor: L.F. Carpenter
    Witnesses: Frank Shattuck, A.W. Lane

GATER, JAMES D.   Written: 9 Mar. 1893   #2315
North East, Erie Co.,   Died: 12 Mar. 1893   Bk. F, Pg. 99
PA   Rec.:   15 May 1893

    Daughter: Mrs. Helen Shearer and her four children
    Sons: James E., Frank I.
    Executor: Daughter
    Witnesses: George Madeira, E.M. Norton both of Healdsburg

GAYNOR, LUCY E.   Written: 22 Jan. 1920   #2605
       Age 87   Filed: 21 Oct. 1926   Bk. 5, Pg. 588

    Nephews: Walter Harry Sturgis, Guy Vans Sturgis
    Executors: Walter Harry Sturgis, Guy Vans Sturgis
    Witnesses: Frank P. Doyle, A.J. LeBaron

GIANELL, GIOCONDA   Written: 31 Oct. 1893   #2870
       Age 67   Died: 7 Apr. 1898   Bk. G, Pg. 166
                           Filed: 16 May 1898

    Sons: Vincenzo Gianella, Agostino Gianella
    Daughters: Terrisa Bisordi, Rosin Trembley
    Grandchild: Names not listed
    Executors: Four children
    Witnesses: D.R. Gale, M.H. Perrman both of Santa Rosa

GIBBONS, EDWARD   Written: 14 Jul. 1883   #1560
Knights Valley Age 65   Died: 30 May 1886   Bk. D, Pg. 242
                           Rec.:   13 Aug. 1886

    Wife: Catherine F.
    Daughter: Emilye Booth (29) wife of Wm. F., Berkeley, CA
    Executors: Wife, J. West Martin of Oakland, CA
    Witnesses: Wm. F. Booth, Frank McDonald of Knights Valley

GIBBS, ELIZABETH A.	Written:	8 Dec. 1887	#1727
	Died:	4 Mar. 1888	Bk. D, Pg. 489-
	Filed:	26 Mar. 1888	590

Daughter: Lizzie Wright Gibbs (about 33), adopted
Brothers: T.B. Albert (about 50) of Canton, Ohio; M. Albert (about 45) of Ohio
Executor: Guy E. Grosse
Witnesses: John Good, A.B. Ware

GIBBS, HENRY	Written:	4 Mar. 1887	#2018
Two Rock Valley	Died:	30 Oct. 1890	Bk. E, Pg. 320
	Rec.:	1 Dec. 1890	

Wife: Mary
Children: Ann Amelia Wooden, Edward Gibbs, Orcelia Purvine, Mary Manly, Elbert C. Gibbs, Frederick H. Gibbs, Carrie E. Gibbs
Executor: Wife
Witnesses: Wm. B. Haskell, F.A. Meyer both of Petaluma

GIBNEY, GEORGE		Written:	30 Dec. 1881	#3330
Cloverdale	Age 46	Died:	16 Jun. 1901	Bk. H, Pg. 60
		Rec.:	22 Jul. 1901	

Former Wife: Martha C. Gibney
Children: Mary A., Martha, Jesse Avis, James Tilden, W.H.
Executor: I.E. Shaw
Witnesses: Wm. E. McConnell, Jas. Anderson

GIBSON, JOHN	Written:	5 Mar. 1889	#2209
Glen Ellen	Died:	7 Apr. 1892	Bk. E, Pg. 604
	Rec.:	23 May 1892	

Wife: Annie E.
Executor: Wife
Witnesses: James A. Shaw, Alfred V. LaMotte

GILBERT, JACOB	Written:	22 Aug. 1874	# 727
	Filed:	29 Jan. 1875	Bk. B, Pg. 133

Wife: Jane A. Gilbert
Sons: Thomas A. Gilbert, Henry D. Gilbert, Platt B. Gilbert
Daughter: Mrs. Cornelia L. Allen
Grand-
Daughter: Jane P. Gilbert
Executors: Sons, Thomas and Henry
Witnesses: E.S. Lippitt, J.R. Jewell

```
GILES, LEWIS R.          Written:  11 Mar. 1873              #1313
Healdsburg               Died:     20 Apr. 1883    Bk. C, Pg. 375
                         Rec.:     10 Jul. 1883
```

Wife:	Purlina A.
Daughters:	Emma Roberts, Helen T. Boon, Frances F. Giles, Georgie --- (?)
Executor:	Wife
Witnesses:	Daniel G. Jewett, G.W. Wertz

Per statement by mother, made 21 May 1883:
Emma (now) Cripps (about 35); Frances (now) Dyer (about 31) of Chicago, Ill.; Georgie Goodspeed (about 29) of Healdsburg; children of Hellen T. Boon (deceased): Eva (9) of Chicago and Jessie (7), Maud (6), May (3) all of Pewaukee, Wisc.

```
GILL, ANN                Written:  11 Oct. 1882              #3424
Petaluma                 Codicil:   1 Aug. 1888    Bk. H, Pg. 105
                         Died:     20 Jan. 1902
                         Rec.:     27 Jan. 1902
```

Children:	Jane C. Skinner, wife of Geo. R.; Sarah F. Aylsworth, wife of Geo. W.; Antoinette J. Gill; Geo. Q. Gill of Tulare Co., Ca.; Lavinia B. Locke, wife of True, of Virginia City, Nev.; Mary B. Taylor (deceased), wife of Frances E., of Tulare Co., Ca.; Elizabeth Cramer (deceased), wife of David R., of Mendocino Co., Ca.
Grand-Children:	Of Mary Taylor: Medora A. Taylor, Chester P. Taylor, John Francis Taylor, Ernest M. Taylor; of Elizabeth Cramer: Albert A. Cramer, David Fleet Cramer, Charles Walter Cramer
Executors:	Four daughters
Codicil Executors:	Sarah F. Aylsworth, Lavinia B. Locke
Witnesses:	Wm. B. Haskell, M.H. Faulkner both of Petaluma
Codicil:	Frank P. Furry, Wm. G. Stahl

```
GILL, SARAH V.           Written:  28 May 1894               #2484
Geyserville              Died:     27 Dec. 1894    Bk. G, Pg. 323
                         Rec.:     17 Dec. 1894
```

Husband:	Jas. W. (former)
Son:	Charles (only child)
Mother:	Eliz. Wisecarver
Executor:	Mother
Witnesses:	B.J. Davis, W.H. Teaby

```
GILLIAM, MITCHAEL        Dated:   8 Nov. 1869              #1257
(MITCHELL)               Died:    26 Jul. 1882    Bk. C, Pg. 266
Green Valley             Rec.:    31 Mar. 1883
```

Wife: Henrietta
Sons: David (minor), Cornelius
Daughters: Lieuhettie (minor), Rebecca (minor), Mary
             Sullivan, Rachel Bowman, Eliz. Ann Crow
Admn: David T.
Witnesses: John Dougherty, Wm. F. Beatty

Note: At the time of David's application for administration he gives names and ages of family members and residence of two who are out of Sonoma Co.:
Widow: Henrietta Gilliam (about 67)
Children: Mary Sullivan (about 44); Rachel Bowman (about 42) of Colfax, Washington Terr.; Cornelius (about 40) of Millville, Shasta Co., CA; Eliz. Ann Crow (about 37); David T. (32); Lieu Hattie Patterson (27); Rebecca Jane Parena (?) (24)

```
GILLISPIE, HENRY         Written: 12 Mar. 1898              #2854
                         Filed:   11 Apr. 1898    Bk. G, Pg. 144
```

Bequest to: Clara E. Davidson
Executor: Clara E. Davidson
Witnesses: John S. Blackburn, Geo. R. Robuson both of Petaluma

```
GIONELLA, LORENZO        Written: 5 Mar. 1892               #2208
Santa Rosa    Age 68     Died:    18 Apr. 1992    Bk. F, Pg.  13
                         Rec.:    16 May  1892
```

Wife: Gioconda
Children: Vincenzo (about 42) of Moore's Sta. Butte Co., CA;
             Agostino (about 40) of Moore's Sta. Butte Co., CA;
             Rosin Tremblay (38) of Sebastopol; Terrisa
             Bissordi (about 30) of Sonoma Co.
Executors: Wife and son Vincenzo
Witnesses: S.P. Whiting, R.W. Elliott

```
GIVENS, ROBERT R         Written: 29 Feb. 1892              #2197
Healdsburg               Died:    7 Mar. 1892    Bk. E, Pg. 505
                         Rec.:    11 Apr. 1892
```

Children: Mrs. Elizabeth N. Nichols, George D. Givens,
             David G. Givens, Anna J. Givens, Grace May Givens,
             Ada Givens (minor)
Brother: Samuel L. of Merced Co. as Ada's Guardian
Executor: M. Raabe of Healdsburg
Witnesses: John N. Ferguson, W.W. Moreland both of Healdsburg

```
GIVLIN, SARAH            Written:  4 Jul. 1889              #1872
Analy Tnsp.              Filed:    8 Jul. 1889

   Sister:      Mrs. Mary Johnson, Mrs. Margaret Cain
   Brosthers:   Owen Rafferty, Patrick, Michael
   Executor:    Patrick Rafferty
   Witnesses:   Mrs. S.J. Folger, J. Mary Rafferty


GLASCOCK, WILLIAM        Witnessed: 16 Feb. 1869            # 408
Healdsburg    Age about  Died:      26 Feb. 1869
              50

   Wife:        Mary Ann
   Executor:    Wife
   Witnesses:   H.M. Willson, Sam H. Rupe


GLENN, JOHN              Written:  1 Oct. 1883              #1374
Santa Rosa               Died:     10 Nov. 1883    Bk. C, Pg. 477
                         Rec.:     10 Nov. 1884

   Wife:        Margaret
   Sons:        Wm. P. of Modesto, CA; James H. (35)
   Daughters:   Sarah J. Barnes (42) of San Francisco;
                Bettie Wynant (38) of Santa Cruz; Mary Parsons
                (33); Lillie May Glenn (17); Harriet Putnam
                (45); children of Alice Wescoatt (deceased):
                Effie Florilla (6), Nelson Glenn (8)
   Executor:    Wife
   Witnesses:   Jas. Wyatt Oates, Louis W. Juilliard


GLENN, MARGARET          Written:  5 Mar. 1895              #2520
Santa Rosa    Age 70     Died:     21 Mar. 1895    Bk. F, Pg. 352
                         Rec.:     8 Apr. 1895

   Children of: Lille Fohrion (deceased daughter)
   Grandson:    Glenn Wescott (son of deceased daughter)
   Son:         Wm. P.
   Exceutor:    Mary F. Parsons
   Witnesses:   James W. Oates, J.W. Jesse


GOFORTH, ELIZABETH A.R.  Dated:    27 Aug. 1900             #3204
                         Died:     3 Sep. 1900     Bk. G, Pg. 458
                         Dated:(?) 17 Sep. 1900

   Friends:     Mrs. Nettie Thompson, Miss Mary E. Slater,
                Mrs. L.M. Rogers, Mrs. M. Forbes, Mr. R.C.
                Moody, F.C. Loomis
   Executor:    Mr. R.C. Moody
   Witnesses:   Nellie J. Coulter, Wm. E. McConnell
```

GOLDBERG, NATHAN   Dated: 11 Jul. 1897   #2986
          Age 73   Died: 7 Feb. 1899   Bk. G, Pg. 263
                          Filed: 15 Feb. 1899

    Wife: Elizabeth Goldberg (formerly Reid)
    Son: Nathan Goldberg
    Executor: Elizabeth Goldberg
    Witnesses: Eleanor Atkinson, P.H. Atkinson

GOOD, JOHN   Written: 5 Dec. 1883   #2222
Santa Rosa   Died: 29 May 1892   Bk. E, Pg. 629
                          Rec.:   20 Jun. 1892

    Wife: Helen M. (2nd)
    Children: James Good of St. Louis, Mo.; Ellen Virginia
                Schaffer of Cincinatti, Ohio; Mrs. Frances
                Isabella Wood of Cincinatti, Ohio; Mrs. Alice
                Maria Foss of Brooklyn, NY; Mrs. Sarah Jane
                Comegys of Keokuk, Iowa; Chas. Anthony Good of
                Cincinatti, Ohio; Mrs. Mary Ann Morey of Santa
                Rosa; John William Good of Moline, Ill.; Harry
                Carlton Good of Vallejo, Ca.; Ellen Josephine Good
                of Santa Rosa; Walter Clifford Good of Santa Rosa
    Executors: Son, Harry Carlton to act in California; son, John
                Wm. to act in Ohio and Illinois
    Witnesses: Thomas Houseworth, Columbus Bartlett both of San
                Francisco
    Codicil: Dated 24 Aug. 1885 adds son, Walter, as additional
                executor

GRAETZEN, STEPHAN AKA   Written: 30 Aug. 1887   #1686
GRATZER   Died: 30 Sep. 1887   Bk. D, Pg. 520
Santa Rosa   Filed: 17 Oct. 1887

    Wife: Kriszintia
    Executor: Wife
    Witnesses: Anton Buhlmann, John Brown

GRAHAM, ANN   Written: 10 Apr. 1871   # 637
                           Died: 17 Apr. 1871
                           Filed: 15 Sep. 1873

    Sons: Thomas (received 10¢), Arthur
    Daughters: Mary L., Ida J.
    Executor: James Learz
    Witnesses: D.M.W. Seaton, J.P. Rodgers

```
GRATER, JOHN F.              Written: 13 Nov. 1893              #2487
Healdsburg      Age 58       Died:    25 Nov. 1894      Bk. F, Pg. 330
                             Rec.:    31 Dec. 1894
```

Wife:	Catherine
Sisters:	Christine Goller, Barbara Funk, Elendra Grater all of Buchenbach, Kunzelsan Wertemberg, Germ.
Nephews:	Henry M. Goller of Concord, Ca.; John Goller of Petaluma; Christ Nicklas of Healdsburg
Niece:	Katarina Walk of Bodenhog, Kunzelsan Wertemberg, Germ.
Bequests to:	Wm. Funk of San Francisco, Mrs. Grace Hammill of Healdsburg
Executor:	J.W. Rose
Witnesses:	N.B. Coffman, C.H. Pond

```
GRAVES, B. F.                Written: 2 Sep. 1901               #3359
Santa Rosa      Age 30       Died:    2 Sep. 1901       Bk. H, Pg. 64
                             Filed:   23 Sep. 1901
```

Wife:	Kittie Ann
Daughters:	Ethelyn P., Lorene May
Son or Brother (?):	Xenophen B.
Executor:	Wife
Witnesses:	Mrs. W.R. Mead, Mrs. Mary E. Kohler, D.R. Gale all of Santa Rosa

```
GRAVES, GEO. WALKER          Written: 6 Apr. 1888               #1971
Petaluma                     Died:    16 May 1890       Bk. E, Pg. 254
                             Rec.:    2 Jun. 1890
```

Wife:	Luella Baber
Children:	Georgie, Hill B.
Executor:	Wife
Witnesses:	M.D. Gosher, Frank W. Shattuck

```
GRAVES, WILLIAM H.           Written: 6 May 1886                #2309
San Francisco                Codicil: 24 Feb. 1891     Bk. F, Pg. 142
                             Died:    7 Apr. 1893
                             Rec.:    21 Aug. 1893
```

Half-Sisters:	Ella Barton, wife of Robert; Anna Benedict, wife of Edwin; Elizabeth Baldwin, wife of Abraham; Nellie Taylor, wife of Alfred
Nephews:	Wm. H. Barton, son of Robert; Edwin Joy
Bequests to:	Mary French, daughter of Abigail J. Wells; Marie Gordon (formerly Fien), formerly a resident of Stuttgart, Germ., now of Lausanne, Switz.; Frank W. and Daisy M., children of M. Gordon
Codicil:	Adds bequest to friend, Thos. B. Bishop of San Francisco
Executor:	Wm. Alvord, Pres. Bank of California, San Francisco
Witnesses:	W.M. Taylor, Andrus B. Howe both of Montclair, NJ

GRAY, GARRETT M.   Dated: 28 May 1897   #3000
            Age 70   Died: 5 Jun. 1897   Bk. G, Pg. 280
                          Filed: 10 May 1899

  Daughters: Frances Agnes Kidd, Millie Lucenda Pfister,
                Lottie L. Hamilton, Maud E. Walsh, Polly Ann
                Adcock, Carrie Gray, Laura Gray, Georgia Gray
  Sons: Samuel D. Gray, William T.B. Gray, Charles Gray
  Executor: Frances Agness Kidd
  Witnesses: T.J. Butts, Miss Laura Simmons

GREATHOUSE, GEO. L.   Written: 2 Mar. 1869   #1017
Ada Co., Idao Terr.   Filed: 15 Jul. 1869

  Wife: Louisa Elizabeth
  Executor: Wife
  Witnesses: Sarah B. Young, Ridgely Greathouse, C.C. Call
                all of Warm Springs, Ada Co., Idaho Terr.

GREEN, GEORGE D.   Written: 1 May 1890   #1968
Petaluma Rancho   Died: 11 May 1890
            Age 50   Rec.:   9 Jun. 1890

  Wife: Not named
  Son: George D.
  Daughters: Mary E.
  Others(?):   John A., Lyman, Jonathon, Sarah Maude
  Executor: Lyman Green
  Witnesses: F.A. Meyer, Wm. B. Haskell

GREEN, H. A.   Written: 27 May 1851 (1857?)   # 48
                          Probate: 30 Oct. 1851(?)

  Wife: Mary
  Son: Wm. Henry (minor)
  Brothers: Israel A., Philip H. both as guardians of Wm.
                Henry while in St. Louis, MO.
  Guardian: Jas. P. Taber, in Sonoma Co.
  Parents: Un-named
  Siblings: Un-named
  Executors: Jas. P. Taber, John Cameron, Peter Campbell
  Witnesses: Martin E. Cooke of Sonoma City, Jos. D. Bristol
                of Napa City

GREEN, WARREN   Written: 6 May 1899   #3291
Preston   Died: 20 Mar. 1901   Bk. H, Pg. 45
                          Rec.:   15 Apr. 1901

  Wife: Stella M.
  Children: Hazel G. Bowers, Isaac Leander, Myrtle, Warren
                Preston, Stella, Emily, Elisah
  Sisters: Delia G. Palmer, Caroline G. Spencer
  Executor: Wife, newphews: (1) P.H. Green, (2) Henry Hubbard,
                (3) Wellington Appleton

```
GREEN, WILLIAM           Written:  25 Oct. 1899          #3085
San Luis, Sonoma Co.     Died:      2 Nov. 1899    Bk. G, Pg. 359
           Age 78        Rec.:     11 Dec. 1899
```

- Wife: Un-named
- Children: Carrie Lund, Katie Wise, Wm. C., Louis K.
- Executor: Louis K.
- Witnesses: Robt. A. Poppe of Sonoma, W.C. Goodman of Schellville

```
GREGORY, ANN             Written:  19 Jun. 1875           # 761
           Age 56        Died:     20 Jun. 1875    Bk. B, Pg. 189
                         Filed:    25 Aug. 1875
```

- Son: Joseph M. Gregory
- Executor: Joseph Kelso of Bellevue, Jackson Co., Iowa
- Witnesses: Samuel Carstens, Michael McMahon

Holds mortgage on land in Washington Township, Jackson Co., Iowa against her

```
GREINER, FREDERICK       Written:  31 Jul. 1901          #3349
San Quentin,   Age 49    Died:      3 Aug. 1901    Bk. G, Pg. 511
Marin Co., Ca.           Filed:    26 Aug. 1901
```

- Sisters: Un-named
- Executor: F. McG. Martin
- Witnesses: F. McG. Martin of Santa Rosa, A. Drahms of San Quentin

```
GRIEST, PETER            Written:   7 Feb. 1884          #1389
Healdsburg     Age 62    Died:     15 Feb. 1884    Bk. C, Pg. 519
                         Rec.:     31 Dec. 1884
```

- Wife: Eliza (50), second wife
- Children: Mary Jane Cook (40), wife of Israel; Rebecca S. Young (35), wife of John; Agnes Black (32), wife of John; Alice Bolles (30), wife of W.A.; Artie (20)
- Grand-Daughter: Priscilla Braunsfield, wife of Wm. Hudson (Huelson ?)
- Executor: Israel Cook
- Witnesses: Jonas Bloom, J.D. Hassett

```
GRIGGS, JOSEPH H.        Dated:     3 Aug. 1895          #2759
           Age 76        Died:     23 Jun. 1897    Bk. G, Pg.  41
                         Filed:    26 Jun. 1897
```

- Grandson: Stewart Griggs, son of Achillas G. Griggs (deceased)
- Daughter: Hattie C. McDaniel, wife of L.J. McDaniel, of Glenn Co.
- Sons: William B. Griggs, Horas (Horace ?) R. Griggs
- Executors: W.B. Griggs, Horas R. Griggs
- Witnesses: W.J. Dogget, W.J. Dogget, Jr.

GROTHAS, FERDINAND Sonoma Age 54	Written: 10 Jan. 1894 Died: 1 Dec. 1899 Rec.: 26 Dec. 1899	#3093 Bk. G, Pg. 367

- Wife: Hannah
- Executor: Wife
- Witnesses: Geo. Breitenbach, Robt. A. Poppe

GROVER, BENJ. FRANKLIN	Written: 20 Apr. 1857 Filed: 8 May 1857	# 50 Bk. A, Pg. 62

- Brothers: Thos. Jefferson, Jas. Madison
- Executor: Cadwell Clark, August Hannah (?)
- Witnesses: Jos. F. Baugh, John D. Snider (?)

GRYFF, JOHN A. Geyserville	Written: 11 Aug. 1886 Died: 22 Mar. 1898 Filed: 11 Apr. 1898	#2857 Bk. G, Pg. 148

- Wife: Maria M. Gryff
- Trustees: John P. Medan, Geo. W. Critchfield
- Niece: Mary Stetler of Marin Co.
- Executors: John P. Medan of San Francisco, Geo. W. Critchfield of Geyserville
- Witnesses: Henry P. Wade, Otto --- Suders (Suden?) both of San Francisco; E.A. Medan, R.H. Hinreichsen

GRYFF, MAGDALENA Geyserville	Written: 3 Jun. 1898 Died: 6 Jan. 1899 Filed: 30 Jan. 1899	#2961 Bk. G, Pg. 240

- Husband: John A. (deceased)
- Niece: Maria Stetler Gianola
- Executor: Niece
- Witnesses: Otto T--- Luden (?) of San Francisco, Emma Rose of Geyserville

GUERNE, HENRIETTA	Written: 26 Jul. 1886 Died: 24 Oct. 1890 San Francisco Rec.: 24 Nov. 1890	#2016 Bk. E, Pg. 317

- Children: Emilie Middleton, Louisa G. Fensier, Daniel, August L., George E., estate of daughter Julia Heald (deceased)
- Executors: Son Geo. E. Guerne, son-in-law Thomas T. Heald
- Witnesses: Louisa Fensier, Pierre Philippe Briol

GUIDOTTI, FRANCESCO   Written: 25 Nov. 1891   #3395
Santa Rosa   Age 49   Died: 26 Nov. 1901   Bk. H, Pg. 91
                          Rec.:   30 Dec. 1901

   Wife: Teresa
   Executor: Wife
   Witnesses: W.A. Werneke, Pietro Pedrini

GUM, ISAAC   Written: 3 Apr. 1890   #2379
Healdsburg   Died: 21 Dec. 1893   Bk. F, Pg. 210
                          Rec.:   12 Feb. 1894

   Wife: Clara
   Sons: Willis, Schuyle (Schuyler ?) Colfax, John Frank
   Daughter: Nellie Hazel
   Executor: Wife, Schuyle C.
   Witnesses: Wm. B. Whitney, J.B. Pine

GUMMER, FRED CHANNING   Written: 6 Apr. 1901   #3420
Healdsburg   Died: 18 Jan. 1902   Bk. H, Pg. 110
                          Rec.:   3 Feb. 1902

   Wife: Emma
   Executor: Wife
   Witnesses: J.W. Hensinger, J.T. Baker
                 Holographic

GUNNING, ANN   Written: 16 Mar. 1885   #1464
Petaluma   Filed: 6 Apr. 1885

   Niece: Sarah McPherson, wife of Joseph Atkinson
   Executors: John Corbett, Rev. W.H. Darden
   Witnesses: T.J. Cavanagh, John Cavanagh

GUTSCHEURITTER,   Written: 9 Apr. 1890   #1957
DOMENIQUE   Died: 16 Apr. 1890   Bk. E, Pg. 243
Kenwood Tnsp.   Rec.:   12 May 1890

   Bequest to: Beloved friend, Edward Clark
   Executor: Ed. Clark
   Witnesses: Wm. E. Call, N. Francoeur

GUYOT, CHARLES R. (?)   Written: 27 May 1901   #3520
Sonoma   Died: 16 Sep. 1902   Bk. G, Pg. 517
                          Rec.:   21 Oct. 1902

   Daughter: Mary Delphine Blanche Schmidt
   Sons: Edward Geo., Leo Hugh, Chas. Leonce of Dixon,
                 Lee Co., Ill., Emile Oliver
   Executor: Daughter
   Witnesses   Robt. A. Poppe, Jonathon Hunter

```
GWYNN, EDWARD              Written:  22 Dec. 1887              #2076
              Age 55       Filed:    25 May  1891
                           Denied Probate

    Wife:         Eunice
    Executor:     Wife
    Witnesses:    J.H. Neyce, A.D. Laughlin


GWINN, JOHN E.             Written:  29 Jan. 1885              #1939
Petaluma     Age over       Died:    15 Apr. 1890          Bk. E, Pg. 220
              40

    Wife:         Mary Ann
    Sisters:      Mary of Boston, Mass.; Rebecca of Boston, Mass.
    Son:          John Henry (minor)
    Brother:      William of Cambridge, Mass.
    Executor:     Wife
    Witnesses:    Wm. B. Haskell, W.H. Zartman


HACKETT, JOHN JAMES        Written:  27 Feb. 1895              #2518
Bodega Tnsp.                Died:     7 Mar. 1895          Bk. F, Pg. 347
                            Rec.:    25 Mar. 1895

    Sisters:      Margaret of Dublin, Jane of Brussels, Minnie of
                  Dublin, Bessie of Dublin
    Brothers:     Joseph, address unknown; Brian of Australia
    Bequests to:  Lottie E.W. Stump, Walter G. Stump both children
                  of Sam'l. W. Stump of Bodega; Susan C., wife of
                  Sam'l. Stump; Jas. Walter Mc Caughey of Bodega
    Executors:    Sam'l. W. Stump or Dan'l. Quinlan
    Witnesses:    Wm. S. Roe, Gilman B. Tibbetts


HAEHL, HENRY               Written:  27 Jan. 1890              #1927
Cloverdale   Age 48         Died:    29 Jan. 1890          Bk. E, Pg. 204
                            Rec.:     3 Mar. 1890

    Son:          Harry
    Daughter:     Amy Mary
    Guardian:     of above: Mrs. Lizzie Schweitzer
    Executor:     Mrs. Lizzie Schweitzer
    Witnesses:    H.H. McKoon, R.S. Markell


HAEHL, JOHN JACOB          Written:  17 Dec. 1881              #1392
Cloverdale   Age 82         Died:    16 Feb. 1884          Bk. C, Pg. 532
                            Rec.:     2 Jan. 1885

    Refers to "Beloved Wife"
    Sons:         Conrad, Jessie(?), Cornelius, Laurence, Jacob,
                  Henry, John
    Daughters:    Catherine Anker (deceased), Margareth Zumpel,
                  Elizabeth Schweitzer, Barbara Schweitzer
                  (deceased)
    Executors:    Wm. Herman Andree, Gaspar Hunziker
    Witnesses:    R.S. Markell, John Geiser (Geisek?)
```

```
HAERING, JOSEPH            Written:  27 Oct. 1885           #1634
San Francisco              Died:     19 Apr. 1887    Bk. D, Pg. 437
                           Petaluma
                           Rec.:     23 May 1887
```

    Wife: Charlotte
    Mother: Un-named, living in Arleshein, Baseland, Switz.
    Executor: Joseph Fetz
    Witnesses: Columbus Bartlett, Miss Emmie Mahl

```
HAGEN, HENRY               Written:  27 Aug. 1890           #3041
              Age 73       Died:      8 Jul. 1899    Bk. G, Pg. 322
                           Filed:    24 Jul. 1899
```

    Wife: Mary Hagan
    Bequests to: Vicenzo Gianello
    Sons: Robert Hagan, Louis Hagan
    Daughters: Teresa Hagan, Frances Hagan, Mary D. Gianello
                  Jane Hagan, Agnes Hagan
    Exeuctors: John Goss, A.B. Ware
    Witnesses: John Goss, A.B. Ware

```
HAGEDOHM REINE             Written:   5 May 1885            #2272½
Petaluma Tnsp. Age 46      Died:     22 Nov. 1892    Bk. F, Pg.  48
                           Rec.:     16 Jan. 1893
```

    Husband: William
    Children: Pauline, Johanna, Herrmann, William
    Executor: None named
    Witnesses: Adam Schaefer, C.Tempel

```
HAHMANN, FEODOR GUSTAV    Written:  18 Jul. 1868            #1350
              Age about   Died:      2 Oct. 1883    Bk. C, Pg. 439
              45          Filed:    29 Oct. 1883
```

    Wife: Henrietta A. (present)
    Children: Henry, Charlotte, Paul, Paulina, Clara, Martha
    Executors: Jabez or Edward Howes of San Francisco, Hugo
                 Schenk of San Francisco, John T. Fortson of
                 Sonoma, CA
    Witnesses: Wm. L. Anderson, E.T. Farmer
    Codicil #1: Change of exectors
    Codicil #4: Names sisters Louisa and Clara

```
HAIGH, MARY                Written:  11 Jul. 1884           #1412
Healdsburg    Age 67       Died:     15 Jul. 1884    Bk. C, Pg. 584
                           Rec.:     11 Aug. 1884
```

    Children: Frances Broback (45), wife of Charles of
                 Jacksonville, Ore.; George W. (40); Robert (37);
                 Mary Alice Seawell (33), wife of George; Frank
                 (29); Edwin (26)
    Executor: Edwin
    Witnesses: John Gamble, Andrew Shriver

HAILMAN, JANE R.			Written:	26 Jul. 1884		#1677
	Age 74		Died:		3 Sep. 1887	Bk. D, Pg. 502
			Rec.:		3 Oct. 1887

Son:	Benj. F. Johnson (55) of Cincinatti, Ohio
Daughter:	Henriette P. Soden of Covington, KY
Grandsons:	Benj. F. Johnson, Foster Arnold
Grand-Daughter:	Maggie F. Johnson
Daughter-in-Law:	Carrie wife of G.W. (deceased)
Grand-Children:	Pennoek Soden, James Hailman Soden, Laura Hailman Soden, William Soden, Henriette Soden, Alfred Johnson
Executor:	Milo S. Davis
Witnesses:	Thos. C. Goodfellow, Sarah E. Williamson

HALL, ELIZABETH P.		Written:	9 Mar. 1883		#1306
				Died:		17 Apr. 1883	Bk. C, Pg. 360
				Rec.:		3 Jul. 1883

Sons:	Geo. H., Presley M., Janus W.
Daughters:	Mary C. Foushee, Prudence Lake, Sarah Mapes, Luzann Ross, Lizzie Belle Hall
Executor:	Geo. H. Hall
Witnesses:	Jas. H. McGee, T.A. Peck

HALL, SAMUEL			Written:	23 Dec. 1880		#1134
				Died:		24 Dec. 1880

Wife:	Samantha Hall
Executor:	None appointed
Witnesses:	Julius A. Davis, Climena Davis, Sally T. Holmes

HALPIN, WILLIAM			Written:	5 Nov. 1885		#2838
				Died:		26 Jan. 1898	Bk. G, Pg. 115
				Filed:		7 Mar. 1898

Wife:	Rose Halpin
Daughters:	Mary Halpin, Margaret Halpin, Ann Halpin, Lizzie Halpin, Catherin Halpin, Alice Halpin
Son:	Thomas Halpin
Executor:	Rose Halpin
Witnesses:	William Morrisey, August Voss

HAMMY, CATHERINE		Written:	24 Apr. 1893		#2320
Analy Tnsp.	Age 65	Died:	28 Apr. 1893	Bk. F, Pg. 127
		Rec.:	22 May 1893	

Husband:	George
Sister-in-Law:	Jane Sheridan
Nephews:	Thos. J. Sheridan, John S. Sheridan
Children:	Of nephew, Thomas B. Tallant (deceased)
Executor:	Husband
Witnesses:	J.P. Gannon, James McChristian both of Sebastopol

HAMMY, GEORGE	Written:	17 Mar. 1899	#3463
Sebastopol	Died:	23 Apr. 1902	Bk. H. Pg. 121
	Filed:	26 May 1902	

Wife:	Delphine
Half-Brother:	--- Hammy of Churwalden, Switzerland
Brothers:	John Hammy of Switzerland; Lucien Hammy of Nauvoo, Illinois; Hermann Hammy of Keokuk, Iowa; Christian Hammy (deceased) of Wisconsin
Executor:	Wife or W.T.J. Orr of Santa Rosa
Witnesses:	George P. Baxter, F.W. Gill both of Sebastopol

Mentions children of brothers, but no names; mentions John Hammy's children living in Calif.; mentions Hammy Ranch in Ocean Tnsp., Sonoma Co.

HANNAH, JOHN		Written:	25 Nov. 1882	#1737
Petaluma	Age 64	Died:	14 Apr. 1888	
		Rec.:	7 May 1888	

Sister:	Sarah Shipman of Appleton, Wisc.
Brother:	Robert
Nieces:	Helen M. Hannah, Sarah Hannah
Children:	Of brothers: William, James, Mathew
Executor:	Thos. Hopper
Witnesses:	H.E. Lawrence, T.C. Schloper

HANNATH, ELIZA		Written:	23 Aug. 1880	#1544
San Francisco	Age 68	Died:	28 Mar. 1886	Bk. D, Pg. 185
		Rec.:	25 May 1886	

Husband:	Chas. J. (deceased)
Step-Daughters:	Elizabeth Weightman, Mary Atkinson
Daughters:	Caroline Wood, Laura Brooks, Harriet Baxter, Helena Fitton, Malvina Bryant's (deceased) children
Son:	George Gass and his children Willie and Minnie Gass
Executors:	Sons-in-law, Sutcliffe Baxter and Edward Fitton
Witnesses:	S.G. Murphy, A.F. Miner

HANS, HERMANN   Written: 21 Aug. 1885   #1495
Cloverdale   Age 39   Died: 6 Sep. 1885   Bk. D, Pg. 90
                       San Francisco
                       Rec.:   28 Sep. 1885

  Brother: Hanry Hans of New York City
  Uncle: Henry Hans of Lintig, Germ.
  Bequests to: Hermann Heidonn, Benj. F. Cushing
  Executor: Claus Wreden of San Francisco
  Witnesses: Frank Spencer, Jas. F. Hoadley, Sr.

HARDIN, HENRY   Written: 29 Sep. 1859   # 149
Johnson Co., Mo.   Probate: 12 Nov. 1859
Native of Jefferson Co.,
Ky.

  Wife: Mary
  Daughters: Irene, wife of Wm. H. Rodgers; Mary Jane, wife of
                          Roland Hughes; Julia A., wife of Wm. E. Bradley;
                          Sarah Ann, wife of E.D. Harris; Ann Eliza, wife of
                          Wm. J. Cox
  Sons: Wm. J., Henry A., James A.
  Executors: Sons, both residents of Sonoma Co.
  Witnesses: Mark York, Jas. H. Lawrence

HARLOW, JAMES   Written: 25 Jan. 1882   #1212
Bloomfield   Died: 30 Jan. 1882   Bk. C, Pg. 178
                           Filed: 6 Mar. 1882

  Wife: Cleora A. (deceased)
  Children: James S., Maggie B., Annie M., Hattie N.
  Brother-in-
  Law: Saurin (?) W. King of Whitefield, Maine, guardian
                          of children
  Executor: Wm. Jones
  Witnesses: Perry C. Smith, John A. McAlister

HARMON, LUTHER N.   Written: 24 Nov. 1879   #1060
                           Filed: 19 Jan. 1880   Bk. C, Pg. 81

  Daughter: Amanda Jane H. Stafford of Santa Ana, Los Angeles
                          Co., Ca.
  Bequests to: Henry H. Harmon, Jonathan Harmon and daughter
  Executor: Daughter
  Witnesses: William Sexton, Elizabeth Staedler (?)
                          Real property in Santa Ana, Los Angeles Co., Ca.

HARRIS, SARAH E.		Written:	9 May 1886	#1551
Sonoma	Age 64	Died:	10 May 1886	Bk. D, Pg. 228
		Rec.:	28 Jun. 1886	

- Sons: Eugene Flint, Purdy Flint both of Yakima, Wash. Terr.; Granville S. Harris, Thomas S. Cooper, John R. Cooper all of Sonoma Valley
- Daughters: Barbara Campbell, wife of Geo., of Cambria, Ca.; Emma McDonald, wife of J.R.(?)
- Executors: Thos. S. and John R. Cooper
- Witnesses: H.H. Davis, B.F. Campbell, L.B. Lawrence

HASKELL, ABIGAIL A.		Written:	30 Aug. 1883	#1393
Petaluma	Age 62	Died:	13 Jan. 1884	Bk. C, Pg. 539
		Rec.:	3 Jan. 1885	

- Husband: Barnabas
- Son: William B.
- Daughter-in-Law: Emma A.
- Father: Aner(?) Grover (deceased)
- Executor: Son
- Witnesses: Mrs. Jenette E. Woodworth, Miss Phebe S. Colby

Property in Hartford Co., Mass. and Hill Co., Tex.

HASKELL, BARNABAS		Written:	-- Jun. 1885	#1610
Petaluma	Age 68	Died:	20 Jan. 1887	Bk. D, Pg. 411
		Rec.:	28 Feb. 1887	

- Wife: Died 1884
- Son: William B.
- Bequests to: Mrs. Adaline Chapman of East Hartford, Conn.; Alfred Kelly
- Grand-Daughter: Euna G.
- Niece: Mrs. Sarah Pitkin, wife of Ralph, of Hartford, Conn.
- Executors: I.G. Wickersham, Jos. Campbell
- Witnesses: H.H. Atwater, J. Campbell

HARTMAN, W. D.		Written:	17 Apr. 1883	#1945
Healdsburg		Died:	27 Jan. 1890	Bk. E, Pg. 217
		El Dorado Co.		
		Rec.:	17 Apr. 1890	

- Trustees: John Moffet of Healdsburg, Stephen Roberts of San Francisco to benefit Hattie, Indian mother of his children
- Children: Elizabeth R., John A., Geo. W., Arthur
- Executors: Trustees
- Witnesses: W.B. Reynolds of Healdsburg, Geo R. Williams of Oakland

HARVEY, JOEL   Written: 6 Aug. 1873   # 644
            Age 72   Died: 27 Aug. 1873
                         Filed: 20 Oct. 1873

    Wife: Lydia
    Daughters: Mary (?) McCleave, wife of H.P.; Susan E. Freeman
                 (deceased), wife of John M.
    Sons: L.B., Harvey, R.A.
    Executors: Sons
    Witnesses: O.W. Craig, G.L. Wratten

HASTINGS, ISAAC   Written: 23 Aug. 1870   # 536
Bennett Valley   Died: 27 Mar. 1872   Bk. A, Pg. 277

    Wife: Agnes
    Son: Hartwell G.
    Daughter: Of Hartwell, by first wife: Lucida Agness
    Children: John Westley of Texas; Sam'l Donthard of Mo.;
                 Emily, wife of Joseph Hastings; Delay Fletcher;
                 A.R.; Jesse Axley; Hartwell G.
    Executor: Hartwell Hastings
    Witnesses: Murray Whallon, Sam'l Batten, Adelia A. Whallon

HATCH, C. P.   Written: 17 Jul. 1888   #2299
Petaluma   Age 74   Died: 18 Mar. 1893   Bk. F, Pg. 188
                         Rec.:   26 Dec. 1893

    Wife: Lucretia Ann
    Nieces: Eunice Eliza, Carrie Lucinda, Lydia Lillie
    Executor: Wife
    Witnesses: F.A. Meyer, Wm. B. Haskell

HAYES, SAMUEL M.   Dated: 18 Mar. 1871   # 481
                         Died: 20 Apr. 1871

    Children: Un-named
    Witnesses: A.M. Church, E. Skaggs, Jr., Geo. W. Watson
                 Requested that Masons and Odd Fellows Orders of
                 Healdsburg take charge of his children

HEALD, DANIEL G.   Written: 10 Nov. 1897   #2807
Petaluma   Age 71   Died: 19 Nov. 1897
                         San Francisco
                         Filed: 20 Dec. 1897

    Wife: Elizabeth Heald
    Sons: George W. Heald, Edwin D. Heald
    Daughters: Sarah E. Heald, Mary L. Heald
    Executor: Wife
    Witnesses: Wm. B. Haskell, Thos. C. Denny both of Petaluma

```
HEALD, ELIZABETH            Written:  19 Nov. 1856              #   54
                            Filed:     4 Dec. 1856
```

Sons:	Thomas, Samuel, Harmon, Jacob
Daughter:	Sarah Shaw
Other:	(?)Mary Eliz. Ridenhour
Executor:	Son, Thos.
Witnesses:	J.S. Ormsby, Cha. W. Armes

```
HEATH, BARBARA M.           Written:   9 Mar. 1885              #1514
Healdsburg     Age about    Died:     20 Sep. 1885     Bk. D, Pg. 140
                35          Filed:    14 Jan. 1886
```

Son:	Herbert McE.
Executors:	Aunt, Mrs. Alice McDonald of Mystic Bridge, Conn.
Agent:	John Gamble, Principal of Litton Springs College
Witnesses:	A.B. Coffman, M.D.; Dr. M.C. Farrar

```
HEBRON, HENRY               Dated:    18 Feb. 1898              #2898
                            Filed:    11 Jul. 1898
```

Friend:	Edward Grove
	Rose, wife of George A. Davis, of Pleasonton, Alameda Co., Ca.
	Holographic

```
HEGELER, JOHN HENRY         Written:   4 Apr. 1873              #  612
JACOB                       Died:      9 Apr. 1873     Bk. C, Pg.  46
                            Filed:     2 Jun. 1873
```

Wife:	Un-named
Son:	John Hegeler
Daughter:	Mary C. Powers
Son-in-law:	David Powers
Executors:	John Hegeler, David Powers
Witnesses:	H.J. Smith, William Norton

```
HEGELER, MARIA              Written:  28 Apr. 1873              #  611
                            Died:      1 May  1873     Bk. C, Pg. 462
                            Filed:     2 Jun. 1873
```

Husband:	John H.J. Hegeler (deceased)
Children:	John H. Hegeler; Mary Powers, wife of David
Executors:	A.S. Purrine, Norman Smith
Witnesses:	John Vanderleith, Chas. Romer of Bodega

```
HEISEL, PAUL                Written:    2 Mar. 1890           #1937
Santa Rosa      Age 61      Died:       8 Mar. 1890      Bk. E, Pg. 214
                            Rec.:      31 Mar. 1890
```

- Wife: Ellen (former)
- Children: Katie, William, Teresa, Joseph, Paul Jr., Nellie, John (minor), Carrie (minor)
- Executor: S.I. Allen
- Witnesses: C.W. Hawkins, Martin Miller

```
HEMBREE, ANDREW THOMPSON   Written:   12 Feb. 1870           # 657
                           Died:       5 Nov. 1873
                           Filed:     15 Dec. 1873
```

- Wife: Corrinda (Lorrinda?)
- Adopted Son: Andrew J.
- Executor: Wife, son
- Witnesses: T.B. McCutchan, David Mc. McCutchan

```
HEMENWAY, GEORGE           Written:   20 Oct. 1900           #3414
Santa Rosa      Age 80     Died:      10 Jan. 1902      Bk. H, Pg. 100
                           Rec.:      31 Jan. 1902
```

- Bequest to: Dora Story Bush
- Executor: Dora S. Bush
- Witnesses: Wm. F. Cowan, Mrs. Hannah M. Dickerson

```
HENDLEY, HARRIET E.         Written:   17 Nov. 1883           #1461
Santa Rosa      Age about   Died:      -- Feb. 1884      Bk. D, Pg. 37
                46          Rec.:      31 Jun. 1885
```

- Husband: John (deceased)
- Children: Frank P., William G.
- Guardians: Appointed, D.N. Carithers, Geo. W. Davis
- Witnesses: James W. Oates, Louis, W. Juilliard

```
HENLEY, JONATHON S.         Written:    2 Apr. 1885           #1998
Sacramento      Age 63      Died:      15 Jul. 1890      Bk. E, Pg. 299
                            Sonoma Co.
                            Rec.:      25 Aug. 1890
```

- Brother: Luther R. of Washington Co., Tenn.
- Children: Of brothers Luther R. and Isaac B.
- Executors: Elihu S. Henley, Sanford B. Henley
- Witnesses: S. Solon Holl, L.S. Taylor both of Sacramento

```
HENNESSY, DANIEL          Written:  11 Aug. 1866            # 325
                          Died:     -- Aug. 1866    Bk. A, Pg. 159
                          San Francisco at St. Marys
                          Rec.:     14 Feb. 1867

    Wife:       Johanna
    Sons:       James, Patrick Daniel
    Daughter:   Mary, wife of George Estes(?)
    Witnesses:  John McCullough, James Kernan


HENRY, JAMES              Written:  18 Apr. 1870            # 453
                          Filed:    3 Sep. 1870

    Daughter:    Margate A.C. Howe
    Son-in-law:  Robert Howe
    Sons:        William, James Henry
    Executors:   Daughter, son-in-law both of San Emigdio Creek,
                 Timber Cove
    Witnesses:   C.S. Williams, John Funk


HESKETH, WILLIAM M.       Written:  30 Apr. 1896           #2633
                          Died:     30 Apr. 1896   Bk. F, Pg. 525
                          Filed:    29 Jun. 1896

    Bequest to:  Dr. E. Lagan of Petaluma
    Executor:    Dr. E. Lagan
    Witnesses:   W.H. Hanger, --- Hanger both of Petaluma


HESS, FREDERICK           Written:  4 Mar. 1880            #1757
Petaluma                  Died:     19 Jun. 1888   Bk. D, Pg. 618
                          Filed:    25 Jun. 1888

    Wife:       Louisa Hess
    Daughter:   Gertrude Hess
    Step-
    Daughter:   Sophie Wright
    Executor:   Louisa Hess
    Witnesses:  Frank W. Shattuck, John Bauer both of Petaluma


HESTER, JOHN H.           Written:  2 Apr. 1881            #1156
              Age about   Died:     4 Jun. 1881    Bk. C, Pg. 138
              50          Filed:    1 Aug. 1881

    Executor:   Kelly Tighe
    Witnesses:  John B. Smith, W.R. Campbell
```

HIGBY, WILLIAM			Written:	5 Jun. 1886			#1700
		Age 73	Died:	27 Nov. 1887	Bk. D, Pg. 552
			Rec.:	27 Dec. 1887

- Wife: Ellen Maria (deceased by Dec. 1887)
- Nieces: Maria L. Hoffnagle, Harriet Knowlton both of Essex Co., NY
- Executors: Wife for California property; nephew, Edmund S. Higby, Essex Co., for New York property
- Witnesses: G.A. Tupper, J.W. Davis
- Next of kin: Per court document: Wm. Jr. (21), Joseph (19), Ellen (17), Eben (15), Saide (11), Ruth (8)

HIGGINS, ASA						#3268

Will missing

HIGGINS, WALTER B.		Written:	23 Oct. 1895		#2612
				Died:	8 Feb. 1896	Bk. F, Pg. 484
				Rec.:	2 Mar. 1896

- Wife: Cornelia
- Executor: Wife
- Witnesses: J.L. Dinwiddie, H.P. Brainerd

HIGUERA, NICHOLAS			20 Apr. 1851			# 51
Napa County			Probate:	14 Apr. 1853	Bk. A, Pg. 63

- Daughters: Martha Frias de Higuera, Encomo --- Cacho Higuera
- Executor: Norman G. Silya Riva
- Witnesses: Johnson Horrell, John B. Horrell

HILBERER, MARIE A.		Written:	23 Apr. 1887		#2550
Geyserville	Age 44		Died:	9 Jul. 1895	Bk. F, Pg. 397
				Rec.:	5 Aug. 1895

- Husband: Phillip
- Executor: Husband
- Witnesses: W.B. Reynolds, H.K. Brown both of Healdsburg

HILL, SARAH			Written:	4 Apr. 1890		#2472
				Died:	15 Sep. 1894	Bk. F, Pg. 316
				Rec.:	19 Nov. 1894

- Daughters: Emily, Jemima A. Yarbrough
- Executors: Hamilton B. Litton, R. Lee Yarbrough
- Witnesses: Wm. F. Russell, Ben S. Wood

```
HILL, WILLIAM MC PHERSON   Dated:     2 Nov. 1896              #2814
Sonoma Valley              San Francisco          Bk. I, Pg. 92
                           Died:     19 Nov. 1897
                           Filed:     3 Jan. 1898

    Wife:          Annie Elmer Hill
    Executors:     Wife; son, Robert Potter Hill
    Witnesses:     John Thomas Scott


HINKSTON, GREENBURY        Written:   1 Jan. 1892              #2171
Petaluma                   Died:      4 Jan. 1892   Bk. E, Pg. 610
                           Rec.:     10 May  1892

    Sister:        Filena Colton
    Brothers:      Samuel, John
    Nephews:       Frances, Mayer
    Brother-in-
    Law:           J.M. Palmer of Petaluma
    Bequests to:   Mrs. Adithas Dryer; her son, Water (Walter?) Mize
    Executors:     D. Hemenway, J.P. Rodgers
    Witnesses:     W.H. Hicks, J.P. Rodgers


HINKSTON, HARLOW           Written:  29 Apr. 1880              #1142
Petaluma                   Filed:    21 Mar. 1881   Bk. C, Pg. 121

                   J.M. Palmer
    Children:      Filena Colton of Kansas; Greenbury Hinkston,
                   Samuel M. Hinkston, Joseph R. Hinkston, John
                   Hinkston all of Sonoma Co.; Mrs. Lucy Ann Palmer
                   of San Francisco
    Executor:      J.M. Palmer
    Witnesses:     Frank W. Shattuck, A. Henry


HINKSTON, NANCY            Written:  25 Apr. 1874              #1441
Petaluma

    Daughters:     Lucy Ann Palmer, Filena Colton
    Sons:          Joseph, Greenberg, John, Samuel
    Executor:      Son, Samuel
    Witnesses:     C.G. Bryant, D.M.W. Seaton both of Petaluma


HINMAN, MILES              Dated:    19 Jan. 1893              #2755
                           Died:     24 May  1897   Bk. G, Pg. 45
                           Filed:    12 Jul. 1897

    Step-
    Daughter:      Addie A. Atwater, daughter of late wife
    Executor:      Addie A. Atwater
    Witnesses:     D.D. Hemenway, Geo. W. Lamoreaux both of Petaluma
```

HINSHAW, WILLIAM CARTER   Written: 7 Feb. 1890   #2362
Petaluma   Died: 2 Nov. 1893   Bk. F, Pg. 182
                           Rec.:   4 Dec. 1893

   Aunt: Miss Lou J. Carter
   Executor: Aunt
   Witnesses: F.A. Meyer, Wm. B. Haskell

HIRTH, GEORGE   Written: 12 Jul. 1897   #2915
                           Died: 17 Aug. ----   Bk. G, Pg. 206
                           Filed: 12 Sep. 1898

   Brother: Albrecht Hirth of Carlsruhe, Germany
   Nephew: Albrecht Hirth, son of Frederick Hirth
   Sister-in-
   Law: Susan Hirth, wife of Frederick Hirth
   Brothers: Frederick Hirth of Santa Rosa, Christian Hirth of
                 San Jose, Gotlob Hirth of Petaluma
   Executor: Frederick Hirth
   Witnesses: Paul T. Hahman, Ben S. Wood

HITCHCOCK, HOLLIS   Written: 13 Dec. 1895   #2599
                           Died: 3 Jan. 1896   Bk. F, Pg. 453
                           Rec.:   20 Jan. 1896

   Nephew: H.M. LeBaron
   Brothers: Children of Benjamin (deceased), Samuel, children
                 of Hiram (deceased)
   Sisters: Lucy, Eliza Ann, children of Pamelia (deceased)
   Executors: Henry E. Lawrence, Geo. P. McNear, H.M. LeBaron
   Witnesses: L.C. Lane of San Francisco Co.; M.D. Merritt, Geo.
                 R. Williams both of Oakland

HOADLEY, JAMES F. SR.   Written: 16 Aug. 1888   #2109
Cloverdale   Died: 17 Aug. 1891   Bk. E, Pg. 457
                           Rec.:   17 Oct. 1891

   Wife: Harriet C.
   Children: Elias Augustes, Harriet M. Whitney, James Francis,
                 Ida L. Humbert, George H. (minor)
   Executors: Sons, Elias and James
   Witnesses: Chas. E. Humbert, Simon Pinchower

HODGDON, MATILDA C.   Dated: 8 Sep. 1887   #3013
Booth Bay, Maine   Died: 3 Dec. 1892   Bk. G, Pg. 283
            Age 84   Filed: 29 May 1899

   Daughter: Of Joseph Campbell (deceased) of Booth Bay, Maine
   Grand-
   Daughter: Carrie S. Read, now Carrie S. Cook, wife of
                 Charles H. Cook
   Executor: Carrie S. Cook
   Witnesses: E.N. Kellogg, U.J. Hussey

HOEN, BERTHOLD Windsor	Written: Age about Died: 60 Rec.:	24 Apr. 1882 7 Aug. 1885 7 Sep. 1885	#1493 Bk. D, Pg. 87

- Wife: Mary Anderson Hoen
- Children: Mary Elizabeth (16), Bertah (15), Ernest Martin (13), Carl Anderson (11)
- Executor: Wife
- Witnesses: John Brown, D.W. Burrel

HOEN, ERNEST Baltimore, MD	Written: Died: Filed:	9 Jun. 1893 16 Jun. 1893 23 May 1898	#2875 Bk. G, Pg. 184

- Wife: Frances Elizabeth
- Executor: Wife
- Witnesses: A.G. Hoen, Ernest Hoen, Jr.

HOGAN, ALICE F. Santa Rosa	Written: Died: Rec.:	5 Oct. 1889 7 Oct. 1889 4 Nov. 1889	#1895 Bk. E, Pg. 168

- Bequest to: Mrs. Catran, Nr. County Farm; Francis Knecht; two daughters of Mrs. Catran
- Admn: Clement Gardner
- Witnesses: Lizzie Quinlan, Clement Gardner

HOFFSTETER, B.	Written: Died: Rec.:	23 Nov. 1889 14 Oct. 1894 10 Dec. 1894	#2479 Bk. F, Pg. 334

- Daughters: Henriette Antoinette Schirmer, Emilie Mathilde
- Grand-Daughters: Eleonore and Jeanne daughters of son, Bernard L.B. Joseph Hoffstetter
- Executor: Emile Schirmer, son-in-law
  Holographic

HOLLAND, HUGH L. Santa Rosa	Written: Died: Filed:	10 Nov. 1875 12 Nov. 1875 20 Dec. 1875	# 781 Bk. B, Pg. 217

- Wife: Mary L.
- Children: Nettie ---, Cora L.
- Executor: Wife
- Witnesses: John Brown, S.A. Rendall, Sallie I. Davis

HOLLGREVE, HENRY   Written: 7 May 1864   # 253
          Age 68   Probate: 6 Jun. 1864   Bk. A, Pg. 120

    Brothers: Fredrick Anton, Clemens both residents of Germany
                  (town un-readable)
    Sister: Josephine resident of Germany
    Executors: Conrad Bruns, Albert Wissell
    Witnesses: H. Brons (Bruns?), Wm. Huefner

HOLMAN, ISAAC A.   Written: 16 Nov. 1859   # 164
                          Probate: 23 Apr. 1860

    Wife: Nancy
    Admn: Wife
    Witnesses: G.R. Codding, Miles Hinman

HOLSER, CONRAD   Written: 31 May 1866   # 320
                          Died: 8 Aug. 1866 (on or about)
                          Filed: 1 Oct. 1866

    Wife: Sarah
    Executor: Sarah Holser
    Witnesses: D.D. Carder, F.F. Fine both of Petaluma

HOOD, GEORGE   Dated: 26 Mar. 1879   #2821
                          Died: 31 Dec. 1897   Bk. G, Pg. 104
                          Filed: 25 Jan. 1898

    Wife: Julia Hood
    Children: Isabella Hood, James Hood, Robert Hood,
                John Hood, William Hood, Margaret Allison
                Hood, George Hood, Alexander Hood, Benjamin H.
                Hood
    Executor: Julia Hood; alternates: James, Robert & John
                Wood (?), sons
    Witnesses: Wm. E. McConnell, Jno. Tyler Campbell

HOOTEN, JESSE   Dated: 19 Feb. 1868   # 385
                          Died: 21 May 1868
                          Filed: 29 Jun. 1868

    Wife: Elisabeth Hooton
    Sons: Martin V. Hooton, James J. Hooten
    Grandson: James J. Miller
    Grand-
    Daughter: Sarah Frances Babb
    Executor: None named
    Witnesses: Cardwell Clark, I.N. Stapp, James C. Cook

```
HOPPER, MARGARET A.        Dated:   30 Dec. 1884              #3217
Knights Valley             Died:    23 Aug. 1900   Bk. G, Pg. 407
                           Filed:   22 Oct. 1900
```

Husband:	Wesley L. Hopper
Sons:	Henry L. Hopper, William Thomas Hooper
Daughter:	Annie Myrtle Hopper
Executors:	Josiah H. Benson, William Benson
Witnesses:	Thos. Rutledge, Wm. E. McConnell

```
HOSATTE, JEAN BAPTISTE     Dated:   14 Dec. 1886              #2820
San Francisco              Died:    30 Dec. 1887   Bk. G, Pg. 119
                           Filed:   15 Feb. 1898
```

Wife:	Francoise Aimee Hosttee nee Maleuvre Fanny Villian nee Maleuvre, wife of Jean Baptiste Villian; Aline Berthe Depuy nee Maleuvre, wife of Jean Baptiste Dupuy
Executor:	Francoise Aimee Hosattee
Witnesses:	L. Regand, J.H. Blood

```
HOSKING, ELIZABETH         Written: 28 Jul. 1893              #2714
San Francisco   Age 67     Died:    28 Feb. 1897   Bk. G, Pg.  22
                           Filed:   28 Feb. 1897
```

	Widow of William Hosking, formerly a resident of Collinsville, Solano Co. Elizabeth, a native of Smithborough, County Monaghan, Ireland, maiden name was Elizabeth Gordon
Daughter:	Mary Jane Elizabeth Hosking (22)
Niece:	Mrs. Lizzie Hemphill, wife of Willie Hemphill, of Danville, Contra Costa Co.; daughter of brother, Robert Gordon
Nephew:	Robert Cunningham, son of sister, Mary Cunningham
Guardian:	Of Mary Jane Elizabeth Hosking, Mathew Presho
Executor:	Robert Cunningham
Witnesses:	C.W. Cross, Fred L. Gadsby

```
HOTELL, DAVID              Written: 17 Nov. 1866              # 332
                           Died:    29 Nov. 1866  Bk. Wills Pg. 172
                           Probate: 3 Jan. 1867
```

Wife:	Polly Holeman Hotell
Daughters:	Nancy Maria Rice, Sarah Jane Stine, Marium Damaris Hotell, Betsey Ann Hotell, Lucinda Goodno Hotell, Mary Irene Hotell
Sons:	Jas. Sam'l Hotell, Wm. Cornelius Hotell, David Edwin Hotell
Executors:	Isiah Thomas of Green Valley, Jacob Rambo
Witnesses:	Jacob Rice, R.L. Woodworth, Sarah Rambo

HOWARD, SQUARE DEALING   Written: 11 Feb. 1898   #3102
Cloverdale Tnsp.   Died: 15 Dec. 1899   Bk. G, Pg. 379
         Age 72   Rec.:   15 Jan. 1900

   Wife: Alice
   Children: Marshal, Orville, Dell, Elvira
   Executor: Wife
   Witnesses: Geo. B. Baer, C.B. Shaw

HOWES, WILLIAM F.   Written: 6 Sep. 1876   #1048
Dennis, Barnstable Co.,   Died: 4 Nov. 1878   Bk. C, Pg. 68
Mass.   Filed: 15 Dec. 1879

   Wife: Margarette J. Howes
   Son: Stephen M. Howes of Rockland, Plymouth Co.
   Daughter: Bertha Howes (minor)
   Executors: Stephen M. Howes, Margarette J. Howes
   Witnesses: Sabra Howes, Thomas S. Howes, Mary G. Howes, John
                W. Howes

HUGHES, JOHN C.   Dated: 6 Apr. 1854   # 50
                          Died: -- Apr. 1854   Bk. A, Pg. 62
                          Filed: 24 Jul. 1854

   Wife: Jane Hughes
   Sons: James L. Hughes, Rowland Hughes, William Hughes,
                Daniel Hughes, Francis M., George M.
   Daughters: Sono-- Hughes Brown, Elisabeth Hughes, Susan C.
                Hughes
   Admn.:   Jane Hughes
   Witnesses: A.A. Guernsey, Warham Easley

HUGHES, FRANCES   Written: 1 Dec. 1881   #1230
JOSEPHINE (GROS)   Died: 4 Apr. 1882   Bk. C, Pg. 221
Petaluma

   Friends: Mrs. Henrietta Cantel, wife of Louis; Louis
                Gregoire of San Francisco
   Executor: Louis Cantel
   Witnesses: Wm. B. Haskell, C.S. Farquar

HUMBERT, ELMIRA   Written: 7 Dec. 1891   #2420
Santa Rosa   Died: 10 May 1894   Bk. F, Pg. 252
                          Rec.:   18 Jun. 1894

   Daughters: Frances Yercie(?), Ladema Cary, Clarry Cary
   Executor: M.C. Wilcox
   Witnesses: Hiram Cole, Rosa H. Halbert

HUMPHREYS RICHARD JAMES	Written:	1 Feb. 1888	#1750
Age 42	Died:	26 May 1888	Bk. D, Pg. 605
	Filed:	13 Jun. 1888	

Bequest to: James L. Patterson, Supt. of "Rimover (Runover?) Mining Co.", Calico, San Bernardino Co., Ca.

HUNGER, FELIX	Written:	18 Feb. 1881	#2476
Sonoma Valley	Died:	29 Nov. 1894	Bk. F, Pg. 327
Dairyman	Rec.:	31 Dec. 1894	

- Wife: Maria
- Executor: Wife
- Witnesses: W. McPherson Hill, Humphry Hill

HUNGERBUHLER, ULRICH	Written:	13 Jan. 1894	#3106
	Died:	30 Dec. 1899	Bk. G, Pg. 382
	Rec.:	22 Jan. 1900	

- Mother: Susana
- Sister: Mrs. Susana Kellenberger
- Brother: Johannes
- Executors: Andrew Frei, J.C. Rued both of San Francisco
- Witnesses: J--- Mahler, second witness un-readable

HUNT, CHARLES	Written:	26 Sep. 1872	# 580
	Died:	24 Oct. 1872	
	Filed:	3 May 1875	

- Son: Charles A. (youngest of family)
- Daughters: Cordelia Hammer of Salt Lake City, Luella Acuff of Napa Co., Lucy Hunt of Petaluma, Ida Hunt of Salt Lake City
- Executor: H.B. Hasbrouck
- Witnesses: Frank W. Shattuck, A. Henry

HUNT PHOEBE	Written:	12 Dec. 1882	#1335
Grand Jaggen,	Rec.:	23 Jul. 1883	Bk. C, Pg. 414
Digby Co., N.S.			
Widow			

- Daughters: Caroline Hunt, wife of William; Ann S. Cronien, wife of Michael; Margaret Nichols, wife of John; Phoebe; Patience; Elizabeth of Boston
- Sons: Joseph of Boston, Mass.; John; William; Masrassa Hunt (deceased) of Petaluma
- Executors: Wm. L. Hunt, Joseph Hunt
- Witnesses: James Franklin of Hill Grove, Digby Co., N.S.; J.M. Viets

HUNT, THOMAS ROWLAND   Dated: 2 Nov. 1899   #3222
                        Died: 7 Oct. 1900   Bk. G, Pg. 470
                        Filed: 29 Oct. 1900

  Wife: Isabel Georgina Hunt
  Children: Dorothy Gladys Hunt, Muriel Penelope Hunt, Hilda
               Winifred Hunt
  Executor: Isabel Georgina Hunt
  Witnesses: F. McG. Martin, A.B. Ware

HUNTER, ELIZABETH A.   Written: 2 Jan. 1872   # 525
                        Died: 2 Feb. 1872
                        Filed: -- Mar. 1872

  Niece: Cynthia Jemima Cross
  Sons: Olin McKendry Hunter, Wilber Lowe Hunter
  Guardian: Of sons, David S. Dickson
  Witnesses: Frank W. Shattuck, J.L. Trefrin

HUNTER, JAMES   Written: 16 Apr. 1868   # 380
                        Died: 1 May 1868   Bk. A. Pg. 307
                        Probate: 15 Jun. 1868

  Wife: Elizabeth Ann
  Children: Wilber Lowe Hunter, Olive McKendre Hunter
  Executor: Wife
  Witnesses: Andrew Mills, Frank W. Shattuck

HUSSEY, EDWARD   Written: 17 Feb. 1887   #1691
Petaluma   Age 57 Died: 2 Nov. 1887   Bk. D, Pg. 532
                or 54   Filed: 5 Dec. 1887

  Wife: Ellen Hussey
  Son: Edward Martin Hussey (minor)
  Daughters: Catherine Florence Hussey (minor), Margaret Anna
               Hussey (minor), Ella Frances Hussey (minor)
  Executors: Ellen Hussey, John Hussey, James F. Cleary
  Witnesses: John Cavanagh, H.H. Atwater both of Petaluma

HUTCHENS, HORATIO   Written: 2 Sep. 1881   #1188
Healdsburg   Filed: 9 Nov. 1881   Bk. C, Pg. 160

  Bequests to: Mary Wiley, wife of Dean Wiley; Nancy Jane Poggi,
               wife of Sorophina Poggi
  Executor: Peter Grise
  Witnesses: L.A. Norton, George Miller

HUTCHINSON, A. F.	Written:	15 Mar. 1875	# 742
	Died:	-- Mar. 1875	Bk. B, Pg. 161
	Filed:	25 Mar. 1875	

- Wife: Mary Hutchinson of Mechanicsburg, Cahmpaigne Co., Ohio
- Son: Willon Hutchinson of Mechanicsburg, Champaigne Co., Ohio
- Executors: Henry Wise, Joseas(?) Davis
- Witnesses: E. Seegelken, William Strong

HUTCHINSON, HENRY HUNT	Dated:	10 Oct. 1893	#3205
County of Derby England	Died:	26 Jul. 1894	Bk. G, Pg. 453
	Filed:	6 Sep. 1900	

- Wife: Un-named
- Daughters: Constance Margaret Hutchinson (spinster), Beatrice
- Sons: Ernest, Alfred, Wolfred Thomas
- Friend: James Harwood
- Fabian Society of London; collegues of Society: William H. DeMattos, William Clarke and Edward R. Pease
- Executors: Sidney Webb, Constance Margaret
- Witnesses: John Harwood, Philip Harwood both of Derby

HYATT, JOHN B.		Written: 29 Oct. 1891	#2567
Cloverdale	Age 64	Died: 29 Aug. 1895	Bk. F, Pg. 418
		Rec.: 30 Sep. 1895	

- Wife: Margaret
- Half-Brother: Josephus L. Patterson of St. Charles Co., Mo.
- HalfSister: Sarah Eliz. Hyatt of St Charles Co., Mo.
- Sisters: Martha J. Patterson (widow) of St. Louis, Mo; Margaret Ann Hyatt of St Louis Co., Mo.
- Executor: E.B. Clark of San Francisco
- Witnesses: C.B. Shaw, Simon Pinschower
- Codicil: Dated 21 Jul. 1893 adds Mrs. Emily Preston

HYDE, JAMES		Written: 27 Oct. 1894	#2634
	Age 67	Died: 6 May 1896	Bk. F, Pg. 506
		Filed: 9 May 1896	

- Sister: Cathrine Hyde of Oakland, Ca.
- Nieces: Mrs. Jennie Collins, wife of Thomas, of San Francisco; Nora County of San Francisco
- Brother: Philip Hyde of San Francisco
- Cousin: Patrick Hyde
- Executor: Patrick Hyde
- Witnesses: John W. Keegan, Peter Towey

HYNES, JAMES J.   Dated: 18 Jan. 1882   #1225
Petaluma   Died: 12 Mar. 1882   Bk. C, Pg. 202
                         Rec.:   15 Mar. 1883

  Wife: Alma R. Hynes
  Children: Wilrick Hynes, Laura A. Hynes
  Children: By first wife: Mary A. Stroud, David Hynes,
               Ida Hynes, John P. Hynes, James E. Hynes
  Executor: Alma R. Hynes
  Witnesses: E.S. Lippitt, Henry Locknane

HALL, SAMUEL   Written: 23 Dec. 1880   #1134
                         Died: 24 Dec. 1880

  Wife: Samantha Hall
  Executor: None
  Witnesses: Julius A. Davis, Climena Davis, Sally T. Holmes

HALPIN, WILLIAM   Written: 5 Nov. 1885   #2838
                         Died: 26 Jan. 1898   Bk. G, Pg. 115
                         Filed: 7 Mar. 1898

  Wife: Rose Halpin
  Daughters: Mary Halpin, Margaret Halpin, Lizzie Halpin,
               Catherin Halpin, Alice Halpin
  Son: Thomas Halpin
  Executor: Rose Halpin
  Witnesses: William Morrisey, August Voss

ITIN, JOHN   Dated: 28 May 1897   #2757
                         Died: 10 Jun. 1897   Bk. G, Pg. 32
                         Filed: 28 Jun. 1897

               Lydia Hefty
               Matthais Itin of St. Paul
               Mary Bauer
  Executors: John Bauer, Fred Hefty, Jr.
  Witnesses: J.W. Jesse, James W. Oates

INK, WALTER P.   Dated: 15 May 1899   #3024
                Age 80   Died: 16 May 1899   Bk. G, Pg. 294
                         Filed: 19 Jun. 1899

  Wife: Hannah
  Brothers: Ira of Chesterville, Ohio; Charles (deceased in
               New York); Theron (deceased in CA)
  Sisters: Jane Overturf of Missouri, Cornelia Ann Fisk of
               Illinois, Marilla of Ohio, Permelia Harvey
               (deceased in Michigan)
  Nephew: Walter Ink of Ohio, son of Theron
               Walter Henry & Nina Plaskett Wardell (relation-
               ship not stated)
  Witnesses: M.L. Pettit, I.S. Lewis

```
INMAN, AARON C.          Written:  12 Oct. 1883           #1404
Fulton        Age 68     Died:     31 Mar. 1884
                         Filed:    14 Jun. 1884
```

Son: Benjamin F. (deceased)
Daughters: Sarah Ann Scott, wife of Wm. L.; (and un-named
             children); Lavina Parks of Kansas city, Mo.; Mary
             E. Weaver of San Francisco
Executor: Wm. Scott
Witnesses: O.H. Hoag, E.J. Fowler

```
INMAN, HIRAM KING        Written:  24 Sep. 1881           #1262
Vallejo Tnsp. Age 71     Died:     27 Aug. 1882    Bk. C, Pg. 291
                         Rec.:     3 May 1883
```

Wife: Nellie (deceased)
Children: None
Nephews   Wm. Francis Mathers, son of sister, Martha;
              Andrew J. Blackwell, son of sister, Eliz.;
              Geo. W. Guinn, son of sister, Ellen; Bradford
              Inman, half-brother to Bradford
Children: Of niece, Sarah Inman
Sister-in-
Law: Isabella Frost
Executor: James Lawlor
Witnesses: P.H. Lawlor, Peter Lawlor, James Lawlor

```
IRWIN, NEWTON CANNON     Written:  9 Nov. 1899            #3438
Gualala, Ca.  Age 77     Filed:    8 Mar. 1902     Bk. H, Pg. 111
```

Wife: Mariah
Son: Joseph Wesley Irwin
Stepsons: John Selden Hayden, Samuel Richmond Hayden
Daughters: Christina Grimes of Cedar Co., Mo.; Orleana Ann
             (deceased); Mary Lucinda Roux; Paulina Mills;
             Emily Hannah Roux
Executor: John Wesley Irwin
Witnesses: Anthony Poff(?) of Salt Point Tnsp., Ca.; Arthur
             C. Walls M.D. of Cazadero, Ca.

```
JACKSON, EUNICE          Written:  19 May 1883            #1982
Petaluma                 Died:     8 Jun. 1890     Bk. E, Pg. 293
                         Rec.:     21 Jul. 1890
```

Husband: Lorenzo (deceased)
Children: Anna, Mary, Eunice, Lorenzo, Frances, Lucinda
             Laird (deceased), wife of Chas.
Executor: Son, Frances
Witnesses: Lewis J. Winans, Wm. B. Haskell

JACKSON, LORENZO   Written: 16 Mar. 1867   # 340
                          Died: 24 Mar. 1867
                          Filed: 6 May 1867

  Wife: Eunice
                 Eight minor children
  Executor: N.H. Galusha

JACKSON, MARTHA JANE   Written: 12 Aug. 1876   #2189
Santa Rosa   Died: 30 Aug. 1876
                          Rec.:   21 Mar. 1892

  Daughter: Roseann Crist, wife of Wm.
  Son-in-law: William Crist
  Daughter: Bell Sorey Banneyburg, wife of Jourden, of San
                 Luis Obispo Co.
  Sons: John B., Wm. C., Thos. J., Walter K.
  Grand-
  Daughter: Martha C. Crist
  Executor: Wm. Crist
  Witnesses: John Brown, Jane Geiger

JACKSON, WILLIAM   Written: 11 Feb. 1868   # 379
                          Filed: 4 May 1868

  Wife: Julia Ann
  Executor: Wife
  Witnesses: John G. McManus, J.J. Morris both of Healdsburg

JACOBS, ELI   Written: 14 Sep. 1889   #1928
Santa Rosa Tnsp.   Filed   6 Jan. 1890
                          Age about 69

  Bequests to: Gionette, daughter of Barclay Hendley; daughter
                 and son of friend, Edward W. Davis; George, son
                 of A.B. Nalley; Lee and Dot, children of C.G. Ames
  Executors: Geo. W. Davis, A.B. Nalley
  Witnesses: J.W. Ragsdale, Arthur L. Harris

JAMES, CHARLES GUSTAVUS   Written: 29 Sep. 1888   #1781
Forestville   Died: 4 Oct. 1888   Bk. E, Pg.   1
                          Probate: 12 Nov. 1888

  Wife: Henrietta
  Witnesses: Robert Weir, Michael Walsh

```
JENSEN, JACOB WILHELM    Written:  18 Sep. 1889                #2097
             Age 68      Died:     30 Jun. 1891    Bk. E, Pg. 410
JENSEN MARIA P.          Jacob
             Age 62      Rec.:     14 Sep. 1891
```

All property to survivor, and at survivor's death to
Children: Maria Nicolina, Ingeborg, Niels, Anna Louise
Witnesses: A. Norstadt, Geo. Harting

```
JEWELL, ISAAC R.         Written:  28 May 1888                 #2061
                         Died:     16 Mar. 1891    Bk. E, Pg. 379
                         Rec.:     13 Apr. 1891
```

Wife: Ruby Ridley
Children: Ella Jewell Flint, George C. Jewell, Jesse J.
            Jewell, Sallie Jewell, Elliott J. Jewell,
            Samuel R. Jewell
Executors: Wife, Geo. C., Jesse J.
            Holographic

```
JOHNSON, ANDREW          Written:  21 Jun. 1899                #3046
Bodega Bay   Age 70      Died:     22 Jul. 1899    Bk. G. Pg. 311
                         Filed:    14 Aug. 1899
```

Sons: John P., Andrew B., Peter F.
Daughter: Rosanna Furlong
Daughter-in-
Law: Hattie Johnson (Mrs. Andrew B.)
Executors: Sons, Peter F. and John P.
Witnesses: Geo. W. Stump of Bodega Bay, CA; Daniel Quinlan
                of Bodega, CA

```
JOHNSON, ALMON T.        Dated:    29 Jan. 1898                #2988
                         Died:     12 Feb. 1899    Bk. G, Pg. 265
                         Filed:    6 Mar. 1899
```

Wife: Mary Ann Johnson
Son: John E. Johnson and John's three children
            Frederick, Frank and Demas
Brother: William Johnson
Grandson: Almon T. Johnson
Executor: Mary Ann Johnson
Witnesses: Wm. B. Haskell, Thos. C. Denny

```
JOHNSON, THOMAS          Written:  26 May 1870                 #1658
Cloverdale   Age 63      Died:     10 Jun. 1887    Bk. D, Pg. 466-
                         Filed:    1 Aug. 1887                  468
```

Wife: Eleanor (82)
Executor: Wife, Henry Kier
Witnesses: J.G. Heald, T. Marble, W.M. Howell

```
JOHNSTON, MISS MARY        Written:   11 Aug. 1891              #2099
Santa Rosa                 Died:      12 Aug. 1891    Bk. E, Pg. 406
                           Rec.:       7 Sep. 1891
```

Sisters:	Mrs. Marth- Stubblefield, Mrs. Nancy Stubblefield
Nieces:	Mary, Laura J. Ora Belle, Mary Esther Blatchley, Florence J.
Nephews:	John Henry, William, Frank
Bequests to:	John Rice Craig, Mary E. Craig, Martha Ann Ware, Wm. McAfee
Cousin:	Joseph Johnston and wife, June Johnston
Executor:	Friend, Henry Raney
Witnesses:	Wm. E. McConnell, H.F. White

```
JONES, DAVID W.            Written:   28 Aug. 1892              #2286
              Age about    Died:      26 Dec. 1892    Bk. F, Pg.  60
              66           Filed:     18 Jan. 1893
```

Bequest to:	Mrs. Janney Hewgitt, wife of John
Brothers:	William (deceased) of Parish of Gold Cliff, Monmouth Shire, Wales, a stonemason; Edward (64) of Parish of Witson, Monmouth Shire, Wales, a stonemason
Nieces:	Un-named
Nephews:	Un-named
Executor:	Sigurd A. Ringstrom
Witnesses:	G.W. Lane of San Francisco, John W. Wilson of Sonoma City

```
JONES, THOMAS J.           Written:   19 Feb. 1887              #1627
Windsor       Age 62       Died:      27 Mar. 1887    Bk. D, Pg. 417
                           Rec.:      13 Apr. 1887
```

Wife:	Clarissa J.
Brother:	R.M. of Sherman, Tex.
Sister-in-Law:	Mary S.(?) of Jackson Co., Tenn.
Executors:	Wife, James W. Oates
Witnesses:	B.F. Bonnel, T.J. Gaines of Healdsburg

```
JONES, WM. M.              Written:    9 Jul. 1889              #1883
              Age 81       Died:      11 Aug. 1889    Bk. E, Pg. 145
                           Rec.:       2 Sep. 1889
```

Daughters:	Josephine B. Jones, Julia A. Hines, Caroline W. Montgomery
Sons:	Absolom T., John M.
Executor:	Wm. E. McConnell
Witnesses:	John Walker of Sebastopol, John F. Boyce of Santa Rosa

JORDON, JOSHUA	Written:	5 Jun. 1873	# 642
	Died:	16 Sep. 1873	
	Filed:	13 Oct. 1873	

- Wife: Adelia
- Sons: Addison Dana, Leslie Alex., Frank
- Executor: Leslie A. Jordon
- Witnesses: Wm. H. Trimble, H.K. Brown (Borwin)

JOYCE, ANN	Written:	19 Apr. 1873	# 618
Petaluma	Died:	11 May 1873	
	Filed:	23 Jun. 1873	

- Husband: Thomas
- Children: Un-named
- Executor: Hubert Naughton
- Witnesses: Frank W. Shattuck, Kelly Tighe, Bridget M. Costello

JUSTI, CHARLES	Written:	29 Jun. 1869	#1488
Signed: CARL FREDRICH	Died:	5 Jul. 1885	Bk. D, Pg. 81
AUGUS JUSTE	Rec.:	17 Aug. 1885	
Glen Ellen	Age 62		

- Wife: Mary (Maria) (59)
- Children: Charles (38), August (36), Hulda (32), Hannah Merlin-Jones (25), Otilda R. (24), Leopold Walter (20), Frederick (18)
- Executor: Wife
- Witnesses: F.G. Hahman, James T. Hardin

JUSTI, MARIE CHRISTINE	Written:	3 May 1899	#3031
Age 73	Died:	4 Jun. 1899	Bk. 4, Pg. 299
	Filed:	3 Jul. 1899	

- Daughters: Hulda Justi, Hannah Merlin-Jones
- Sons: Charles R. Justi, Leopold Justi
- Grandsons: Charles Justi, William Justi
- Grand-Daughter: Hobarta Merlin-Jones
- Executor: Leopold Justi
- Witnesses: Robert A. Poppe of Sonoma, CA; William J. Behler of Glen Ellen, CA

KASELAW, JOHN	Dated:	30 Dec. 1886	#3162
CHRISTOFFER	Died:	27 May 1900	Bk. G, Pg. 432
San Leandro	Age 63		

- Wife: Bertha
- Daughters: Mathilda, Adda, Bertha all adults
- Executor: Bertha
- Witnesses: L.F. Rendenpaker, August Bjorkman of San Leandro

KAUFFMAN, FRANK ANTONE   Dated: 18 Oct. 1881   #1185
                          Filed: 29 Oct. 1881   Bk. C, Pg. 158

  Wife: Cathrine Kauffman
  Children: Charles Kauffman, Lewis Philip Kauffman,
               Frank Kauffman, Minie (Minnie?) Kline,
               John Kauffman
  Executor: Charles Kauffman
  Witnesses: Alexander Wiley, Bernard Hoffstetter

KAUFMANN, CATHERINE   Written: 13 May 1882   #1406
Santa Rosa   Age 64   Died: 14 Jun. 1884   Bk. C, Pg. 558
                          Filed: 14 Jul. 1884

  Husband: Frank Anton (deceased)
  Sons: Frank (32), John (26)
  Daughter: Mrs. Minnie Klein (30)
  Executor: Son, Frank
  Witnesses: E.P. Colgan, Darwin C. Allen

KEARNS, JAMES   Written: 21 Aug. 1884   #1619
Petaluma   Age 64   Died: 16 Feb. 1887   Bk. D, Pg. 390
                          Rec.:   21 Mar. 1887

  Nephews: Peter & Bernhard, sons of deceased brother,
               Thomas of San Francisco
  Nieces: Rose & Bridget, daughters of Thos.
  Brother: Bernhard of San Francisco
  Sisters: Mary, Bridget, Margaret of New York city; Ann
               of Co. Antrim, Ire.
  Executor: Father James Cleary
  Witnesses: E. Rogers, J. Campbell

KELLOGG, WARREN S.   Written: 13 Jan. 1873   # 619
                          Died: 10 May 1873

  Wife: Frances Eliz.
  Executor: Wife
  Witnesses: Geo. Mulligan, J.W. Clack

KELLY, MARK   Written: 13 Dec. 1879   #1059
                          Filed: 13 Jan. 1880   Bk. C, Pg. 78

  Wife: Rebecca J. Kelly
  Children: Nelly D. Skelton of Alabama, John Maynard Kelly,
               Martha A. Kelly, William S. Kelly, Kate Kelly,
               Francis Kelly, Anna A. Kelly, Mark Kelly Jr. of
               this state
  Executor: Appointed; William Kelly a minor at time will was
               written
  Witnesses: John Wheaton, John Thomas Wheaton

KELLY, MARY CECILIA   Written: 15 May 1893   #3235
Brisbane, Queenland,   Codicil: 25 Jan. 1898
Australia   Filed: 5 May 1902
Music teacher

   Husband: Joseph Kelly of Sydney, New So. Wales,
                Australia, separated by Protection Order
                14 Aug. 1882
   Sons: Joseph Kelly, Francis Kelly
   Brother: Thomas Aloysius Pole of Leicester, England
   Sister: Agnes Pole of Brisbane, Australia
   Trustee: The Queensland Trustees, Ltd.
   Witnesses: P.J. O Shea of Brisbane, Australia; Chas. Eden (?)
                of Brisbane, Australia; John George Brown,
                Deputy Registrar of Titles
   Codicil
   Witnesses: P.J. O Shea of Brisbane, Australia; J. Allan
                Duncan of Brisbane, Australia

KENNEDY, JAMES   Written: 16 Jan. 1871   #1062
                             Died: 21 Jan. 1880   Bk. C, Pg. 83
                             Filed: 18 Oct. 1881

   Wife: Electa Kennedy
   Executor: Electa Kennedy
   Witnesses: Jasper J. Lindsay, Bradford Bell

KENNEDY, MARIAH   Written: 30 Mar. 1886   #1539
Sonoma   Age 76   Died: 2 Apr. 1886   Bk. D, Pg. 218
                             Rec.:   23 Jun. 1886

   Grand-
   Daughter: Annie M. Church
   Daughters: Mary Otis Webb, Margaret Ann Church
   Admn: Annie M. Church
   Witnesses: J.G. Smyth, Obed Charb

KENNY, MARGARET   Dated: 20 Jul. 1900   #3190
                             Died: 3 Aug. 1900   Bk. G, Pg. 448
                             Filed: 4 Sep. 1900

                Mrs. Annie J. Carey
                Rose Carey
   Executor: D. J. Healey
   Witnesses: F.A. Meyer, Thomas Dortmund

KESSER, LOUIS SR.   Written: 1 Sep. 1892   #2563
Santa Rosa   Age 70   Died: 7 Aug. 1895   Bk. F. Pg. 411
                             Rec.:   10 Sep. 1895

   Wife: Pauline
   Children: Alma, Louis Jr.
   Executor: Wife or son
   Witnesses: H.M. Forsyth, F.G. Nagle

KIER, HANS HENRY AKA   Written: 12 Dec. 1898   #3392
HARRY   Died: 26 Nov. 1901   Bk. H, Pg. 85
                          Filed: 16 Dec. 1901

    Sisters: Christina Jorgerson, Thrina Hansen
    Niece: Carrie Jorgersen
    Bequests to: Amy Haehl, Harry Hael, Gorge Hanson, Kate Anker,
                  Sina (?) Braint, Bergitha Ludwig of Seattle, WA,
                  Peter H. Ludwig, Mary Nelson, Josie Hanson,
                  Annie Elizabeth Schieffer
    Executors: Peter H. Ludwig, William Schieffer of Santa Rosa
    Witnesses: Holographic

KIMBALL, J. T.   Written: 16 Jul. 1865   # 287
                          Probate: 30 Jul. 1865

                  John F. Jarvis
    Executors: J.B. Hinkle, John F. Jarvis
    Witnesses: B.F. Smith, C.H. Nins

KIMBLE, HARRISON   Written: 20 Feb. 1893   #2353
Sebastopol   Died: 13 Aug. 1893   Bk. F, Pg. 176
                          Rec.:   6 Nov. 1893

    Wife: Majesta
    Children: J. Whiting Kimble of Sebastopol, Mary F. Clark
                  of Chico, Liston Kimble of Los Angeles, Charles
                  Kimble of Sebastopol
    Executors: Three sons
    Witnesses: John S. Saunders, Fred H. Luth

KIMBLE, MARY ANN   Dated: 19 Mar. 1900   #3179
          Age 40   Died: 20 Jun. 1900   Bk. H, Pg.   2
                          Filed: 9 Jul. 1900

    Husband: J.W. Kimble
    Children: Thomas H. Kimble, Mary M. Kimble, Francis L.
                  Kimble (minor), Delia C. Kimble (minor),
                  Annie May Kimble (minor), Theresa T. Kimble
                  (minor) Edward W. Kimble (minor), Frederick
                  P. Kimble (minor)
    Executor: Mary M. Kimble
    Witnesses: Wm. T. Searles, George P. Baxter

KING, MATHEW WALLACE   Written: 9 Feb. 1893   #2324
Santa Rosa   Died: 9 May 1893   Bk. F, Pg. 130
                          Rec.:   24 May 1893

    Wife: Un-named
    Son: Henry
    Executors: Wife and John P. Overton
    Witnesses: Holographic

```
KISER, JOHN P.              Written:   2 Sep. 1875              # 776
Petaluma                    Died:     14 Sep. 1875       Bk. B. Pg. 208
                            Filed:     1 Nov. 1875

    Wife:         Mary E. (who has left me)
    Son:          Abraham Cooper (minor)
    Daughter:     Henrietta (minor)
    Daughter:     Of wife Mary E., Ida
    Brothers:     Abraham, Mathew, Aaron
    Executor:     Brother, Abraham
    Witnesses:    E.L. Lippitt, John Fritsch


KITTREDGE, WILLIAM T.       Written:   2 Jan. 1892              #2151
Santa Rosa                  Died:      3 Jan. 1892       Bk. E, Pg. 505
                            Rec.:     18 Jan. 1892

    Wife:         Deceased
    Sister:       Laura K. Jenny of Kansas City, MO
    Brother-in-
    Law:          C.H. Cook of Sonoma Co.
    Children:     Of Fred Kittredge of Minn.
    Executor:     Wm. D. Reynolds
    Witnesses:    Guy E. Grosse, J.H. Boswell


KLINE, JACOB J.             Dated:    19 Nov. 1881              #1196
             Age 43         Died:     19 Nov. 1881       Bk. C, Pg. 170
                            Rec.:     27 Dec. 1881

    Wife:         Minnie Kline
    Children:     Isabelle Kline, Lena Kline, Charles Kline,
                  Frank Kline
    Executor:     Minnie Kline
    Witnesses:    J.F. Boyce, A.J. Musselman


KNIGHT, LUTHER              Written:  13 Jul. 1893              #2350
Glen Ellen   Age 66         Died:      6 Sep. 1893       Bk. F, Pg. 165
                            Rec.:      9 Oct. 1893

    Son:          William Horton Knight
    Daughter:     Mary A. (?) Miner of Glen Ellen
    Executors:    Daughter, Mary and Chas. F. Doe of San Francisco
    Witnesses:    H.H. Davis M.D., Robt. A. Poppe both of Sonoma


KNOWLES, JAMES H.           Written:  23 May 1895               #2552
Blucher Valley              Died:     14 Jul. 1895       Bk. F, Pg. 408
                            Rec.:     10 Aug. 1895

    Wife:         Clarissa A.
    Sister:       Mary Ogden of Waterburg, Conn.
    Grand-
    Daughter:     Mary Knowles
    Grandson      James Knowles
    Son:          Wm. H.
    Executor:     Wife
    Witnesses:    Wm. B. Haskell, Wm. R. Overholser
```

KOGER, WILLIAM   Dated: 9 Feb. 1856   # 58
            Age 59   Died: 16 Feb. 1856   Bk. -, Pg. 6&7
                         Filed: 7 Mar. 1856

    Daughters: Mary Bice, Martha Dillingham, Adeline Koger
    Wife: Matilda
    Executor: Matilda
    Witnesses: H.P. Mollison, Thomas McClish

KOHLE, CATHERINE   Written: 6 Feb. 1885   #1470
Santa Rosa   Age 55   Died: 8 May 1885   Bk. D, Pg. 66
                         Rec.:   6 Jul. 1885

    Husband: A. (deceased)
    Daughters: Louise Kate Kohle (21), Augustina Kohle (14)
    Son: Wm. H. Quinlan (23)
    Executor: Louise Kate
    Witnesses: John F. Boyce, John Brown

KOLMER, JOSEPHA   Dated: 3 Feb. 1865   # 274
Salt Point Tnsp.   Died: 22 Feb. 1865   Bk. A, Pg. 129
                         Filed: 5 Apr. 1863(?)

    Daughter: Caroline Howard
    Son: John Kolmer
    Executor: F. Helmke
    Witnesses: J.W. Phinny, William Rogers

KOPF, WILHELM   Written: 17 Mar. 1892   #2203
Santa Rosa   Age 67   Died: 20 Mar. 1892   Bk. E, Pg. 603
                         Rec.:   25 Apr. 1892

    Wife: Katharine
    Children: Adolph A., William, Carl L., August J. Louisa
                V. Fenkhausen, wife of Walter
    Executor: Wife
    Witnesses: D.F. Moltzen of Santa Rosa, W. Fenkhausen of
                San Francisco

KRAFT, ROSOMOND   Written: 4 Jan. 1887   #1604
Santa Rosa   Died: 20 Jan. 1887   Bk. D, Pg. 351
                         Rec.:   5 Feb. 1887

    Children: Nellie May, Jesse Athol, Emma Agnes, Violet (all
                under 14 years of age per J. Booth)
    Executor: Father, Jesse Booth
    Witnesses: H.C. Petray, Henry R. Bull

```
KRON, ELIZABETH        Written:   2 Sep. 1890 I              #2969
Petaluma      Age over  Written:  17 Sep. 1892 II
              60        Codicil:  31 Oct. 1893
                        Filed:    25 Jan. 1899 I
                        Filed:    25 Jan. 1899 II
```

Daughter: Mary Schmidt (Mrs. George)
Grand-
Daughters: Lizzie Schmidt, Millie Schmidt, Emma Schmidt
Grandson: John Kron Schmidt
Son-in-law: George Schmidt
Mentioned: Prof. F.A. Cromwell
Executors I: H.H. Atwater
Executor &
Trustee II: D.B. Fairbanks
Witnesses I: Thomas Maclay, Wm. B. Haskell both of Petaluma
Witnesses II: Jerome T. Gardner, F.A. Meyer both of Petaluma

```
KRUSE, JAMES            Written:  20 Jan. 1879              #1510
Mark West Creek         Died:     20 Oct. 1885     Bk. D, Pg. 133
              Age 50    Rec.:      7 Dec. 1885
```

Wife: Mariana (48)
Children: John (27), Anna Foss (24), Frederick (19),
               Charles (17), James (15), Henry (12), August (10)
Executors: F.G. Hahman, Geo. P. Noonan
Witnesses: Jno. P. Overton, Henry W. Hudson

```
KUCHEL, JACOB           Dated:     6 Apr. 1900              #3170
Ruby Hill, Eureka Co.,  Died:     30 Apr. 1900     Bk. H, Pg. 12
Nevada        Age 54    Filed:     9 Jul. 1900
```

               Henry Kuchel of No. 40, Foster St., New Haven,
               Connecticut
               Mrs. Edward Kummer of Petaluma, CA
               Mrs. George Gimbel of Butzbach, Hesse-Darmstadt,
               Germany
               Miss Greta Gimble of Butzbach, Hesse-Darmstadt,
               Germany
Executors: Henry Kuchel, Edward Kummer
Witnesses: H.C. McTernay, George A. Bartlett both of
               Eureka, Nevada

```
KYLE, THOMAS            Written:  28 Jan. 1898              #2863
                        Died:     28 Mar. 1898
                        Filed:     9 May  1898
```

Wife: Marinda Kyle
Son: John G. Kyle
Daughters: Mary M. Kyle, Effie M. Kyle, Philana Nash,
               Beatrice J. Gunn (deceased)
Grand-
Children: Louise Gunn, Ray Gunn
Executor: Wife
Witnesses: W.D. Reynolds, Wm Prindle

LACQUE, BRUNNELL	Written:	7 Jul. 1880	#2006
Santa Rosa Tnsp.	Died:	12 Sep. 1890	Bk. E, Pg. 312
	Rec.:	6 Oct. 1890	

- Wife: Anna
- Children: Un-named
- Executor: Wife
- Witnesses: J. Latture of Hollister, CA; Nelson Carr, Hannah L. Carr both of Santa Rosa

LA FRANCHI, BATTISTA	Dated:	5 Nov. 1893	#2749
	Died:	6 May 1897	Bk. G, Pg. 38
	Filed:	28 May 1897	

- Wife: Giacomina LaFranchi
- Sons: Achille LaFranchi, Ottorino LaFranchi, Arthur LaFranchi, Oliver LaFranchi
- Executor: Giacomina LaFranchi
- Witnesses: E.B. Martinelli of San Rafael, John Zeller of Reclamation, Sonoma Co.

LALLEMENT, JEAN NICOLAS	Written:	21 Jun. 1875	#1049
San Francisco/Des	Filed:	15 Dec. 1879	
Ardennes, France			

- Wife: Marie Francoise Adolphine Lallement nee Parent
- Daughter: Marie Donatienne Lallement
- Executor: Wife
- Witnesses: Wm. H. Aiken, J.H. Blood
- Codicil Witnesses: V.G. Robin, Pietro Martinoni

LAMBERT, HENRY F.		Written:	8 Jan. 1889	#1830
Healdsburg	Age 67	Died:	21 Feb. 1889	Bk. E, Pg. 89
		Rec.:	26 Mar. 1889	

- Niece: Emma Gibson
- Nephew-in-Law: Silas Gibson
- Sister: Maria Bells
- Children: Of brother Joseph J. Lambert; of brother Chas. L. (deceased) namely Jane Laveel; of brothers R.F., W.S. & Geo. L.
- Grand-Children: Of Chas. L.; Ellen Augusta & Geo.
- Executor: Silas Gibson
- Witnesses: C.W. Weaver, Jasper McCracken

```
LANCEL, ANSELME          Written:    2 Dec. 1888           #2108
Occidental    Age 63     Died:       9 Sep. 1891    Bk. E, Pg. 452
                         Rec.:       5 Oct. 1891
```

- Wife: Melanie (Hubert)
- Children: Levin Amel--- (oldest son); Eugene Henry (2nd son); Paul Luc-- (3rd son); Benjamin; Juliette Melanie (oldest daughter); Gabrielle Dina (2nd daughter); Jeanne Henrietta; Ason Jean
- Executor: First Judge of Sonoma Co. Superior Court
- Witnesses: Holographic

```
LANE, EMMA D.            Written:   26 Dec. 1885           #1519
Petaluma                 Died:      12 Jan. 1886    Bk. D, Pg. 146
                         Filed:      8 Feb. 1886
```

- Son: Lincoln (8½)
- Trustee: Sister-in-law Sarah Lane of Brooklyn, NY
- Witnesses: Wm. B. Haskell, Wm. A. Chapman

```
LANG, JAMES P.           Written:   20 Feb. 1890           #1992
San Francisco            Died:      22 Jun. 1890    Bk. E, Pg. 296
                         Rec.:      28 Jul. 1890
```

- Wife: Katie
- Children: Susie B., Katie A., William, James B., Joseph S.
- Executor: Wife
- Witnesses: Jos. B. Chardin, Geo. F. Hoeffer

```
LANGDON, ELIZA JANE      Written:   30 Jun. 1863           #1046
                         Filed:     19 Nov. 1879    Bk. C, Pg.  65
```

- Husband: Charles W. Langdon
- Daughter: Eliza Caroline (infant)
- Brothers: George Forshew of Hudson, NY; Frank Forshew of Hudson, NY
- Sisters: Alma B. Graff (Mrs. Milton) of Hudson, NY; Sarah A. Faxen(?) (Mrs. Elisha) of Stowington, Conn.; Caroline A. Allen (Mrs. Charles H.) of Napa City, CA
- Previous marriage to Robert R. Pierpont of Napa City CA
- Son John Pierpont (deceased)
- Executor: Charles W. Langdon
- Witnesses: Rob Cronche (?), J.C. Penwell of Napa City, CA

```
LANSBURY, WILLIAM H.     Written:   21 Mar. 1864           # 593
                         Filed:      5 Jul. 1864
```

- Wife: Eliz. H.
- Daughters: Sarah Caroline, Rhoda T., Louise K. Levalley
- Son: B.F.
- Executor: O.C. Hooper
- Witnesses: J. Ramey, S.B. Robeson

```
LARSEN, OLEF                 Written:   7 Dec. 1868              # 401
                 Age 44      Died:     15 Dec. 1868
                             Probate:   1 Jan. 1869

   Wife:         Caroline
   Children:     Edwin Olef (6), Charles Emil (3), Magnus (1)
   Executor:     Wife
   Witnesses:    G.T. Pauli, C. Dyer of Sonoma


LATAPIE, EDWARD              Died:      9 Nov. 1881              #1044
                             Rec.:     27 Oct. 1881   Bk. C, Pg.  59

   Wife:         Elnora Latapie
   Mother:       Sophie Latapie
   Executor:     Elnora Latapie
   Witnesses:    J.B. Southard, Mat Aikin


LATIMER, L. D.               Written:  21 Sep. 1899              #3374
Windsor, Sonoma Co.,         Died:     25 Sep. 1901   Bk. H, Pg.  66
CA                           Filed:    21 Oct. 1901

   Wife:         Mentioned but not named
   Sons:         Lorenzo P.N., Hugh N.N.
   Grandsons:    Harry Dow Latimer, Lorenzo Phelps Latimer
   Executors     Sons
   Witnesses:    Holographic


LAUGHLIN, JAMES H.            Written:  20 Feb. 1890             #2194
Mark West                     Died:     25 Feb. 1892   Bk. E, Pg. 575
                              Rec.:     21 Mar. 1892

   Wife:         Frances E.
   Children:     Mrs. Sarah Addie Thomson, Annie A. Laughlin, J.
                 Henry, Frank W., Grant A., Clyde H.B.
   Executors:    Wife & son J. Henry
   Witnesses:    Frank Briggs of Fulton, C.T. Mathisen of Mark West


LAURITSON, CHRISTINA         Written:  15 Feb. 1888              #2448
MARIA                        Died:      4 Nov. 1894   Bk. F, Pg. 320
Santa Rosa       Age 35      Rec.:     10 Dec. 1894

   Husband:      John
   Executor:     Husband
   Witnesses:    John Brown, T.W. Leavenworth
```

```
LAVIN, JAMES                    Written:  26 May 1888              #2060
Petaluma        Age over  Died:    5 Mar. 1891       Bk. E, Pg. 372
                50        Rec.:    6 Apr. 1891

     Wife:         Mary
     Son:          James J.
     Sister:       Susan Trimble, wife of Patrick
     Niece:        Maggie Lavin, daughter of deceased brother
                   Dominick
     Step-
     Daughter:     Alice Soldate, wife of John
     Executor:     Son, James J. Lavin
     Witnesses:    Wm. B. Haskell, F.A. Meyer


LA VINE, NELLIE MALVINIA Written: 23 Aug. 1880                     #1117
                         Filed:   19 Oct. 1880

     Husband:      Frank
     Executor:     Husband
     Witnesses:    O.B. Shaw, Mary L. Shaw


LAWLER, PATRICK           Written:  12 Sep. 1879                   #1681
         Age 66           Codicil:  12 Jan. 1887       Bk. D, Pg. 514-
                          Died:      9 Sep. 1887                    519
                          Filed:    25 Oct. 1887

     Wife:         Bridget
     Sons:         James Lawler, Patrick H. Lawler, Dennis Lawler,
                   John Lawler, Peter Lawler
     Daughters:    Mary E. Lawler Studdert, Bridget F. Lawler
                   Hardin, Lucy M. Lawler Rogers
     Executors:    Wife & James Lawler, son
     Witnesses:    Charles L. Ackerman, Walter D. Mansfield, Holland
                   Smith, Chas.(?) Carpy


LAWTON, JOHN              Written:  25 Sep. 1882                   #1854
Sebastopol      Age 42    Died:     20 Jan. 1886       Bk. E, Pg. 118
                          Filed:    29 May 1889

     Wife:         Fannie H.
     Children:     Un-named
     Executor:     Wife
     Witnesses:    Israel Lawton, Wm. D. Lawton both of Oakland, CA


LEARD, R. A.              Written:   2 Dec. 1871                   # 617
                          Died:     14 May 1873
                          Filed:    24 May 1873

     Wife:         Phoeba
     Executor:     Wife
     Witnesses:    Albert Wright, W.S. Canan
```

LEARY, JAMES   Written: 17 Aug. 1873   # 638
                             Died: 18 Aug. 1873
                             Filed: 15 Sep. 1873

              No wife mentioned
Children: Arthur Walter, Ida Jane both adopted
Executor: Joseph Vandermooth (?)
Witnesses: John Cavanaugh, Eugene Campbell

LEAVENWORTH, THADDEUS W. Written: 30 Jul. 1883   #2317
Sonoma Co.   Died: 30 Jan. 1893   Bk. F, Pg. 116
                        Rec.:   8 May 1893

Wife: Cornelia T.
Sister: Charlotte Brown of Honeyoye Falls, NY
Bequests to: Hattie Cary, Walter M. Cary, Jas. H. Cary, James
              C. Cary
Executors: Wife & Jas. C. Cary
Witnesses: G.F. Cowdery, E.J. McCutchen both of San Francisco

LEE, DANIEL   Written: 7 Jul. 1883   #1347
Donohue   Died: 13 Jul. 1883   Bk. C, Pg. 425
Mechanic   Rec.:   8 Oct. 1883

Wife: Mary Teresa
Daughters: Catherine, Mary Margaret
Son: Daniel P.
Executor: Wife
Witnesses: Edwin Reynolds, C.H. Mould

LEEK, JOSEPHINE   Written: 3 Jul. 1888   #1823
           Age 58   Died: 28 Jan. 1889   Bk. E, Pg. 43
                             Filed: 13 Feb. 1889

Husband: Wm. G. (deceased)
Daughter: Eliza Ann Fowler
Sons: John J., Geo. W., Chas. E., Ira G.
Executor: John J.
Witnesses: W.P. Overland, C.A. Hoffer

LEEK, WILLIAM C.   Written: 13 Aug. 1886   #1574
Santa Rosa Age 62   Died: 14 Sep. 1886   Bk. D, Pg. 287
                             Rec.:   4 Oct. 1886

Wife: Josephine
Sons: J.G. Leek, Geo. W., Charles E. Ira G.
Daughter: Eliza A. Fowler, wife of A.F.
Executor: Ira Leek, Eliza Fowler
Witnesses: O.A. Hoag, Dr. J.B. Pressley

```
LEINHARD, RUDOLF          Written:   27 Mar. 1891              #2066
Healdsburg    Age 34      Died:       4 Apr. 1891     Bk. E, Pg. 385
Home Bakery
```

- Father: Joseph of Uerkhein, Switz.
- Mother: Maria of Uerkhein, Switz.
- Executor: John F. Grater
- Witnesses: T. Coman, J.T. Coffman

```
LENNOX, JOHN              Dated:    13 Apr. 1858              # 115
                          Filed:     1 Jun. 1858     Bk. A, Pg.  46
```

- Wife: Louisa Lennox
- Sons: Robert Lennox, James Harrison Lennox (minor), John Alexander Lennox (minor)
- Executors: Robert Lennox, Granville P. Swift
- Witnesses: Geo. L. Wratten (?)

```
LEVY, LOUIS               Dated:     8 Nov. 1871              # 512
                          Died:      9 Nov. 1871     Bk. A, Pg. 247-
                          Filed:    13 Nov. 1871                 249
```

- Brothers: Un-named
- Sisters: Un-named
- Executor: Abraham Morris
- Witnesses: Frank W. Shattuck, T. Phillips

```
LEWIS, JERE               Dated:     8 Jun. 1897              #2977
                          Died:      5 Jan. 1899     Bk. G, Pg. 253
                          Filed:    27 Feb. 1899
```

- Sons: C.M. Lewis, C.M.V. Lewis
- Daughter: Elizabeth A. Stanger, her husband A.H. Stanger
- Wife: Elizabeth Lewis
- Executors: C.M. Lewis, A.H. Stanger
- Witnesses: Frank Burr, J.M. Hickey

```
LEWIS, RICHARD E.         Written:  28 Jun. 1894              #2436
Healdsburg    Age 65      Died:     30 Jun. 1894     Bk. F, Pg. 293
```

- Wife: Nancy Jane
- Children: Rachel Susan, Rebecca Ann, Sarah Adeline, Cassia Sylvania, Marth Augusta, Lena May, Prudence Mable
- Step-Daughters: Mary E. Poe, Mary E. King
- Executor: Wife
- Witnesses: Wm. Mothorn, W.W. Moreland

LIBBY, CLARAC MARIA   Written: 31 Jan. 1902   #3434
HELENA nee BERGLUND   Died: 12 Feb. 1902   Bk. H, Pg. 113
                             Filed: 24 Mar. 1902

   Bequests to: Mrs. J.H. McLeod; Dr. J.H. McLeod; Mrs. Schudy (?)
             of 314 3rd St., Santa Rosa; Nora Schudy; Mrs.
             Michelsen; Mrs. J.N. Mitter (?) of 1941 Fillmore
             St.; Mrs. Mogensen of Berkeley, CA; Mrs. C.
             Jorgensen of 1114 Alabama St., San Francisco;
             Edward Michelsen
   Brothers: Alfred Berglund of Stockholm, Sweden; Hugo ---
   Sister: Ellen
   Mentioned: Simpson & Roberts contractors of 3rd St., Santa
              Rosa
   Witnesses: J.H. McLeod, J.E. Gracier

LIEBIG, AUGUST FREDERICK Written: 27 Jun. 1874   #1847
Salt Point Tnsp.   Died: 13 Mar. 1889   Bk. E, Pg. 107
                          San Francisco
                          Filed: 29 Apr. 1889

   Wife: Anna Helene
   Executor: Wife
   Witnesses: Theodore H. Hittell, H. Ludolph

LIKINS, ELIZA ANN   Dated: 1 May 1900   #3270
                             Died: 8 Feb. 1901   Bk. H, Pg. 35
                             Filed: 4 Mar. 1901

   Husband: Levi Likins
   Son: J.L. Likins
   Grand-
   Children: Frank J. Likins, Walter L. Likins, Ernest Likins
              all sons of J.L. Likins
   Executor: J.L. Likins
   Witnesses: Calvin Seites, W.W. Moreland

LINDSAY, J. J.   Written: 26 Jan. 1892   #2374
Windsor   Died: 2 Dec. 1893   Bk. F, Pg. 204
                             Rec.:   8 Jan. 1894

   Wife: Esther A.
   Children: Walter C., Estella B., Maggie F., Adin A.
   Executors: Wife; son, Walter
   Witnesses: Sanford B. Henley, W.J. Mitchell, J.F. Philpott
              all of Windsor

LINDSEY, THOMAS S   Written: 7 Sep. 1866   # 371
              Age About Died: 12 Jan. 1868 (about)
              40

   Wife: Sarah A.
   Executor: Wife
   Witnesses: I.G. Wickersham, Alex McCune

LINEBAUGH, JOHN   Written: 5 Feb. 1890   #2143
                         Died: 9 Dec. 1891   Bk. E, Pg. 540
                         Rec.:   9 Feb. 1892

    Wife: Carrie Virginia (2nd)
    Daughters: Sarah Elizabeth Parish, Mary Jane Low
    Sons: Robert, Henry
    Witnesses: J.C. Sims, Geo. Pearce both of Santa Rosa

LINUS, JOHN   Dated: 9 Apr. 1861   # 245
                Age 41   Filed: 30 Jan. 1864   Bk. A, Pg. 109

    Sisters: Margaret Castle, wife of John Castle of MO;
                Sarah Catherine Cass, wife of Mr. Cass of
                Muskigum Co., Ohio
    Uncle: John W. Dunn of Lickins Co., Ohio
    Executor: Charles Patton
    Witnesses: S. Payran (?), Fredric Alberding, Charles Patton,
                Thos. W. ---weil, R.H. Crane

LINVILLE, BYRAM   Written: 13 Nov. 1897   #3403
Cloverdale   Age 76   Died: 26 Nov. 1901   Bk. H, Pg. 101
                         Rec.:   31 Jan. 1902

    Wife: Elizabeth
    Children: Valentine (?) Z. of Calaveras Co., CA; Jasper
                A. Linville of Calaveras Co., CA; Pleasant Day
                Linville of San Francisco; Permelia H. Monday
                of Los Angeles; Eliz. N. Wisecarver of Calaveras
                Co., CA; Mary Ada Wisecarver of Sonoma Co.;
                Clement Roy Linville of Cloverdale
    Grand-
    Children: Maud Ingram, Frank Linville
    Executors: Clement Linville, Mary Ada Wisecarver
    Witnesses: Fred. W. Brush, Geo. E. Brush

LITTLE, THOS. C.   Written: 19 May 1873   # 636
                         Died: -- Jul. 1873
                         Filed: 12 Sep. 1873

    Father: John of Colchester Tnsp., Essex Co., Ontario,
                Canada
    Mother: Mary of Colchester Tnsp., Essex Co., Ontario,
                Canada
    Sister: Mary Jane Burgess of Sonoma
    Executor: John Schwartz
    Witnesses: Frank W. Shattuck, Jane E. Schwartz

LODGE, JOHN D.   Written: 8 Mar. 1893   #3077
Santa Rosa   Age 69   Rec.:   2 Nov. 1899

  Wife: Martha
  Children: Jennie Harris, wife of Wm. H. of Los Angeles;
              David E. Lodge of Healdsburg; Tillie A. Prince,
              wife of Morris of Santa Rosa
  Executor: Wife
  Witnesses: John P. Overton, C.A. Hoffer

LONG, WILLIAM   Written: 18 Jul. 1866   # 695
                             Died: 14 Jun. 1874
                             Filed: 13 Jun. 1874

  Wife: Polly
  Children: Isaac; Mary Rice, wife of John; Rachel Ward,
              wife of Albert T.; Jane Taylor, wife of Charles.
  Heirs: Of George; Of Eliz. Struck of MO.
  Executors: Wife, L.T. Hall
  Witnesses: H.M. Willson, J.G. McManus

LONG, REBECCA   Written: 24 Jun. 1899   #3038
                  Age 65   Died: 27 Jun. 1899   Bk. G, Pg. 304
                             Filed: 17 Jul. 1899

  Husband: Henry Long
  Daughters: Larina L. Bristow, Ellen Hayes, Emma Gendelc,
              Sarah Long
  Sons: Frederick Long, Charles W. Long
  Executor: Larina Bristow
  Witnesses: C.H. Thompson, Amanda C. Sonders, Josephine K.
              Abendroth

LOOMIS, PHOEBE JANE   Dated: 9 May 1898   #2884
Widow   Died: 21 May 1898   Bk. G, Pg. 192
                             Filed: 31 May 1898

  Sisters: Hannah Aryelia Bonter, wife of Wm. D. Bonter of
              Belleville, Province of Ontario; Susan Peck, wife
              of S.S. Peck of Petaluma; Eliza Lettitia Simmour
              of Colorado
  Executor: Col. D.B. Fairbanks of Petaluma
  Witnesses: Wm. B. Haskell, Thos. C. Denny

LOONEY, ROBERT   Written: 10 Oct. 1882   #1552
Petaluma   Died: 16 May 1886   Bk. D, Pg. 236
                             Rec.:   28 Jun. 1886

  Wife: Sarah
  Next of Kin: Mrs. Addie Bostwick, Mrs. Vera Doty, Mrs. Nevada
                Rudolph, Mrs. Lillie Cheney
  Executor: Wife
  Witnesses: E.L. Lippitt, Chester F. Wright

```
LOONEY, SARAH              Written:   11 Sep. 1886            #1618
Vallejo Tnsp.  Age about   Died:      21 Feb. 1887   Bk. D, Pg. 385
               60          Rec.:      21 Mar. 1887
```

Daughters: Addie L. Bostwick, Nevada Rudolph, Vera M. Doty,
               Lillie M. Cheney
Grand-
Children: Robert Haywood, Albert Haywood
Executors: Thos. H. Cheney, Albert Doty
Witnesses: Wm. P. Edwards, John Riewerts

```
LOPEZ, MARIA YGNESIA       Dated:     6 Jan. 1849              #   1
```

Parents: Juan Francisco Lopez, Feliciana Arbaez Difrintoz
Husband: Joaquin Carrillo (deceased)
Children: Josepha Carrillo, Ramona Carrillo, Maria de la Lus
               Carrillo, Francisco Carrillo, Joaquin Carrillo,
               Ramon Carrillo, Juan Carrillo, Delorez Carrillo,
               Julio Carrillo, Marta Inana Carrillo, Felicidad
               Carrillo
Witnesses: Joaquin Carrillo, Julio Carrillo

```
LOSEE, HANNAH              Written:   19 Sep. 1891            #2131
Sonoma Valley              Died:      16 Nov. 1891   Bk. E, Pg. 476
```

Husband: John A. (deceased)
Brother: John Brickwell of Willow River, Pine Co., Minn.
Sisters: Elizabeth Hawkins of Birkenhean, Auckland, N.Z.;
               Caroline Stone of High Wycombe, Buckingham, Eng.
  (?) :   Edward A. Losee of Brooklyn, N.Y.; J.P. Losee
               of St. Joseph, MO.
Executor: John R. Cooper
Witnesses: Robt. A. Poppe, R.E. Perkins both of Sonoma City

```
LOSEE, JOHN AREA           Written:   17 Apr. 1879            #2064
Sonoma         Age 58      Died:       3 Apr. 1891   Bk. E, Pg. 308
                           Rec.:      25 May  1891
```

Wife: Hannah
Executor: Wife
Witnesses: Charles M. Harvey, Thomas Spriggs Cooper

```
LOUCKS, A. H.              Written:   27 Feb. 1886            #1538
Santa Rosa                 Died:      16 Mar. 1886   Bk. D, Pg. 169
                           Rec.:       5 Apr. 1886
```

Wife: Sarah J.
Daughters: Kate R. Myrick, Jennie G. Morely
Executor: Wife
Witnesses: James McReynolds, A.D. Laughlin

LOVEJOY, MARY GOULD		Written:	7 Jan. 1872				# 666
				Died:	10 Jan. 1872
				Filed:	16 Feb. 1874

   Husband:		Dr. John
   Bequests to:	Mrs. Kate H. Lovejoy, wife of Dr. Allen P; Miss
			Annie Gray of San Francisco; Mrs. Lois W. Smith of
			No. Edgecomb, Maine; Dr. Allen P. Lovejoy
   Executor:	Dr. Allen P. Lovejoy
   Witnesses:	Joshua Snow, Mrs. L.A.A. Hatch (Lucretia)

LOWELL, SAMUEL D.		Dated:	14 Mar. 1861				# 191
				Died:	20 Apr. 1861		Bk. A, Pg. 76
				Filed:	6 Jun. 1861

			No family heirs
			George Storey, Thomas VanWinkle
   Executor:	George Storey
   Witnesses:	A.C. Bledsoe, C.W. Broback, J.G. Dow

LUCAS, ELIZABETH		Written:	4 Jun. 1887			#1786
				Died:	19 Oct. 1888		Bk. F, Pg. 3
				Rec.:	13 Nov. 1888

   Husband:	Frederick G. (deceased)
   Sons:		Caleb S., Frank R., Fred G., Charley C.
   Daughters:	Cornelia Jones, wife of William of Baltimore;
			Nellie B.
   Executor:	L.W. Burris
   Witnesses:	N.H. Frazier, Victor Piezzi

LUCAS FREDERICK G.		Written:	7 Mar. 1887			#1629
Shipmaster	Age 62		Died:	28 Mar. 1887		Bk. D, Pg. 420
				Rec.:	25 Apr. 1887

   Wife:		Elizabeth W. (50)
   Daughter:	Nellie B. (10)
   Next of Kin:	Frederick G. (29) of Baltimore, Md.; Frank (26)
			residence unknown; Caleb (20); Charles (17);
			Cornelia Jones (22) of Baltimore, Md.
   Executors:	L.W. Burris, Wm. E. McConnell
   Witnesses:	Victor Piezzi, Thos. B. Miller

LUCAS, JOHN			Written:	10 May 1872			# 593
				Died:	23 Jan. 1873
				Filed:	3 Mar. 1873

   Wife:		Nancy Tolbert Lucas
   Sons:		James, Lewis, John Henry, Edward, Willis
			(deceased), Jennie & John L. Green, children
			of daughter Nancy Eliza (deceased)
   Executor:	Wife
   Witnesses:	Wm. H. Bond, James Butler, Wm. Churchman

LUDOLFF, HENRY   Written: 24 Mar. 1898   #2946
                Age 78   Died: 23 Nov. 1898   Bk. G, Pg. 231
                         Filed: 12 Dec. 1898

    Sons: Henry O. Ludolff, Robert Ludolff (deceased)
    Grandson: Frederick Ludolff
    Executor: Henry O. Ludolff
    Witnesses: R.F. Crawford, Geo. F. Kohler both of Santa Rosa

LUTTRELL, J. F.   Written: 15 Jun. 1893   #2357
                         Died: 4 Oct. 1893   Bk. F, Pg. 180
                         Sitka, Alaska
                         Rec.:   13 Nov. 1893

    Wife: Semantha J.
    Grandson: John Francis
    Sons: Paul S., Frank M., H.L.
    Bequests to: Hattie, M--tin
                  Holographic

LYMAN, CHARLES   Written: 22 Aug. 1885   #1848
    Petaluma   Age 69   Died: 29 Mar. 1889   Bk. E, Pg. 110
                         Rec.:   29 Apr. 1889

    Sisters-in-
    Law: Lydia Bristol, wife of Lambert of New Haven, Conn;
                  Melinda Lyman, widow of John of Northfield, Mass.
    Daughter: Lydia (adopted), name un-known from orphans home,
                  San Francisco
    Brother: Joseph of Northfield, Mass.
    Bequests to: Julia Harvey, wife of J.C.; Alfred Stebbins of
                  Oakland, CA
    Executor: Alfred Stebbins
    Witnesses: Wm. B. Haskell, John Fritsch

LYNCH, WILLIAM   Written: 10 Dec. 1872   # 591
                Age 35   Died: 16 Jan. 1873
                         Filed: 6 Feb. 1873

    Sisters: Catharine --- , Anne Cleary of San Francisco
    Brother: John Lynch
    Cousin: Michael Lynch of Virginia City, Nev.
    Parents: William Lynch, Catherine Lynch of Maghernageeragh,
                  County Tyrone, Ireland
    Sister-in
    Law: Mary Ann Lynch, wife of brother
    Nephews: Wm. John McGlynn, son of sister; Hugh McGlynn,
                  son of sister
    Niece: Catherine McGlynn, daughter of sister
    Executors: John Lynch of Vallejo Tnsp., Sonoma Co.; Thos.
                  J. Cleary of San Francisco
    Witnesses: Thos. Roach, Herbert Naughten

LYONS, THOMAS M.   Written: 3 Sep. 1889   #3336
                          Died: 6 Jul. 1901   Bk. H, Pg. 58
                          Filed: 8 Aug. 1901

  Wife: Agnes
                Property in Ukiah, Mendocino Co.
  Executor: Wife
  Witnesses: W.D. Reynolds, E.F. Woodward both of Santa Rosa

MADLER, STEPHEN   Written: 2 Jun. 1871   # 492
                          Died: 15 Jun. 187- Bk. A, Pg. 228-
                                                             232
  Children: Anna Frances (minor); Clara Josephine (minor);
                Lizzie Maria (minor), to live with Mrs. Wolf
                until of age; Margretta (minor), to be adopted
                by Wesley Mock with father's consent
  Executors: Wesley & Edward Mock
  Witnesses: Theodore Mock, William Mock

MAGG, FRANCIS FREDERIC   Written: 1 Jul. 1886   #1566
Petaluma   Died: 28 Jul. 1886 Bk. D, Pg. 251
                          Rec.:   13 Sep. 1886

  Wife: Sarah
  Daughter: Lena Frey
  Executors: Wife, Anton Meyer
  Witnesses: George Densmore, J.J. Edelmann

MALONE, ANNIE MARY   Written: 2 Nov. 1899   #3319
Santa Rosa   Age 78   Died: 25 May 1901 Bk. G, Pg. 490
                          Rec.:   24 Jun. 1901

  Brothers: Peter Malone, Frank, Patrick
  Nieces: Aggie Malone Kilcorse, Susie Malone Claner,
                Kate Malone, Ida Malone
  Nephews: Frankie Malone Claner, John Malone, Stephen
                Malone, John Malone, James Malone
  Executor: Mrs. Harriet R. Tupper
  Witnesses: D.D. Davisson, J.M. Walker

MANION, WILLIAM   Written: 9 Feb. 1887   #1689
Santa Rosa   Died: 11 Oct. 1887 Bk. D, Pg. 526
                          Rec.:   25 Oct. 1887

  Wife: Elizabeth E.
  Son: W.H.
  Daughters: Sarah Frances Wooly, Lilly Belle
  Next of Kin: Luella Manion, Eliz. J.
  Executors: Wife, W.H.
  Witnesses: James H. McGee, J.A. Barham

MANN, ADELIA A.	Written:	1 Jul. 1898	#3470
	Died:	-- May 1902	Bk. H, Pg. 125
	Filed:	9 Jun. 1902	

Niece: Mary Shaver of Missouri
Friend: Mrs. Margaret Wiers of Petaluma, CA
Executor: Margaret Wiers
Witnesses: F.A. Meyer, Wm. B. Haskell both of Petaluma, CA

MANN, WILLIAM D.	Written:	25 Feb. 1868	#1821
San Francisco	Died:	17 Jan. 1889	Bk. E, Pg. 47
	Filed:	18 Feb. 1889	

Wife: Adelia A.
Executor: Wife
Witnesses: Cyrus W. Carmony, E.W. Burr, Jas. O. Dean

MANSFIELD, LYNUS	Written:	19 May 1869	# 413
	Died:	25 May 1869	

Daughter: Angeline Bryant
Executors: Wm. T. Allen, Joseph D. Silvia
Witnesses: Wm. T. Allen, Joseph D. Silvia

MARDIS, JOHN S.	Written:	10 Dec. 1890	#2368
Clinton, Iowa Age 72	Died:	13 Oct. 1893	Bk. F, Pg. 196
		Sonoma Counth	
	Rec.:	2 Jan. 1894	

Wife: Margaret
Son: James of Plymouth Co., IA
Grandsons: John H. Mardis, Edward
Bequests to: Abbie Ellen Tabor; Mamie Montana Holliday;
             Mary E. Allen of Cedar Co., IA; children
             of Matilda Ann Thurman; Richard Thurman;
             Louis W. Mardis and his children of Sac Co., IA;
             Abbie E. Kiles of Plymouth Co., IA
Admin: Jas. W. Allen, Louis W. Mardis
Witnesses: C.G. Peck, L.F. Davis both of Lakeview, Sac Co.,
             IA

MARKLEY, THOMAS COX	Written:	18 Jan. 1888	#2059
Santa Rosa Age 51	Died:	28 Aug. 1890	Bk. E, Pg. 353
		Greenville Co., S.C.	
	Rec.:	23 Mar. 1891	

Wife: Jennie Elizabeth, daughter of Alex. Smith, Esq.
Sister: Jessie M. Markley of Greenville, S.C.
Codicil #1: 13 Oct. 1888 gives full name of sister: Jessie
             Margaret, adds S. Katherine Smythe
Codicil #3: Appoints John Markley Executor
Witnesses: G.W. Oates, W.H. Underhill, A. Hendrickson

MARSHALL, HENRY	Written:	7 May 1891	#2077
Santa Rosa	Died:	8 May 1891	Bk. E, Pg. 393
	Rec.:	1 Jun. 1891	

- Wife: Un-named
- Children: Elizabeth Ann, Emily, Phebe Irene, Charlotte Isabella, Lilly Bertha, Mary Alice, William, Frank
- Executor: Son, William
- Witnesses: Wm. Angwin, C. Feige

MARSHALL, JAMES	Written:	26 Oct. 1896	#2678
	Died:	29 Oct. 1896	Bk. F, Pg. 566
	Filed:	19 Nov. 1896	

- Wife: Rachel Marshall
- Daughters(?): Sarah J. Marshall, Fannie Armstrong Wm. A. Marshall, Mary E. Marshall, Jane M. Bates (probably brothers and sister of James)
- Executor: Rachel Marshall
- Witnesses: Dr. J.F. Boyce, William Martin

MARSHALL, JOHN AKA	Written:	4 Apr. 1890	#2030
JOHN M. DE FRIETAS	Died:	24 Nov. 1890	Bk. E, Pg. 330
Age over 30	Rec.:	29 Dec. 1890	

- Wife: Francisca
- Children: Mary, Manual, Rosa, John Domingo, Joseph, Frank
- Guardian: Of children, brother-in-law, A. E. Rafael
- Executor: A.E. Rafael
- Witnesses: F.A. Meyer, John King

MARSHALL, JOHN	Written:	7 Feb. 1873	#1248
Healdsburg	Died:	11 Jul. 1882	Bk. C, Pg. 244
	Filed:	17 Jul. 1882	

- Wife: Sarah A.
- Executor: Wife
- Witnesses: Minnie Pimm (later McLean) of San Francisco, Chas. K. Jenner

MARTI, MELCHIOR	Dated:	5 Feb. 1897	#2718
Age 52	Died:	20 Feb. 1897	Bk. G, Pg. 14
	Filed:	3 May 1897	

- Wife: Elizabeth Jenny Marti
- Nephew: Rudolph Jenny
- Executor: Elizabeth Jenny Marti
- Witnesses: P.J. Mangan, Clitus Barbour

```
MARTIN, JOHN           Written: 29 Jul. 1889              #3360
Petaluma               Died:    29 Aug. 1901   Bk. H, Pg.  71
                       Filed:   23 Sep. 1901

    Wife:       Ida
    Sons:       Wm. John, Erasmus
                Other children (?)
    Executors:  Wife and son, Wm. John or son, Erasmus
    Witnesses:  W.W. Chapman, F. Zimmerman


MARTIN, RICHARD        Written: 16 Jun. 1873              # 624
MONTGOMERY             Died:    23 Jun. 1873

    Wife:       Ophelia V.
                No provision for son, Arthur Albert
    Executor:   F.G. Hahman
    Witnesses:  Sam'l Potter, E.W. Maslin


MARTIN, SILAS M.       Written:  6 Dec. 1890              #2392
Petaluma               Died:    26 Feb. 1894   Bk. F, Pg. 239
                       Rec.:    16 Apr. 1894

    Children:   Albert P., Martha A. Collins, Mary E. Ables,
                Lutitia J. Wright
    Children:   Of daughter, Zillah E. Collins (deceased)
                namely Frederick H., Nancy E., Gertrude, Zittah
                G., John M.
    Executor:   Thos. J. Ables of Marin Co.
    Witnesses:  Frank C. Purvine, Mrs. Frank C. Purvine


MARTIN, WILLIAM        Written: 19 May  1883              #3258
Petaluma, CA           Died:     6 Jun. 1901   Bk. H, Pg.  26
                       Humboldt Co.
                       Filed:    4 Feb. 1901

    Wife:       Jane
    Executor:   Wife
    Witnesses:  Wm. B. Haskell, F. M. Collins both of Petaluma, CA


MARTINELLI, LORENZO    Written:  6 Sep. 1878              #2314
Marin Co.     Age 43   Died:     2 Apr. 1893   Bk. F, Pg. 119
                       Sonoma Co.
                       Rec.:     8 May  1893

    Wife:       Caroline
    Sons:       Ennio, Arnaldo, Geremia, Erminigildo, Roberto
    Daughter:   Erminia
    Executor:   Wife
    Witnesses:  Wm. B. Haskell, M.H. Faulkner both of Petaluma
```

```
MARTINONI, STEPHEN        Dated:     12 Jul. 1895              #3343
Sonoma          Age 47    Filed:      3 Aug. 1901

  Wife:          Matilda Martinoni
  Daughter:      Rosa Marie Martinoni of San Francisco
  Executor:      Robert A. Poppe
  Witnesses:     Pietro Roveda, Angelo Pera


MASSEY, H. W.             Written:   29 Oct. 1891              #2147
Santa Rosa      Age 58    Died:      25 Nov. 1891     Bk. E, Pg. 501
                          San Francisco
                          Rec.:      11 Jan. 1892

  Wife:          Florence May
  Sister:        Emily E. Massey of Blue Island, Ill.
  Executor:      Wife
  Witnesses:     Geo. R. Williams of Oakland, CA; Hu Jones of
                 San Francisco


MATHEWS, MC KINNEY        Dated:     11 Oct. 1863              # 242
                          Filed:     19 Oct. 1863

  Wife:          Sarah E. Mathews
  Daughter:      Allis Mathews
  Executor:      Sarah E. Matthews
  Witnesses:     C.W. Langdon, Russell Ferguson, M.A. McPear


MATHEWS, SARAH            Written:    3 Mar. 1865              # 279
                          Probate:   22 Apr. 1865

  Husband:       McKinney (deceased)
  Daughter:      Alice McKinney Mathews
  Uncle:         Lowry B. Hall
  Executor:      Lowry B. Hall
  Witnesses:     C.W. Langdon, Prudence J. Hall


MATHIES, HENRICH          Written:   19 Jun. 1877              #1350
Petaluma        Age 44    Died:      21 Sep. 1883     Bk. C, Pg. 430
                          Rec.:      15 Oct. 1883

  Wife:          Lina
  Step-
  Daughter:      Georgina Held (10)
  Sons:          Henri (8), Walter (3), Willie (1)
  Daughter:      Dora (5)
  Executor:      Wife
  Witnesses:     Conrad Poehlmann, Geo. Pearce
```

```
MATLI, NICHOLAS            Written:   31 May  1882          #1270
Sonoma          Age 42     Codicil:   17 Oct. 1882      Bk. C, Pg. 308
                           Died:      23 Oct. 1882
                           Filed:      2 Nov. 1882
                           Rec.:      21 Jun. 1883
```

- Wife: Josephina
- Sisters: Anna Mary Matli Steffi (Mrs. John), Elizabeth Matli (Mrs. Vitale Matli), Catherine Matli all residing in Forazzo, Domodossala, Italy
- Executor: Wife
- Witnesses: R.J. Pauli, F. Albert Pauli, Murray Whallon all of Sonoma, CA

```
MATTEI, GIOVANNI           Written:   21 May  1887          #1760
                Age 55     Died:      16 Jul. 1888      Bk. D, Pg. 614
                           Filed:     23 Jul. 1888
```

- Daughters: Delfina Mattei, Guilia Mattei
- Executors: Delfina Mattei, Guilia Mattei
- Witnesses: Frank Mazzi of 22 Montgomery Ave., San Francisco; Cyril V. Grey of 1304 Post St., San Francisco; Jeremiah Respini of San Antonio Tnsp., Marin Co., CA

```
MATTHIAS, PAUL             Written:   11 Aug. 1897          #2840
                Age 59     Died:       1 Feb. 1898      Bk. G, Pg. 129
                           Filed:     21 Feb. 1898
```

- Wife: Emma A. Matthias
- Sons: Paul Matthias, Theodore Matthias
- Executor: Emma A. Matthias
- Witnesses: Henry G. Matthias, R.F. Crawford

```
MAXWELL, JOHN M.           Written:   10 Mar. 1866          # 678
                           Died:      26 Mar. 1874
                           San Diego Co.
                           Filed:     11 May  1874
```

- Wife: Clara L.
- Executor: Wife
- Witnesses: C. Bruns, G.L. Wratten

```
MAYER, JACOB G.                                              #3171
```

No will

MAYNARD, F. T.   Dated: 13 Apr. 1895   #2924
                          Died: 20 Aug. 1898   Bk. G, Pg. 217-
                          Filed: 26 Sep. 1898   220

    Wife: Mary A. Maynard
    Brother: Henry C. Maynard of Conneant, Ohio
    Son-in-Law: J.F. Fairbanks
    Daughters: Gracie Maynard, Eva Fairbanks, wife of J.F.
    Sons: Rowl (deceased), Harry
    Executors: Aaron Schroyer, friend; Mary A. Maynard
    Witnesses: Wm. B. Haskell, H.P. Brainerd

MC ALLISTER, BENJAMIN B. Written: 9 Oct. 1884   #2148
San Francisco   Died: Sonoma County   Bk. E, Pg. 514
                          Rec.:   18 Jan. 1892

    Wife: Angeline H.
    Children: Angie C., Walter B.
    Executor: Wife
    Witnesses: M. Garcelon, Chas. Sanborn, John J. Cunningham
                  Holographic

MC CALLUM, DUNCAN M.   Dated: 28 Apr. 1876   #1208
Caspar, Mendocino Co.   Died: 28 Apr. 1876   Bk. 1, Pg. 101
                          Filed: 29 Apr. 1876   (Mendocino Co.)

    Wife: Eliza McCallum
    Sons: William McCallum (9), John (8), Jackson (6)
    Daughter: Eliza McCallum (11)
    Father: John McCallum
    Mother: Elizabeth McCallum
    Executors: Eliza McCallum, Jacob A. Jackson, Allan C. Ross,
                  Eugene Brown
    Witnesses: Peter Merriman, W.A. McCornack, Thomas Jones

MC CANN, JOHN   Dated: 1 Jul. 1881   #1164
Mark West   Filed: 21 Jul. 1881   Bk. C, Pg. 150

    Wife: Ella McCann
    Sons: Thomas McCann (eldest), other minor sons
    Daughters: un-named, two
    Executor: Ella McCann
    Witnesses: M.W. Tarwater, Thos. Rutledge

MC CAUSLAND, JAMES   Written: 24 May 1894   #2668
Cloverdale   Age 64   Died: 19 Sep. 1896   Bk. F, Pg. 557
                          Filed: 30 Sep. 1896

    Wife: Lizzie McCausland
    Daughter: Amy McCausland
    Executors: Lizzie McCausland, Geo. W. Burbank, David Burbank
    Witnesses: Wm. McCausland, Geo. B. Baer both of Cloverdale

MC CHRISTIAN, PATRICK	Written:	19 Dec. 1885	#1770
Santa Rosa	Died:	21 Aug. 1888	Bk. D, Pg. 631
	Filed:	20 Oct. 1888	

- Wife: Sarah
- Executor: James McMenamin
- Witnesses: L.W. Burris, G.A. Johnson

MC CHRISTIAN, SARAH	Written:	29 Aug. 1891	#2237
	Died:	30 Jul. 1892	Bk. F, Pg. 23
	Filed:	17 Aug. 1892	

- Nephew: James McMenamin
- Executor: Nephew
- Witnesses: B.M. Nye, Arch M. Johnson, Geo. A. Johnson

MC CLELLAN, EDWARD SMALL	Dated:	7 Sep. 1892	#3197
Age 63	Filed:	27 Aug. 1900	

- Wife: Helen L. McClellan
- Sons: Albert R. McClellan, Edward C. McClellan
- Executor: Helen L. McClellan
- Witnesses: F.C. Nagle, O. DeBendeleben

MC CLUSKY, JOHN	Written:	1 Dec. 1876	#1019
Robinson Tnsp.,	Died:	13 May 1879	Bk. C, Pg. 42
Allegheny Co., PA			

- Sons: Hiram, John N. (?), Henry, Cyrus, William, Mathew N. (?), Samuel (incompetant) with John W. Bell as guardian
- Executor: Son, Henry
- Witnesses: Jas. Scarborough, John Meanor

MC CORKLE, M. K.	Dated:	12 Aug. 1895	#3169
	Died:	6 May 1900	Bk. H, Pg. 6
	Dated:(?)	9 Jul. 1900	

- Niece: Allie James McDill
- Executor: Allie James McDill

MC CRACKEN, JOHN	Written:	24 May 1880	#1427
Brooklyn, NY	Died:	4 Mar. 1884 (prior to)	

                Owner of Los Guilucis Rancho

- **Wife:** Anna P.
- **Children:** John Henry, Anna P., Mary Jenkins, William Denison
- **Bequest to:** Eliza Hood, wife of Wm.
- **Executors:** John H. Lynde, Abel Denison both of New York City
- **Witnesses:** John George Shaw of Los Guilucos, Regina M.T. Buckle of Los Angeles in 1884
- **Codicil:** Removed Lynde and Denison
- **Bequest to:** Sisters, Mary Jenkins and Charlotte MacRae McCracken both of Switzerland
- **Executors:** Son, John H.; Walter T. Hatch

MC CURDY, CHARLOTTE	Written:	8 May 1884		#1536
Petaluma	Died:	12 Mar. 1886	Bk. D, Pg. 182	
Farmer	Rec.:	12 Apr. 1886		

- **Grand-Nephew:** Richard Joseph Smith
- **Grand-Niece:** Sophia Louisa Smith
  Both are children of nephew, Richard John (deceased)
- **Executor:** Friend, David Walls
- **Witnesses:** Frank W. Shattuck, William F. Shattuck

MC CURDY, JOANN (JOANNA)	Dated:	22 May 1880		#1215
Petaluma	Died:	17 Feb. 1882	Bk. C, Pg. 188	
	Rec.:	20 Mar. 1882		

                Mrs. Mary Ann McCurdy of Gardner, Kenne Beck Co., Maine
                Frank Colburn, Clara W. Colburn, and James Colburn children of Captain Samuel S. Colburn of Philadelphia, Pa.

- **Daughter:** Mrs. Carie H. Weston
- **Executor:** Mrs. Carie H. Weston
- **Witnesses:** J.S. Shepherd, J. Snow

MC CURDY, JOHN	Dated:	15 Oct. 1856	# 201
Prisoner in Mexico City	Filed:	30 Sep. 1861	

- **Wife:** Charlotte McCurcy of Petaluma
- **Witness:** John Black at Consulate of U.S. in Mexico 22 Oct. 1856

MC DONALD, ANNE   Written: 3 Feb. 1877   #1084
Mendocino Co. Age about Filed: 4 Apr. 1877
               44   Mendocino Co. Probate Court

   Husband: A.C. McDonald
   Children: Mary Curtis, Alice Byron, George H. McDonald,
                 Lillian McDonald, Flora McDonald, Anne McDonald,
                 Alex C. McDonald
   Executor: A.C. McDonald
   Alternates: James M. Smith, brother; George H. McDonald, son
   Witnesses: J.M. Smith, R. Harrison

MC ELARNEY, FRANK   Written: 15 Sep. 1883   #2292
San Francisco   Age 60   Died: 4 Feb. 1893   Bk. F, Pg. 90
                          Filed: 20 Mar. 1893

   Nephew: Patrick Smith of Cloverdale, Ca.
   Bequests to: Ann Smith (Mrs. Patrick) of San Francisco, James
                 Francis Smith, Frank William Smith, Owen -- Smith,
                 Henry Smith, William Smith, Annie Smith, Mary
                 Smith, Jennie Smith, Catherine Augusta Smith
   Trustees: Patrick Smith, Ann Smith; or James F. Smith, Owen
                 Smith
   Witnesses: Jas. F. Tevlin, Thos. E. Curran, Richard Purcell

MC FARLAND, MALVINA   Written: 20 Dec. 1887   #3242
Petaluma, Ca.   Died: 5 Dec. 1900   Bk. H, Pg. 18
                          Filed: 31 Dec. 1900

   Husband: Alex McFarland (deceased)
   Bequest to: Mrs. Rebecca Wilson, wife of Benjamin Wilson, of
                 C. St., Petaluma
   Daughter: Eliza --- (adopted)
   Executor: Mrs. Rebecca Wilson
   Witnesses: Wm. B. Haskell, Emma A. Haskell both of Petaluma

MC GEE, ROBERT   Written: 25 Feb. 1893   #2347
Bodega Tnsp.   Age 81   Died: 7 Sep. 1893   Bk. F, Pg. 154
                          Rec.:   18 Sep. 1893

   Daughter: Mary Ann Thomas
   Executor: Daughter
   Witnesses: John H. Fowler of Santa Rosa, Thos. Smith of
                 Valley Ford

MC GUIRE, WILLIAM   Dated: 31 Jul. 1869   # 420
CRAYTON   Filed: 16 Aug. 1869

   Wife: Sarah Ann McGuire
   Daughter: Cora Elenor (minor)
   Son: William Clarence (minor)
   Executor: Levi Johnson
   Witnesses: J.N. McGuire, John Dougherty

```
MC KINNEY, ROSCOE        Dated:   21 Dec. 1882              #1285
Guerneville              Died:     5 Jan. 1883    Bk. C, Pg. 332
                         Rec.:    25 Jun. 1883

   Wife:         Susan E. (A.)
   Son:          George (6)
   Executor:     Wife
   Witnesses:    G. Watson, Henry C. Ralston


MC KINNON, WM. W.        Written: 18 Feb. 1858              # 113
                         Filed:    5 May  1858

   Brother:      Charles
   Executor:     Chas. McKinnon
   Witnesses:    L. Lamberton, Wm. Brown, I.G. Wickersham


MC MANUS, JOHN G.        Written: 28 Nov. 1868              #1579
                         Died:    30 Oct. 1883    Bk. D, Pg. 314
                         Rec.:    25 Oct. 1887

   Wife:         Eliza Jane
   Step-
   Daughter:     Ann Eliza McCann (Alderson in 1886)
   Son:          John
   Daughter:     May Ellen
   Executor:     Wife
   Witnesses:    David Bloom, D.F. Speers (?)


MC MENAMIN, MARY         Written: 16 May  1902              #3480
                         Died:    13 Jun. 1902    Bk. H, Pg. 132
                         Filed:   14 Jul. 1902

   Brothers:     John, James, Tom, Michael
   Sisters:      Kate, Rose Lowrey
   Bequests to:  Sebastopol Catholic Church
   Executor:     Patrick McMenamin
   Witnesses:    Annie A. Connolly, Ada R. Fowler


MC MINN, JOSEPH          Written:  4 Dec. 1884              #1447
Sonoma          Age 90   Died:    12 Dec. 1884    Bk. D, Pg.  11
                         Rec.:     5 Jan. 1885

   Wife:         Mary
   Sons:         John, Pascal, Joseph (deceased)
   Daughters:    Lucretia Parker (deceased), Alzira Wallace,
                 Selina Bidwell (deceased), Mary Ann Mathews
   Executor:     Son, John
   Witnesses:    M.G. Richie, John Brown
```

```
MC MINN, MARY              Written:  22 Jul. 1886              #1825
              Age about    Died:     21 Jan. 1889    Bk. E, Pg. 143
              84           Filed:    25 Feb. 1889
```

- Husband: Joseph (deceased)
- Son: John
- Daughters: Lucinda Rodgers, Joshua Martin, Johannah Huff, Elizabeth Richie, Mary Ann Mathews
- Executor: John
- Witnesses: Wm. E. McConnell, Chas. F. Rohrer

```
MC NABB, SAMANTHA F.       Written:  18 May 1878               #1089
```

- Bequests to: Claramon Heflin, niece, of Huntsville, Walker Co., Texas
- Executor: Claramon Heflin
- Witnesses: Of earlier will dated 15 Oct. 1876: Belle Bayley, Mary Williams
- Holographic

```
MC NALLY, MARY             Written:  31 Aug. 1882              #1317
Petaluma                   Filed:    16 May  1883
```

- Husband: Michael
- Daughter: Mary A.
- Son: Matthew
- Executor: L.H. Patty
- Witnesses: Walter S. Hinkle, J.P. Rodgers

```
MC NAMARA, BERNARD         Dated:    4 Aug. 1900               #3194
              Age 66       Died:     5 Aug. 1900     Bk. G, Pg. 447
                           Filed:    14 Aug. 1900
```

- Son: Daniel McNamara
- Sisters: Mary Tighe, Nancy Gray both of Massachusetts
- Executor: Patrick Redm (?)
- Witnesses: J.M. Cassin, R.F. Crawford

```
MC NAMARA, ELLEN C.        Written:  23 Oct. 1879              #2423
                           Died:     29 May 1894     Bk. F, Pg. 255
                           Sonoma Co.
                           Rec.:     25 Jun. 1894
```

- Husband: M.
- Brothers: Edward Currey of Philadelphia, Pa.; Thos. Currey or wife, Margaret
- Niece: Nellei Currey, daughter of Thos.; Maggie Winters, daughter of Kate Nielson (Mrs. John)
- Nephew: Thos. Winters, son of Kate Nielson (Mrs. John)
- Executors: Joseph Aling of San Rafael, Thos. Currey
- Witnesses: Jas. H. Wilkins, Hepburn Wilkins both of San Rafael
- Codicil: 15 Mar. 1887 add Rev. O'Connor of San Rafael
- Codicil: 1891 revokes O'Connor

MC PEAK, MATHEW   Written: 10 Jul. 1872   # 646
          Age 74   Died: 12 Sep. 1873
                         Filed: 13 Oct. 1873

  Wife: Mary
  Sons: Harmon of Missouri, Henry, Anthony
  Daughters: Polly Irwin, Eliz. Blakeley's children
               Laura and Nealy Bates
  Executor: Son, Anthony
  Witnesses: Silas Weller, John T. Fortson

MC PHERSON, CHARLES   Written: 15 Mar. 1875   # 740
PERRY   Died: 22 Apr. 1875   Bk. B, Pg. 154
                         Filed: 26 Apr. 1875

  Sons: Colburn McPherson, Syourgus McPherson, Miller
               McPherson, Stonewall McPherson, Welcome
  Wife: Minerva McPherson
               Oliver McDaniel
  Executor: Frank C. St.Clair of Stanislaus Co.
  Witnesses: Michael C. Bailey, Henry S. Gird

MC PHERSON, STONEWALL   Written: 2 Jan. 1887   #1733
             Age 22   Filed: 30 Mar. 1888   Bk. D, Pg. 591

  Brothers: Ewell McPherson, Early McPherson
  Sisters: Mary McPherson, Annie McPherson
  Half-
  Brothers: Colborn McPherson, Lyourgus McPherson, Miller
               McPherson
  Nephew: Sylvester Simmons
  Bequest to: Olivia McDaniels of Mendocino Co., CA
  Executors: Joseph Fox, Miller McPherson
  Witnesses: James H. Budd, Frank E. Dunlap both of Stockton;
               Joseph Fox, Mrs. Joseph Fox both of Milton, CA

MC PHERSON, THOMAS   Dated: 3 Oct. 1879   #1036
                         Died: 3 Oct. 1879
                         Filed: 21 Oct. 1879

  Brother: Kirk
  Children: Charley (minor), Birdy (minor)

MC REYNOLDS, JACOB   Written: 5 Feb. 1874   # 699
                         Died: 18 Jul. 1874
                         Filed: 24 Aug. 1874

  Wife: Anna C.
  Children: Un-named
  Executor: Sons Jacob & Stephen
  Witnesses: Robertson Heald, C.W. Langdon

MEAD, CATHERINE C.		Written:	4 Aug. 1875	# 759
		Died:	6 Aug. 1875	Bk. B, Pg. 176
		Filed:	16 Aug. 1875	

Children: Wilson H. Mead, William Edward Mead, Willard Ryland Mead, Sarah Ellen Williamson, Alice C. Mead
Executors: Winfield S.M. Wright, Edward Neblett
Witnesses: John G. Pressley, O.L. Allen

MEAGHER, AGNES		Written:	18 Sep. 1889	#1907
	Age 66	Died:	12 Nov. 1889	Bk. E, Pg. 309
		Rec.:	6 Oct. 1890	

Daughter: Nancy Hardin
Sons: William Hardin, George W. Hardin
Executor: Daughter
Witnesses: Murray Whallon, Wm. H. Hedges, H.H. Atwater

MEHRTENS, MARTIN		Written:	25 Aug. 1884	#1572
HEINRICH		Died:	7 Sep. 1886	Bk. D, Pg. 268
Santa Rosa	Age 54	Rec.:	27 Sep. 1886	

Wife: Anna
Children: Adele M.C. (25), Thudy Henrietta (8)
Executor: Adele and Christopher Hacke
Witnesses: E.A. Seegelken(?), A.B. Warn

MELDRUM, DAVID	Dated:	9 Jan. 1888	#3272
	Died:	21 Jan. 1901	Bk. H, Pg. 39
	Filed:	23 Feb. 1901	

Daughters: Rachel J. Leaft, widow of William Leaft; Kate G., wife of Frank Payne; Lucy H. Thomas; Mary E. Shannon
Son: James Meldrum (deceased)
Grand-Children: Walter James Meldrum; Rachael E. Meldrum children of George W. Meldrum (deceased); Joseph W.G. and Meldrum D. Shannon
Executor: Mary E. Shannon
Witnesses: Alexander Dunn, Andrew J. Muir

MERTENS, CHRISTIAN	Dated:	18 Jan. 1864	# 241
	Died:	25 Jan. 1864	Bk. A, Pg. 113
	Filed:	28 Jan. 1864	

Mrs. Welshald, wife of Theodor Welshald
Executor: G.T. Pauli
Witnesses: Charles VanGeldern, Harold L, Kamp

MEYER, BABETTA AKA	Written:	2 Sep. 1892	#2697
MEYERS, BARBETTA	Died:	11 Nov. 1896	Bk. G, Pg. 28
	Filed:	23 Feb. 1897	

- Husband: Jacob F. Meyer
- Executors: J.J. Edelman, Edward Kummer
- Witnesses: A. Morstadt, G.G. Herman

MEYER, WILLIAM	Written:	29 Sep. 1871	# 508
	Died:	2 Oct. 1871	Bk. A, Pg. 236

- Wife: Louise
- Sons: Fred (by first wife), William (20 months)
- Daughters: Augusta (5), Julia (4)
- Executors: Franz Breitenbach, F.A. Pauli, Caspe Schuster
- Witnesses: Luis Fink, L. Litzius

MICHELSEN, LUDWIG	Written:	17 Feb. 1894	#3401
CHRISTIAN	Died:	14 Dec. 1901	Bk. H, Pg. 96
Alexander Valley	Rec.:	13 Jan. 1902	
	Born: 19 Jan. 1824		

- Sister: Anna Margaretha Klintworth
- Niece: Salome Auguste Klintworth
- Brothers: Arnold, Christian August
- Nieces: Margaretha Michaelsen, Salome Elise Michaelsen, Wilhelmine Marie Michaelsen
- Nephew: Johann Hinrich Michaelsen
- Executor: Brother, Christian A.
- Holographic

MIDDLETON, WILLIAM H.	Written:	25 May 1872	# 556
	Filed:	5 Aug. 1872	

- Wife: Emily Middleton
- Children: Un-named (large family)
  Previous marriage with children un-named
- Executor: Emily Middleton
- Witnesses: T.W. Hudson, Thos. T. Heald

MILLER, JOSEPH MORGAN	Dated:	25 Oct. 1872	# 728
	Died:	23 Jan. 1875	Bk. B, Pg. 135
	Filed:	25 Jan. 1875	

- John Walker and wife Elenor
- Mary Josaphene Walker
- Executors: John Walker, John Dougherty
- Witnesses: George J. Reigle, B.G. Doughtery, John Doughtery
- Codicil
- Witnesses: John Doughtery, J.G. Johnson

```
MILLER, CHARLES          Written:  24 Jun. 1874              # 774
Sonoma                   Died:     28 Sep. 1875    Bk. B, Pg. 202
Late of Petaluma         Filed:     1 Nov. 1875
```

- Wife: Caroline (Neeb)
- Daughter: Matilda Molt, wife of John, of San Francisco
- Step-Daughter: Louisa Hess
- Witnesses: L. Ellsworth, D.D. Carder

```
MILLER, DANIEL           Dated:     5 Jun. 1853               # 66
                         Died:      9 Jun. 1853    Bk. A, Pg.  23
                         Filed:    15 Jun. 1853
```

- Nephew: Thomas E. Birch of Clinton Co., Mo.
- Sons: Daniel E., Charle S.
- Daughters: Martha, Mary Ann
- Executor: Robert Crane
- Witnesses: Uriah Groschong, Jonathan Leslie, E.J. Schellhous

```
MILLER, L. W.            Written:  30 Nov. 1875              # 783
Sonoma                   Died:     11 Dec. 1875    Bk. B, Pg. 228
                         Filed:    27 Dec. 1875
```

- Wife: Ina B.
- Sons: Frederick H., George E. (Wales L. Palmer, of San Francisco, to see boys have useful trade)
- Bequest to: W. Wash. Gilam (Gilliam)
- Executor: Wife
- Witnesses: Barclay Henley, C. Bethel

```
MILLER, SAMUEL           Written:   4 Apr. 1861              # 189
                         Probate:   6 May  1861
```

- Wife: Un-named
- Children: Un-named
- Executors: Father, Isaac; brother, Chas.
- Witnesses: J.B. Beeson, second name is cut off page

```
MILLERICK, PHILLIP       Written:   4 Apr. 1880             #1080
Timber Cove, Ca.         Died:     12 Apr. 1880    Bk. C, Pg.  92
                         Filed:    21 Oct. 1881
```

- Nephews: John Millerick, George Millerick
- Guardian: Their father
- Witnesses: John Herbert, George Bogle, Alexander Herbert

MILLS, NANCY H.	Dated:	10 Jun. 1899	#3139
Age 53	Died:	21 Mar. 1900	Bk. G, Pg. 404
	Filed:	9 Apr. 1900	

                E.T. Mills (Emery T.?)
                Delia D. Gerichter & her mother, Rhoda E. Yates
Father: J.T. Flippen
Executors: E.T. Mills, Della D. Gerichter, Rhoda E. Yates

MILLS, NILES	Written:	27 Oct. 1874	# 717
	Died:	26 Nov. 1874	Bk. B, Pg. 125
	Filed:	1 Dec. 1874	

Wife: Helen Mills
Sons: Edward C. Mills, George, Eastern, Albert
Executor: Helen Mills
Witnesses: James M. Charles, D.D. Carder

MITCHELL, ROBT. T.	Written:	6 Aug. 1887	#3108
Age 53	Died:	28 Nov. 1899	Bk. G, Pg. 385
	Rec.:	29 Jan. 1900	

Wife: Sarah J.
Children: Emma C. Wilson, Bertie, William
Executor: Wife
Witnesses: Jas. W. Oates, H.H. Churchill

MIZE, MERRILL	Dated:	4 May 1874	# 731
	Died:	15 May 1874	Bk. B, Pg. 144
	Filed:	12 Feb. 1875	

Wife: Mary Mize
Sons: John A. Mize (minor), Frederic Mize (minor)
Daughter: Julia Mize (minor)
Executor: Mary Mize
Witnesses: John Fulkerson, George W. Moore

MOCK, CHARLES	Written:	1 May 1878	#1132
Petaluma	Died:	11 Dec. 1880	
	Filed:	3 Jan. 1881	

Grand-
Children: Anna Clara, Lizzie Maria, Margueretta all children of Stephen Madler & wife, Frances; Ann, John both children of Thos. Bryant & wife, Julia (Mock)
Bequest to: Helen Thomas
Executors: A.B. Derby, Geo. B. Williams
Witnesses: Jas. L. Munro, Wash. Neil

MOCK, WILLIAM   Written: 20 Aug. 1873   #2860
Petaluma   Died: 2 Apr. 1898   Bk. G, Pg. 154
                       Filed: 18 Apr. 1898

  Wife: Mary B. Mock
  Daughter: Mary Lizzie Goodwin (adopted)
  Executor: Mary B. Mock
  Witnesses: E.S. Lippitt, Frank K. Lippitt, Geo. Harris of
               Petaluma, James McKee Harris of Petaluma, Joel
               Merchant of Petaluma

MOFFET, JOHN   Written: 11 Dec. 1883   #1380
Healdsburg   Died: 1 Jan. 1884   Bk. C, Pg. 490
                       Rec.:   11 Dec. 1884

  Wife: Merca Ann
  Sisters: Lucinta Fairbanks of Petaluma, Julia A. Groves
               of Des Moines, Iowa
  Brother: E. Raines Moffet of Joplin, Mo.
  Children: Of brother Joseph (deceased), namely, E.J., R.A.,
               and Joseph of Augusta, Iowa
  Nephew: Charles Moffet of Sonoma Co.
  HalfSisters: Zorah A. Finck of Augusta, Iowa; Euphemia L.
               Hibler of Bentonville, Ark.; Lillie C. Moffet of
               Augusta, Iowa
  Friend: Wilson Brown of Healdsburg
  Executors: Brother-in-law, H.T. Fairbanks; friend, Jas.
               Samuels
  Witnesses: Thos. T. Riley, Frank W. Shattuck

MOLLOY, EDWARD B.   Dated: 15 Dec. 1866   # 476
                       Died: 26 Jan. 1871
                       Filed: 9 Feb. 1871

  Wife: Mary
  Daughters: Bessie, Minnie
  Executor: Mary Molloy
  Witnesses: Wm. Mulligan, John O. Darrow

MOORE, ELISHA   Written: 20 Mar. 1865   # 295
                       Filed: 29 Aug. 1865

  Wife: Luticia
  Children: Elizabeth Ellen, Perry Charles, Laura, Henrietta
  Son: Francis M. (from former wife)
  Executors: J.B. Beeson, Theodore Dittamore
  Witnesses: J.G. Edwards of Mendocino Co., Theo. Dittamore of
               Sonoma Co.

MORGAN, CHARLES   Dated: 31 May 1866   # 334
                         Died: 2 Jun. 1866   Bk. Wills Pg. 154-
                         Rec.:   12 Feb. 1867   156

    Mother: Jane Morgan of Pennsylvania
    Brother: John Morgan of Warren Co., Pennsylvania
    Executors: John Morgan, George Morgan (also a brother)
    Witnesses: Cornelius Bice, John Clack

MORISON, MELINDA   Written: 8 Dec. 1877   #1045
                         Filed: 18 Nov. 1879   Bk. C, Pg. 61

    Sons: Joseph Morton, A. Jackson Morton, Zacchariah T.
                Morton, Richard Morton, George W. Morton, Wm.
                G. Morton
    Executors: Joseph Morton, Zachariah T. Morton
    Witnesses: E.S. Sippitt, John Fritsch

MORRILL, CHARLES A.   Written: 31 May 1883   #1722
Geyserville   Age 41   Died   21 Feb. 1888   Bk. D, Pg. 594
                         Filed: 30 Apr. 1888

    Wife: Fannie A.
    Children: Lora P., Ernest, Herbert S., John A.
    Admin: Wife
    Witnesses: R. Augusta Pratt, C.L. Bogan

MORRIS, JOHN   Written: 17 Jan. 1880   #1101
                         Filed: 16 Aug. 1880

    Sons: James F. Morris, William R. Morris, Robert W.
                Morris, John P. Morris
    Daughters: Leah I. Woods, Tabitha F. Adams, Elizabeth A.
                Lawson, Rebecca H. Hall, Nancy E. Ellis
    Executors: John P. Morris, Leander G. Ellis

MORSE, EBENEZER E.   Written: 2 Jul. 1869   #1421
San Francisco   Died: 28 Aug. 1884   Bk. C, Pg. 599
                         Rec.:   30 Sep. 1884

    Wife: Sarah
    Children: Emma L., Nellie A.
    Executor: Wife
    Witnesses: Daniel Rogers, James Rogers Booth

MORSE, SUSAN B.   Written: 12 Sep. 1871   # 519
Petaluma   Filed: 24 Jan. 1872

- Daughter: Mary Jane Morse
- Sons: John W. Shoemaker, Henry C. Morse, Geo. W. Morse, Simon L. Morse, Stephen A. Morse, Charles B. Morse, Richard S. Morse, James C. Morse
- Executor: Stephen A. Morse
- Witnesses: I.G. Wickersham of Petaluma, John Fritsch

MORSE, WILLIAM P.   Written: 14 May 1897   #2848
Sebastopol   Age 69 Died: 23 Feb. 1898   Bk. G, Pg. 157
                             Filed: 16 Mar. 1898

- Wife: Mary J. Morse
- Son: Stephen C. Morse
- Daughter: Delia A. Moran
- Executor: Mary J. Morse
- Witnesses: R.F. Crawford, Maggie M. Crawford

MORTON, EDWARD H.   Written: 10 May 1870   #1605
Sonoma   Died: 9 Jan. 1887   Bk. D, Pg. 364
Carpenter   Rec.:   21 Feb. 1887

- Wife: Jennette G.
- Sons: Martin T. (eldest), Henry C. (deceased by 8 Mar. 1884), Howard (youngest) of San Francisco in 1887
- Executor: Wife
- Witnesses: J.P. Cochran, J.F. Stirling

MOWBRAY, JAMES R.   Written: 15 May 1881   #1165
Cloverdale   Age 63 Filed: 8 Jul. 1881   Bk. C, Pg. 153

- Wife: Mary J. Mowbray
- Bequest to: James W. Lanison
- Executor: Marj J. Mowbray
- Witnesses: D.P. Morgan, James K. Polk both of Cloverdale

MULLALY, PATRICK   Intestate   #2235
Analy Tnsp.   Died: 28 Jun. 1892   Bk. 18, Pg. 582
                             Closed: 26 Jul. 1893   Decree of Distribution

- Children: Catherine E. Jones (25), Michael John Mullaly (31), Thos. W. Mullaly (21), Julia Gericke (29) of Sonoma, Richard Mullaly (33) of Solano Co., Mary A. Mullaly (34), Bridget Roach (36) of Marin Co., Edward P. Mullaly (19), Joseph P. Mullaly (17)

MULLER, FRANK		Written: 3 Jan. 1888	#1711
Windsor	Age 45	Died: 23 Jan. 1888	Bk. D, Pg. 566
		Filed: 20 Feb. 1888	

                    Catherine Hooper (41), Margaret Richards (35) both of Cambria Co., Pa.

- **Brother:** Joseph
- **Grand-Children:** Frank, Leo, Alan, Louisa, all children of Joseph and Amanda
- **Executor:** Joseph Muller
- **Witnesses:** Fred King, Amos M. Shane

MULLER, JOSEPH	Written: 23 Sep. 1890	#2007
Windsor	Died: 24 Sep. 1890	
Winemaker	Rec.: 13 Oct. 1890	

- **Wife:** Nancy
- **Children:** Francis Leon, Amanda Louisia, Mary Barbete
- **Executor:** None named, but Nancy to conduct business as usual
- **Witnesses:** Amos M. Shane, John D. Cooper

MULLIGAN, GEORGE V.		Written: 24 Mar. 1894	#2407
Healdsburg	Age 41	Died: 26 Mar. 1894	Bk. F, Pg. 246
		Rec.: 7 May 1894	

- **Wife:** Fanny
- **Children:** George, Walter, Alice
- **Executor:** Wife
- **Witnesses:** Andrew Price, J.T. Coffman

MURPHY, PATRICK	Written: 19 Jan. 1878	#1041
	Died: 29 Oct. 1879	Bk. C, Pg. 54
	Filed: 9 Dec. 1879	

- **Wife:** Mary
- **Daughters:** Katie Murphy (19), Margaret Murphy (16), Mary Elizabeth (15)
- **Son:** John (14)
- **Executors:** Mary Murphy; John Murphy, brother
- **Witnesses:** John Cavanaugh of Petaluma, James Sullivan of Vallejo Tnsp.

```
MURRAY, MARY              Written:  30 Aug. 1884              #1434
Petaluma                  Died:     27 Oct. 1884    Bk. C, Pg. 621
                          Rec.:      9 Dec. 1884
```

Sisters:	Agnes O. Healey, Annie O'Grady
Stepmother:	Bridgett O'Grady of Ireland
Grand-Children:	Michael, Marria, Margarett and Honorai O'Grady
Bequests to:	Lissie, Minnie and Willy Thourigood in Calif.; Arthur Henry Connoly of Petaluma; Theodore Bayliss; Minnie A. Connoly, wife of B.; Sister Mary Catherine of Petaluma; J.F. Cleary of Petaluma; James Crook of Marin Co.; P. Meacham F. Drumgold of New York; J. Cavanagh of Petaluma; I.L. Alamany of San Francisco
Executors:	J.F. Cleary, John Cavanagh
Witnesses:	E.R. McCarthy, John Magrath

```
MURRAY, THOMAS I.         Written:  30 Jun. 1893              #2427
Santa Rosa    Age 32      Died:      6 Jul. 1894    Bk. F, Pg. 296
                          Rec.:     23 Jul. 1894
```

Mother:	Annie F.
Executor:	Wm. F. Lee
Witnesses:	C.S. Farquar, H.L. Tripp

```
MYRICK, D. B.             Written:   8 Jun. 1882              #1252
Geyserville               Died:     27 Jul. 1882    Bk. C, Pg. 249
```

Wife:	Eliza
Executor:	Wife
Witnesses:	A.P. Moore, C.W. Skaggs

```
NANERY, FREDERICK         Written:  24 Oct. 1882              #1537
Petaluma                  Died:     18 Feb. 1886    Bk. D, Pg. 175
                          Rec.:     12 Apr. 1886
```

Wife:	Dora
Children:	Herrmann, Frederick A. Jr., Henry
Executor:	Wife
Witnesses:	Henry Greenwood, John R. Wilson

```
NAU, KUNIGUNDA AKA        Dated:    16 Mar. 1896              #3195
PETER, KUNIGUNDA          Died:      2 Aug. 1900    Bk. G, Pg. 451
                          Filed:    12 Sep. 1900
```

Husband:	Martin Peter
Children:	Barbara Emma Goethe, Charles W. Nau
Executor:	Charles W. Nau
Witnesses:	Wm. E. McConnell, John Anton Kruse

NAU, THOMAS   Written: 7 Feb. 1885   #1476
                         Died: 27 May 1885   Bk. D, Pg. 63
                         Rec.:   22 Jun. 1885

  Wife: Kunnigunda
  Children: Barbara E., Charles W.
  Executor: Wife
  Witnesses: James A. Shaw, James E. Hamilton

NEEB, JOHANNA   Written: 8 Mar. 1871   # 480
                         Died: 7 Apr. 1871 Bk. Wills Pg. 217
                         Filed: 8 May 1871

  Husband: John Neeb (69)
  Daughter: Friederike Fichtner (59), wife of Chas., of San
               Francisco
  Native of Schwartzburg Londershandler, Germany
  Executor: Gustave H. Malech of San Francisco
  Witnesses: Gustave H. Malech, Martin Wigmann, Julius George

NEEB, JOHN   Written: 15 Mar. 1873   # 671
                         Died: 19 Feb. 1874
                         Filed: 23 Mar. 1874

  Wife: Caroline
  Friend: F. Albert Pauli
  Executor: F. Albert Pauli
  Witnesses: Wm. E. McConnell, F. Oette

NEIL, WASHINGTON   Written: 21 Mar. 1879   #1124
Petaluma   Filed: 4 Dec. 1880   Bk. C, Pg. 114

  Wife: Julia A.
  Children: Francis, Daniel Gilman, Charles, Washington,
               Walter Scott, Sonoma, Unchristened infant son
  Executor: Wife
  Witnesses: Ralph Brown, Wm. D. Bliss

NELSON, WILLIAM CLARK   Written: 1 Feb. 1896   #2811
Santa Rosa   Age 55   Died: 25 Oct. 1897
                         Filed: 27 Dec. 1897

  Wife: Comelia Nelson
  Sons: Charles W. Nelson, James Ira Nelson, John Henry
               Nelson
  Daughter: Emma Elizabeth Eugley (Engley)
  Executor: Wife
  Witnesses: John Tyler Campbell, Robert A. King both of
               Santa Rosa

NEWBURGH, EDWARD	Written:	4 Jun. 1892	#2262
	Died:	23 Oct. 1892	Bk. F, Pg. 30
	Filed:	21 Nov. 1892	

- Wife: Fanny
- Sons: Albert, Arthur, William, Henry
- Daughters: Therese Allenberg (Mrs. L.), Estelle
- Executor: Wife
- Witnesses: Holographic

NEWTON, MORRIS	Written:	10 Jun. 1889	#2841
	Died:	23 Dec. 1897	
	Filed:	26 Feb. 1898	

- Wife: California Newton
- Executor: California Newton
- Witness: Frank McCain

NICHOLS, HARRY W.	Dated:	6 Mar. 1866	# 309
	Died:	6 Mar. 1866	
	Filed:	13 Mar. 1866	

- Sisters: Mrs. Louisa E. Clark, Miss Jane Acton Nichols, Sarah Nichols, Ann E. Kennedy; all resided in London, Mrs. Kennedy at Nr 34 South St. Sidney St., Stepney, London, District E
- Associate: Benjamin Ducker
- Executors: James Singley, Noah Van Valkenburg
- Witnesses: Chas. Humphries, H. Flega (?), S. Payran

NORRIS, CHARLES	Written:	22 Dec. 1883	#1384
Age 72	Died:	19 Jan. 1884	Bk. C, Pg. 497
	Rec.:	12 Dec. 1884	

- Wife: Martha E.
- Children: Luke P.H., Theodorus, Mary Jane McPeak, Leroy, Samuel H., James N., Charles, Bertha M., Sarah C. Holden
- Executor: Wife
- Witnesses: Wm. E. McConnell, Clark Wells

NORTHUP, CHARLES H.	Dated:	15 Jan. 1870	# 441
Healdsburg	Died:	2 Apr. 1870	
Minister	Filed:	6 Jun. 1870	

- Wife: Lucia S.
- Daughters: Lulie B., Jessie S.
- Sons: Charles H. Northup, William Arthur Northup
- Executor: A.A. Sargent
- Witnesses: J.B. Smith, W.S. Canan

NORTON, L. A. Healdsburg	Written: Died: Rec.:	27 Jul. 1891 16 Aug. 1891 14 Sep. 1891	#2098 Bk. E, Pg. 413

- Wife: Emma Sarah (second wife)
- Children: Mary Elizabeth (25), Edward Mallory (22), Lewis Adelbert (21)
- Executor: Son, Edward
- Witness: J.S. Young

NUTTING, HERMAN	Written: Probate:	3 Apr. 1856 28 Aug. 1857	# 68 Bk. A, Pg. 32-35

- Wife: Mary M.
- Daughters: --- Maria, Mary Asenath, Rebeca Hildreth
- Sons: Frank Agustus, Horace Clark
- Executors: Mary M., Horace
- Witnesses: Mary M. Nutting, Horace I. Nutting, W.W. Zilhart, A.T. King, Jacob Foutz, Isaac Russell

O BRIEN, ISABELLA	Written: Died: Rec.:	2 May 1895 3 May 1895 27 May 1895	#2529 Bk. F, Pg. 362

- Son: Albert
- Daughters: Isabella, Nellie
- Executor: Isabella
- Holographic

O DONNELL, GEORGE Cloverdale Age 50	Written: Died: Rec.:	18 Apr. 1887 24 Apr. 1887 31 May 1887	#1637 Bk. D, Pg. 448

- Mother: Susan of Burtonport Co., Donegal, Ireland
- Brothers: John of Burtonport Co., Donegal, Ireland; Dennis of San Francisco
- Sisters: Mary Sharkey of Co. Donegal; Bridget Gallagher of Co. Donegal
- Bequests to: Mrs. Louisianna Worth, wife of Clarborne; Geo. Henry Lewes of San Francisco
- Executor: Peter Carberry of Downieville, Ca.
- Witnesses: Rev. John Meiler of Healdsburg, D.F. Spurr of Cloverdale

```
OETTL, FRANZ              Written:  6 Jun. 1881              #1310
Sonoma         Age 64     Died:     2 Apr. 1883    Bk. C, Pg. 364
                          Filed:   28 May  1883
                          Rec.:     7 May  1883
```

- Wife: Augusta
- Sons: Julius (28), Henry (23) both of first marriage; Franz (6)
- Daughters: Mary (21) of first marriage; Bertha (5)
- Executor: Wife
- Witnesses: George W. Clark of Sonoma, Ludwig M. Johannsen

```
OFFUTT, CHARLES           Dated:   13 Aug. 1879              #1025
Petaluma                  Filed:    1 Sep. 1879    Bk. D, Pg. 272
```

- Daughters: Sarah Ann, Mary J., Nancy Ellen
- Sons: John W., Chas. A., Lewis G.
- Executors: John W., Chas. A.
- Witnesses: Frank W. Mathews, John T. Barnes

```
OGAN, DAVID P. W.         Written: 18 Apr. 1872              # 548
                          Died:     6 Jun. 1872    Bk. A, Pg. 301-
                          Probate:  9 Jul. 1872              307
```

- Wife: L.F.
- Children: Kitty Virginia (2), Mary Amy (4), David Parkerson (1)
- Executor: Un-named
- Witnesses: J.B. Boyse (?), C. McGuire, C.W. Langdon

```
O GORMAN, THOMAS          Written:  5 Nov. 1873              # 662
                          Died:    18 Nov. 1873
                          Filed:    5 Jan. 1874
```

- Wife: Ann
- Daughters: Kate, Ann
- Son: John James
- Executor: Kate O'Gorman
- Witnesses: Jesse C. Wickersham, Daniel Brown

```
O KEEFE, DAVID            Written:  2 Jul. 1872              # 574
                          Died:    11 Aug. 1872
                          Filed:    4 Ovt. 1872
```

- Daughter: Margarett Elizabeth O'Keefe
- Guardian: Chas. Lynch
- Executor: Charles Lynch
- Witnesses: Kelly Tighe, Jerry Dwyer

O KEEN, HIRAM   Dated: 18 Feb. 1900   #3154
                             Died: 18 Apr. 1900   Bk. G, Pg. 425
                             Filed: 28 May 1900

    Brother: R.A. Keen
    Executor: R.A. Keen
    Witnesses: Wm. H. Joy, Katie Wieberts

OLIVER, FRANCES A.   Written: 9 Dec. 1892   #3234
 (GAFFNEY)   Died: 15 Jun. 1898   Bk. H, Pg. 20
 Petaluma   Filed: 7 Jan. 1901

    Husband: William M. Oliver
    Brothers: Benjamin Gaffney, Joseph Gaffney, James Gaffney
    Bequest to: Willaim R. Johnston of San Francisco
    Executor: William R. Johnston
    Witnesses: Miss Lizzie Upman of 435 Bush St., San Francisco;
                Richard V. Curtis of 2630 Folsom St., San
                Francisco; M. Cooney of 405 Kearny St., San
                Francisco

OMAN, MALVINA G.   Written: 7 Aug. 1885   #1715
 Stockton, CA   Age 73   Filed: 18 Feb. 1888   Bk. D, Pg. 582

    Bequests to: Hile Gay, son-in-law; Harry Sylvester; Minnie
                 Sylvester; Eliza Oman, sister-in-law
    Daughters: Mrs. Abbie Williams of Petaluma, Ca.; Maryette A.
                 Saere of Madison Co., Montana; Jane Gay of Colusa
                 Co., Ca.
    Sons: George W. Oman of Stockton, Ca.; John Oman of
                 Sprague, Wash. Terr.; Moroni Oman of Crook Co.,
                 OR; Joseph Oman of Stockton, Ca.
    Executors: G.W. Oman, John Williams
    Witnesses: Richard Lauxer, Charles B. Comfort

ORDWAY, WILLIAM   Dated: 17 Sep. 1866   # 333
                             Died: 5 Jan. 1867   Bk. A, Pg. 175-
                             Filed: 1 Apr. 1867   178

    Wife: Arah Ordway
    Daughters: Mary Abby, Martha Jane, Drucilla Hellen all minors
    Executors: Arah Ordway, Courtney Talbot, Arah's brother
    Witnesses: I.G. Wichersham, M. Doyle

ORMERD, ANN AMELIA   Written: 17 Dec. 1891   #2930
 San Francisco   Died: 27 Jul. 1898   Bk. G, Pg. 221
                             Filed: 24 Oct. 1898

    Sons: William Henry, Lawrence Wellington, Reuben Ridgon
    Daughter: Edith Amelia
    Executor: R.L. Rigdon of San Francisco
    Witnesses: J.K. Johnson of 830½ Bush St., San Francisco;
                Miss Lillian R. Freeman of 77 Elizabeth St.,
                San Francisco

```
OTIS, ISAAC                    Written:  24 Aug. 1888              #2583
                               Died:     10 Oct. 1895   Bk. F, Pg. 437
                               Filed:     8 Nov. 1895

    Mother:     Ann Otis
    Nephews:    Frderick W. Otis, Leonard Joseph Otis, Lewis
                Samuel Otis
    Executor:   Ann Otis
    Witnesses:  A.B. Ware, R.M. Swain, Frank A. Brush


OTIS, MARY J.          Written:   8 Dec. 1884              #1716
Petaluma      Age 73   Died:      2 Dec. 1887   Bk. D, Pg. 580
                       Filed:    12 Mar. 1888

    Sons:        Philo J. of Selma, Fresno Co., Ca.; Charles W.
    Daughters:   G.H. Otis of Selma, Ann (Laird?) of Santa Cruz,
                 Ca.
    Witnesses:   Sarah C. Pierce, M.M. Codding, M.C. Chapman


OTTMER, V. S.                  Written:  22 Jun. 1895              #2590
Burns, Ore.                    Filed:     9 Dec. 1895
                               Denied Probate

                Jennie L. Campbell


OVERHOLSER, A. W.      Written:  26 Jun. 1884              #1408
Petaluma      Age 55   Died:     26 Jun. 1884
Owned meat market      Rec.:     21 Jul. 1884

    Children:   Wm. R. Overholser, India Smith, Josiah Iredale
                Overholser, Alonzo Burton Overholser, Hattie
                E. Overholser, Charles Overholser, Clarence
                Overholser
    Executor:   Wm. R.
    Witnesses:  John P. Rodgers, J. Wallace MacWhinnie


OVERTON, A. P.                 Written:  30 Mar. 1898              #2872
                               Died:     13 Apr. 1898   Bk. G, Pg. 171
                               Filed:    16 May  1898

    Wife:       Jennie A.
    Sons:       T.T. Overton, John P. Overton
    Daughter:   Jessie Livernash
                A.P. Overton Co., Inc.
    Executor/
    Trustee:    John P. Overton
    Witnesses:  Thos. Rutledge, M.H. Dignan both of Santa Rosa
```

OWENS, JOHN B.   Dated: 12 Oct. 1865   # 373
Round Valley, Mendocino   Died: 1 Dec. 1866
Co.   Rec.:   8 Apr. 1867
                            Mendocino Co.

  Wife: Susan C.
  Son: Henry C.
  Daughter: Harriet E. Owens
  Executor: S.D. Baechtel of Little Lake
  Witnesses: C. Heberle, H. Brown

PALMER, ELIAS B.   Written: 7 Jun. 1887   #2259
Valley Ford   Filed: 27 Oct. 1892

  Wife: Mary Jane
  Son: Ellsworth
  Executor: Wife
  Witnesses: F.A. Meyer, Wm. B. Haskell

PALMER, WILLIAM   Written: 30 Jul. 1881   #1182
                            Filed: 22 Oct. 1881   Bk. C, Pg. 156

  Wife: Margaret
  Children: John A., Wm. J., Mary E., Edward L., Geo. F.,
              Annie C., James H.
  Executor: Wife
  Witnesses: I.G. Wickersham, M. Walsh

PARISH, WILLIAM   Written: 20 Nov. 1890   #2053
Sonoma   Age 65   Died: 9 Feb. 1891   Bk. E, Pg. 366
                            Rec.:   23 Mar. 1891

  Sons: William John, James
  Executor: Henry Weyle
  Witnesses: Allen A. Converse, David Calloway

PARKER, ELIZABETH   Written: 23 Mar. 1889   #1897
Petaluma   Age over   Died: 22 Jul. 1889   Bk. E, Pg. 176
              40   Rec.:   18 Nov. 1889

  Husband: Deceased
  Son: George J.
  Daughter: Jeannette B. Perry, wife of James, of Petaluma
  Executor: Daughter
  Witnesses: Wm. B. Haskell, H.E. Lawrence

PARSONS, CHARLES S. Petaluma	Written: Died: Rec.:	25 Oct. 1882 25 Oct. 1882 21 Jun. 1883	#1269 Bk. C, Pg. 303

- Wife: Minerva F.
- Children: Charles A., Ella E.
- Executor: Wife
- Witnesses: F.W. Shattuck, L.H. Patty, Geo. C. Parsons

PARSONS, HARRIET Santa Rosa	Written: Died: Filed:	14 Feb. 1887 16 Dec. 1888 31 Dec. 1888	#1809 Bk. E, Pg. 35

- Husband: Isaac
- Son: John Isaac
- Nephew: Louis P. Goodyear of Kansas
- Bequests to: Wm. Parsons Read, Harriet Cordilia Read
- Executors: Husband, son
- Witnesses: Wm. Prindle, W.D. Reynolds

PARSONS, ISAAC	Written: Codicil: Died: Filed:	14 Feb. 1887 27 Dec. 1888 24 Nov. 1892 30 Nov. 1892	#2273 Bk. F, Pg. 37

- Wife: Harriet
- Son: John Isaac
- Daughter: Mary Fidelia Read (deceased)
- Grandson: William Parsons Read (minor)
- Grand-Daughter: Harriet Cordelia Read (minor)
- Executors: Son, wife
- Witnesses: Wm. Prindle, W.D. Reynolds
- Codicil: L.W. Burris, G.A. Tupper

PARSONS, MINERVA M. Sebastopol	Written: Died: Rec.:	1 Dec. 1892 5 Dec. 1892 16 Jan. 1893	#2275 Bk. F, Pg. 54

- Husband: James M.
- Daughter: Elzann Cox of Oregon, Holt Co., Mo.
- Executors: Husband, Thos. G. Wilton
- Witnesses: John Saunders, W.W. Parr, Chas. Solomon

PARTING, ALICE Santa Rosa	Age 33	Written: Died: Filed:	12 Nov. 1894 13 Nov. 1898 27 Dec. 1898	#2949 Bk. G, Pg. 235

- Mother: Eunice Parting of Santa Rosa
- Sister: Margaret Edith Parting of Santa Rosa
- Aunt: Eusardia Nicholas of Santa Rosa
- Executor: Frederick D. Webley of Santa Rosa
- Witnesses: Louis Cowles, K. Nagasawa both of Santa Rosa
  Holographic

PATCHETT, JOHN ARMSTRONG Written: 1 Jan. 1903   #3555
Annapolis   Age 61   Died: 13 Jan. 1903   Bk. G, Pg. 551
                             Rec.:   6 Feb. 1903

    Wife: Mary O. (present wife)
    Children: Of previous marriage: Benj. E., Mary Alice Mason,
                Bertha Bondshu, Emma Minerva; by Mary: Franklin
                Arthur, Olive May, Albert Passmore, Mary Esther,
                Irene Amy, John Moyer, Roy Carpenter, Dosha
                Isabelle, Walter Cecil, Ulysses Arnold
    Executors: Wife; Benj. E., son
    Witnesses: O.O. Jeffers, John Murphy

PATTERSON, REBECCA   Written: 27 Apr. 1869   # 412
                           Filed: 22 Jun. 1869

    Children: Martha Ann White, Caroline P. Miller, William
                Patterson, Joseph Patterson, Mathew Spencer
                Patterson (deceased) of Indiana
    Executor: Greenberry Miller
    Witnesses: J.M. Lymones, Frank W. Shattuck

PATTERSON, WILLIAM H.   Dated: 30 Jul. 1867   # 346
                           Filed: 2 Jul. 1867

                Gen Tounsend (Townsend)
    Executor: Tounsend
    Witnesses: Daniel H. Jones, S.C. Florence, Z. Middleton

PATTON, MARY SUSAN   Dated: 26 May 1881   #1158
Vallejo Tnsp.   Filed: 13 Jun. 1881   Bk. C, Pg. 140

    Father: Rodney A. Todd
    Mother: Nancy Carolina Todd both of Stockton
    Brothers: George W. Todd, James M. Todd, Benjamin F. Todd
                (minor)
    Sister: Violella L. Todd (minor) all of Stockton
    Executor: Richard H. Crane
    Witnesses: John H. Stelter, Henry Parkerson

PATTY, L. H.   Written: 12 Apr. 1893   #2541
                Age over   Died: 26 May 1895   Bk. F, Pg. 377
                50   Rec.:   18 Jun. 1895

    Wife: Adelia H.
    Son: Levi H. (under 25)
    Brother: Albert Patty of Chacinto, Kansas
    Sisters: Malinda Cooper of Chattanooga, Tenn.; Catherine
                Walden of Chacinto, Kansas; Mary A. Whitney of
                San Francisco
    Witnesses: Daniel Brown, F.A. Meyer both of Petaluma

PAULI, F. ALBERT	Written:	21 Aug. 1882	#1624
Sonoma Age 51	Died:	7 Mar. 1887	Bk. D, Pg. 428
	Rec.:	18 Apr. 1887	

- Wife: Emilie
- Children: Gustave A. (7), Ferdinand R. (5), Alfred H. (2), Francis A. (unborn at time will was written)
- Executor: Wife
- Witnesses: Murray Whallon, Jacob Aherns

PAULI, G. T.	Written:	10 Jan. 1880	#1070
	Filed:	17 Mar. 1880	Bk. C, Pg. 88

- Daughters: Caroline Pauli, Paulina Pauli, Eloisa Pauli
- Sons: Robert J. Pauli, Albert Pauli, Emil Pauli
- Brother: F.A. Pauli
- Guardian: Caroline Pauli for Eloisa (minor); F.W. Pauli for Robert, Albert & Emil (in case of death of F.W. Pauli then F.G. Hahman)
- Executors: F.A. Pauli or friend, F.G. Hahman; Caroline Pauli
- Witnesses: G.W. Sparks, F. Grothaus

PAXTON, HANNAH H.	Written:	11 Oct. 1894	#3505
Healdsburg	Codicil:	24 Jan. 1899	Bk. H, Pg. 146
	Died:	30 Aug. 1902	
	Rec.:	29 Sep. 1902	

- Sisters: Miss Mary M. McClellan, Ruth McClellan
- Sons: Blitz W., Charles E.
- Grandson: John A.
- Grand-Daughter: Roma W.
- Executors: Both sons; sister, Mary
- Witnesses: Annie Rodda, Jas. W. Oates
- Codicil: Jas. W. Oates, Oscar Mathews

PAXTON, JOHN A.	Written:	15 Sep. 1885	#1755
San Francisco	Died:	10 May 1888	Bk. D, Pg. 612
	Filed	27 Jun. 1888	

- Wife: Hannah H.
- Sisters-in Law: Mrs. Ruth McClellan, Mrs. Mary Margaret McClellan
- Sons: Charles E., Blitz W.
- Sister: Mrs. Eliz. Ann Jordan of Lexington, Va.
- Nieces: Mrs. Isabella P. Steel of Lexington, Va.; Miss Eliz. Ann Wright
- Nephew: Paxton Wright
- Executors: Wife, John Garber
- Witnesses: Seldon S. Wright, W.T. Coleman

Two codicils

PAYNE, WILLIAM W.   Written: 28 Feb. 1880   #1085
                           Filed: 1 Jun. 1880   Bk. C, Pg. 93

    Wife: Mahalath Payne
    Sons: William Payne, James H. Payne (deceased),
                   Tilpman H. Payne (deceased)
    Daughters: Minerva Todd, Ruth Bever
    Son-in-law: John W. Todd
    Grandson: Edward H. Payne
    Witnesses: A. Wright, Thos. Riley

PEOPLES, NATHAN   Written: 1 Apr. 1871   #1213
         Age 61   Died: 23 Jan. 1882   Bk. C, Pg. 183
                           Filed: 6 Mar. 1882

    Wife: Rachel Peoples
    Daughters: Hannah B. Withington, wife of James Withington,
                   of White Pine Co., Nev.; Sarah Amanda Patton,
                   wife of Samuel Patton, of Shelby Co., Mo.
    Sons: Jackson M. Peoples of Monroe Co., Mo.; Nathan W.
                   Peoples
    Executor: Rachel Peoples
    Witnesses: Arthur E. Shattuck, Frank W. Shattuck

PERRY, MARY A.   Dated: 17 Feb. 1901   #3273
                           Filed: 26 Jul. 1901   Bk. G, Pg. 503

                   Gussie Santos
                   Wm. L. Sales, guardian of Gussie
                   Gertie Justin
                   Rev. Cleary
                   Mary Santos
                   Frank Justin
    Brothers: Three
    Sisters: Three
    Executor: --- McNear
    Witnesses: F.A. Meyer, F.A. Leal

PETER, JOHN   Written: 31 Dec. 1863   # 72
                           Died: 11 Apr. 1864   Bk. A, Pg. 116
                           Probate: 13 May 1864

    Daughters: Patsy Lanham, Margi White, Eliz. Walker, Nancy
                   Coffer
    Sons: Hartford (and his two children, John Henry & Mary
                   E.), Silas, Meriman Peter, Jordan Peter, Horace
                   Peter, Samuel Peter, John Thos. Peter
    Executor: Jordan Peter
    Witnesses: I.G. Wickersham, Wm. Bennett

(150)

```
PETERS, JURGEN            Written:  21 Mar. 1882           #2214
Petaluma Tnsp.  Age 54    Died:     17 Jan. 1892    Bk. E, Pg. 625
Born Witzwort, Island     Rec.:     31 May  1892
Fohr

    Wife:       Margaretha Magalena Dorothea
    Children:   Christian Julius Peters, Heinrich Peters, Hermann
                C. Hansen, Emma C.M. Hansen
    Witnesses:  Martin H. Flohr, Heinrich M. Feddersen


PETERSON, ANNA CARRIE     Dated:    15 Feb. 1899           #3157
Bodega Tnsp.              Died:     17 May  1900    Bk. G, Pg. 428
                          Filed:    11 Jun. 1900

    Brother:    Charles John Peterson
    Niece:      Hannah Speckter (King)
    Executors:  H.P. Brainhard, John Speckter
    Witnesses:  Mrs. B. Harrington of Occidental, Wm. J.
                Cunningham, J.P. of Bodega


PETIT, JACQUES            Written:   5 Sep. 1888           #1775
Healdsburg      Age 67    Died:     14 Sep. 1888    Bk. D, Pg. 628
                          Filed:    15 Oct. 1888

    Wife:       Henriette
    Children:   Of deceased sister: Louise Favre; of deceased
                brother: Louis Petit
    Executor:   Wife
    Witness:    J.W. Rose


PFISTER, MARY             Written:   2 Jan. 1896           #2682
                          Died:     15 Oct. 1896    Bk. F, Pg. 573
                          Filed:    24 Dec. 1896

    Daughters:  Julia A. Robinson, Bertha E. Pfister, Martha A.
                Pfister
    Sons:       John E. Pfister, Conrad C. Pfister, Volney J.
                Pfister, Nelson B. Pfister, Franklin P. Pfister
    Executor:   Conrad C. Pfister
    Witnesses:  D.R. Gayle, Leo Paul Bonjour


PHILBEE, JAMES            Written:  24 Jul. 1882           #1338
Santa Rosa      Age 65    Died:     12 Jul. 1883    Bk. C, Pg. 416
                          Rec.:      6 Aug. 1883

    Wife:       Sarah Jane
    Son:        Frank (about 8)
    Stepson:    Martillus Ramey
    Daughters:  Nicena Ellison, Mary Ellen Philbee, Margaret Jane
                Philbee
    Executor:   Wife
    Witnesses:  John T. Campbell, William F. Russell
```

PHILBEE, SARAH JANE　　　Written: 19 Nov. 1895　　　　　　　　#2607
　　　　　　　　　　　　Died:　　2 Feb. 1896
　　　　　　　　　　　　Filed:　 5 Feb. 1896

　Son:　　　　　Frank Philbee
　Daughters:　 Mary Ellen Harris of Oakland, Ca., Rachel N.
　　　　　　　　Ellison, Margaret J. Kelly
　Grandson:　 Albert Newton Ramey of Livermore, Ca.
　Guardian:　 Josephine Alice Miller of Livermore, Ca.
　Executor:　 John Harris of Oakland, Ca., son-in-law
　Witnesses:　 Alonzo T. Peery, D.R. Gale

PHILBROOK, HENRY　　　　　Written: 8 Jun. 1897　　　　　　　#2920
WHITNEY　　　　　　　　　Died:　 1 Jul. 1898　　Bk. G, Pg. 211
　　　　　　　　　　　　Filed:　 19 Sep. 1898

　Wife:　　　　 Elizabeth Philbrook
　Daughters:　 Nancy Barlow of Spencerville, Ohio; Martha Ford
　　　　　　　　of Napa Co., Ca.; Lucinda Williams of Mendocino
　　　　　　　　Co., Ca.
　Sons:　　　　 David Cyrus Philbrook, Enos A. Philbrook, James
　　　　　　　　Barnabas Philbrook
　Executors:　 David Cyrus Philbrook, Enos A. Philbrook, James
　　　　　　　　Barnabas Philbrook
　Witnesses:　 John S. Saunders, Jabez B. Sullivan both of
　　　　　　　　Sebastopol, Ca.

PHILIPS, NANCY M.　　　　 Written: 24 Mar. 1894　　　　　　　#2403
Healdsburg　　Age 66　　 Died:　 6 Apr. 1894　　Bk. F, Pg. 228
　　　　　　　　　　　　Rec.:　 30 Apr. 1894

　Sons:　　　　 James H., Frank C.
　Grandson:　 Harold F.
　Grand-
　Daughter:　 Fannie P.
　Executor:　 J.W. Rose
　Witnesses:　 C.W. Weaver, C.H. Pond

PHILLIPS, ELIZABETH J.　 Dated:　 4 Jun. 1900　　　　　　　 #3265
　　　　　　　　　　　　Died:　 27 Jan. 1901　 Bk. G, Pg. 484
　　　　　　　　　　　　Filed:　 25 Feb. 1901

　Husband:　 Henry C. Phillips
　Grand-
　Daughter:　 Ethel Elledge, Polly M. Cook
　Daughters:　 Polly A. Ervin, Nancy E. Finney, Rebecca E.
　　　　　　　　Willson, Martha J. Elledge
　Sons:　　　　 Francis M. Cook of Tulare Co.; Jacob S. Dobkins;
　　　　　　　　George A. Cook, Isaac Cook
　Executor:　 Martha J. Elledge
　Witnesses:　 E.M. Norton, S.L. Wattles

PHILLIPS, MARGARET	Written:	6 May 1882	#1273
Petaluma	Died:	8 Nov. 1882	Bk. C, Pg. 320
	Rec.:	23 Jun. 1883	

Daughters:	Debbie & Tillie Phillips both of Petaluma and both adopted
Nephew:	William Johnson of San Francisco
Nieces:	Lizzie Brown of Petaluma, Louisa Branch of Lakeville
Sisters:	Bridget Guilfoyle of San Francisco, Mary Gason of Ireland, Johannah Guilfoyle of Australia, Ann Hoary of Canada
Brothers:	Patrick Guilfoyle of Sonoma Co., Michael Guilfoyle
	Rev. Father Cleary of Petaluma
	Sister Mary Catharine of Petaluma
	Miss M.F. Mogan of Petaluma
Executor:	Col Peter Donahue
Witnesses:	Frank W. Shattuck, Wm. F. Shattuck

PHILLIPS, LOTTIE P.	Dated:	11 May 1898	#2895
	Died:	12 Jun. 1898	Bk. G, Pg. 200
	Filed:	18 Jul. 1898	

Children:	Amelia Ann Phillips (23), Mary Ellen Phillips (19), Maud Rea Phillips (16), Georgie Duvall Phillips (10)
Executor:	Amelia Ann Phillips, Mary Ellen Phillips
Witnesses:	S.O. Heaton, Geo. R. Somes

PIEHL, EDWARD HEINRICH	Dated:	29 Jun. 1900	#3176
	Died:	30 Jun. 1900	Bk. G, Pg. 440
	Filed:	23 Jul. 1900	

Wife:	Katharine Piehl
Daughter:	Lilian Piehl
Executor:	Katharine Piehl
Witnesses:	F.H. Rosenbaum, Belle Lawrence, John R. Hebe (?)

PIERCE, ABRAM J.	Written:	7 May 1882	#1318
Petaluma	Died:	27 Apr. 1883	Bk. C, Pg. 380
	Rec.:	10 Jul. 1883	

Wife:	Mary J.
Son:	William S.
Executor:	Wife
Witnesses:	F.P. Wickersham, I.J. Wickersham

PIERCE, SARAH C.   Written: 15 Nov. 1884   #2135
Petaluma   Codicil: 30 Jul. 1885   Bk. E, Pg. 479
                     Died: 28 Nov. 1891
                     Rec.:   28 Dec. 1891

- Husband: Solomon (deceased)
- Grandson: Wm. S. Pierce (minor)
- Niece: Phoebe Colby
- Bequest to: Mary Colby, widow of Geo.
- Codicil: Brother, Abram S. Jewell
- Executors: Hiram T. Fairbanks, Isaac R. Je--ll, Wm. B. Haskell
- Witnesses: Wm. H. Haldane of New York City, Llewellyn E. Carpenter of Jersey City, N.J.
- Codicil: Wm. B. Haskell, Wm. A. Chapman both of Petaluma

PIERCE, WILLIAM S.   Written: 28 Feb. 1895   #2521
Petaluma   Died: 20 Mar. 1895   Bk. F, Pg. 356
                     Rec.:   15 Apr. 1895

- Step-Mother: Mary Jane Pierce
- Executor: Mary J. Pierce
- Holographic

PIEZZI, GIUSEPPE   Dated: 15 Aug. 1898   #2911
                     Died: 16 Aug. 1898   Bk. G, Pg. 209
                     Filed: 13 Sep. 1898

Descendant of Giovan Antonio of Giurmaglio, Canton Tessin, Switzerland. Will written in St. Mary's Hospital in San Francisco

- Niece: Elisa LaFranchi, wife of Maurizio
- Brothers: Dominico Piezzi of Giurmaglio, Serafino Piezzi of Santa Rosa
- Executor: Victor Piezzi of Carillo, Sonoma Co.
- Witnesses: Geo. F. Cavalli, G.E. Porta both of San Francisco

PINA, ANTONIO   Dated: 10 Apr. 1853   # 71
                     Filed: 20 Apr. 1863

- Daughter: Maria Ant (?)
- Others: Jesus Pina, Francisco Pina, Luis Pina, Clara Pina, Natividad Pina, Mr. Pauli, Don Pedro Bojorques, Mrs. Guadalupe West, Mr. Juan Guaco, Don Ramon Sanchez, Don Faciendo Garcia, Don Joaquin Bororquez, Mr. Llonso, Mr. Santa Ana, Mr. Juan Bejarano, Salvador Mendez, Don Ramon Carrillo, Don Julio Carrillo, Don Juan Silvas
- Executor: M. Guadalupe Vallejo
- Witnesses: A.P. Chapman, Robert Ward

PINA, GERMAN		Written: 17 Jun. 1847	# 70
		Probate: 8 Sep. 1852	

Son of Don Lazaro Pina & Dona Placida Villela (deceased)

- Brothers: Four
- Sister: One
- Executor: Jose DeJesus Pina
- Witnesses: Jose Santellan, Jose DelaRosa, Antonio Ortega

PLAGE, HELENE		Written: 14 Aug. 1878		#1903
Sonoma	Age 50	Died: 29 Sep. 1889		Bk. E, Pg. 182
		Probate: 2 Dec. 1889		

- Niece: Helene Dresel
- Nephews: Carl Dresel, and Gustave, children of sister, Johanna; Emil Dresel, son of sister, Bertha
- Executor: Julius Dresel, brother-in-law, of Sonoma, Ca.
- Witnesses: Louis Beckers, of New York, Jacob Gundlach

PLASKET, ALICE		Written: 4 Dec. 1886	#1638
Cloverdale	Age 32	Died: 8 Jan. 1887	
		Rec.: 23 May 1887	

- Husband: Peter
- Children: Un-named
- Executor: Husband

PLUMLY, MARCHANT WILSON	Written: 2 Nov. 1889	#1904
Salt Point Tnsp.	Died: 5 Nov. 1889	Bk. E, Pg. 185
	Rec.: 2 Dec. 1889	

- Bequests to: H.A.F. Coward; Beulah Broyles, daughter of Mrs. H.A. Howard; Mrs. David P. Peters; James Henry; John Ruoff of Timber Cove; J.L. Brooks; Mrs. Wm. Bolder of Salt Point Tnsp.
- Witnesses: John L. Brooks, Horace H. Howard both of Fort Ross

PLUNKIT, ELEANOR		Written: 20 Apr. 1891	#2114
Sebastopol	Age 66	Codicil: 20 Aug. 1891	Bk. E, Pg. 485
		Died: 7 Oct. 1891	
		Rec.: 29 Dec. 1891	

- Sister: Rosanna Gascard of Modoc Co., Ca.
- Son: John Plunkit (16), adopted
- Bequest to: Minnie Faylor of Guerneville, wife of Orson
- Codicil: Newphew, John Plunkit; friends Mrs. Sidney Yeagley and Mrs. Mary Wood
- Executor: Sister
- Codicil: W.C. Grainger
- Witnesses: Jno. Brown, John Goss both of Santa Rosa
- Codicil: Sidney Yeagley, Jas. Coleman

POCAI, SEBASTIANO	Written:	9 Feb. 1891	#2067
Guerneville Age 31	Died:	24 Feb. 1891	Bk. E, Pg. 376
	Rec.:	27 Apr. 1891	

Son of Ferdinando & Catterina (deceased)

- Brother: Felice
- Nephews: Antonio, Raffaelo
- Witnesses: Amadeo Baesi, Arcangelo Christofani

POOL, JOHN	Written:	23 Nov. 1880	#1131
Guerneville	Filed:	27 Dec. 1880	

- Wife: Lyddia Pool
- Children: Un-named
- Executor: Lyddia Pool
- Witnesses: Henry Beaver, John Robinson

POOLE, JARED F.	Written:	13 Apr. 1899	#3419
Age 74	Died:	8 Jan. 1902	Bk. H, Pg. 107
	Rec.:	3 Feb. 1902	

- Daughter: Harriet A. Moran (only child)
- Brother: Anderson T. of Martha'a Vineyard, Mass.
- Executor: Harriet Moran
- Witnesses: J.G. Pierce, Jas. A. Strider

POPPE, J. A.	Written:	25 Apr. 1872	#1051
Sonoma City	Died:	4 Dec. 1879	Bk. C, Pg. 76
	Filed:	19 Dec. 1879	

- Wife: Catharina Poppe
- Children: Charles Poppe, Robert Poppe, Emma Poppe, Kate Poppe, Julius Poppe
- Executor: Catharina Poppe
- Witnesses: O.W. Craig, Geo. W. Clark

POST, RACHEL	Written:	2 Feb. 1878	#1163
Petaluma	Filed:	13 Jul. 1881	Bk. C, Pg. 148

- Bequest to: Louisa Casto
- Grand-Children: Of daughter Addie Ann P. Reyerson of Solano Co.; son of James & Ann Ryerson now in New York City
- Executors: Geo. Lamereaux, Thos. Jeff. Graham
- Witnesses: D.D. Carder, N.W. Scudder

```
POTTER, CHARLES S.          Written:  29 Sep. 1892              #2468
Sonoma Tnsp.    Age 58      Died:      2 Oct. 1894      Bk. F, Pg. 312
                            Oakland, CA
                            Rec.:     16 Nov. 1894

    Wife:       Elizabeth A.
    Children:   Maggie Nesbit, Joseph H. Potter, Adelaide, Aggie,
                Lottie, Charles W., Emily, Nellie
    Executor:   Wife
    Witnesses:  C.L. Colvin, J.C. Plunkett both of Oakland, Ca.


POWER, THOMAS J.            Written:  13 Jun. 1870              #1734
                            Died:     12 Jan. 1888      Bk. D, Pg. 598
                            Filed:     7 May  1888

    Wife:       Mary S. Power
    Witness:    Sarah Shane


PRESSLEY, JOHN G.           Written:   6 Feb. 1889              #2548
                Age 56      Died:      5 Jul. 1895      Bk. F, Pg. 386
                            Rec.:     29 Jul. 1895

    Wife:       Julia B.
    Brother:    William Burrows
    Executor:   Wife
                Holographic


PRESTON, RICHARD MILNE      Written:   8 Mar. 1882              #1228
San Luis Obispo             Died:     22 Mar. 1882      Bk. C, Pg. 217
                Age 40      Filed:    18 Apr. 1882

    Daughter:   Lida Halman Preston
    Son:        Abram Pierce Preston
    Wife:       Lida Preston
    Executor:   Wife
    Witnesses:  Wm. E. McConnell, J.M. Roney


PRINCE, PETER               Written:  11 Jan. 1892              #2195
Santa Rosa      Age 55      Died:      3 Mar. 1892      Bk. E, Pg. 599
                            Rec.:     15 Apr. 1892

    Wife:       Charlotte
    Children:   Sidney, Theodora, Melville, Sanford H., Elede,
                Kionel D., Milton D.
    Executor:   Wife
    Witnesses:  S. Moral, A.D. Laughlin
```

```
PRINDLE, WILLIAM            Dated:   16 Feb. 1877              #3121
                            Died:     4 Feb. 1900    Bk. G, Pg. 415
                            Filed:   23 Apr. 1900
```

- Wife: Nellie L. Prindle
- Children: Fred Albert Prindle, Marian Ella Prindle
- Executor: Nellie L. Prindle
- Witnesses: Sheldon Armstrong, F.M. Caldwell

```
PRITCHARD, JOSEPH           Written: 21 Dec. 1901              #3445
Shelville, Ca.              Died:    20 Mar. 1902    Bk. H, Pg. 118
                            Filed:   14 Apr. 1902
```

- Brother: George Pritchard of London, Canada West
- Executors: M.T. Akers of Shelville, Ca., R.A. Poppe of Sonoma
- Witnesses: Holographic

```
PROVO KLUIT, ADRIAAN OR     Written: 20 Apr. 1891              #2310
KLUIT, ADRIAAN PROVO        Died:    12 Mar. 1893    Bk. F, Pg. 103
Hayward, Ca.    Age 44      Sonoma Co.
                            Rec.:     6 May  1893
```

- Wife: Frances Emma Cross ProvoKluit
- Daughters: By Johanna Louisa ProvoKluit: Adriana Johanna Louise, Henriette
- Executor: Sam'l J. Allen of San Francisco
- Guardian: Of daughters, Sam'l J. Allen
- Witnesses: Charles Prowse, R. Reid both of Hayward

```
PROWS, DANIEL W.            Dated:   18 Jun. 1894              #2876
           Age 72           Died:    23 Apr. 1898    Bk. G, Pg. 181
                            Filed:   23 May  1898
```

- Relatives: Alice West (formerly Lang) of California; William Prows of Utah; Mary Jane George of Utah; Simeon Prows of Florida; James Prows of Kentucky; and the children of Thomas Prows of Virginia
- Brothers: Alma Prows of Sonoma Co., Ca.; Sylvester Prows of Sonoma Co., Ca.; Joseph Prows of Kentucky
- Sisters: Mary Ann Barlow of Sonoma Co., Ca.; Elizabeth Martin of Kentucky; Mary Ellen Turner of Kentucky
- Executors: Alma Prows, Sylvester Prows
- Witnesses: J.D. Silvia, Jr.; W.W. Moreland both of Healdsburg

```
RAFAEL, MANUEL IGNACIO    Written:   25 Jun. 1889              #2492
Petaluma      Age 72      Died:      3 Dec. 1894      Bk. F, Pg. 341
                          Rec.:      28 Jan. 1895
```

Wife:	Ignatio
Daughters:	Margaretta, Jessie
Grand-Children:	August, Antonie, Joseph all sons of daughter, Marie Fernands (deceased)
Bequests to:	M.E. Rafael, Antoine, Joseph, children of Rosa Frates, Ceatono Rafael, John Rafael
Executor:	Wife
Witnesses:	F.A. Meyer, Manuel J. d'Avellar

```
RAGLE, GEO. J.            Written:   1 Dec. 1883               #2371
                          Died:      11 Dec. 1893     Bk. F, Pg. 210
                          Rec.:      2 Jan. 1894
```

Wife:	Margaret J.
Son:	Alexander (adopted)
Executor:	Wife
Witnesses:	Wm. E. McConnell of Santa Rosa, W.J. Hunt of Sebastopol

```
RAINS, ANNA               Written:   -- Nov. 1886              #1826
                          Died:      17 Aug. 1888    Bk. E, Pg.  97
                          Rec.:      8 Apr. 1889
```

Husband:	Gallant (deceased)
Son:	John
Witnesses:	W.P. Thompson, Philip Morshead

```
RAMBO, ANN                Written:   13 May 1872               # 550
                          Filed:     1 Jul. 1872
```

Sons:	A.J. Rambo, John L. Rambo, James H. Rambo, L.A. Rambo
Daughter:	Lovina F. Wilson
Executor:	Wm. Wilson
Witnesses:	B.B. Berry, J.H. Rambo

```
RAMBO, MILTON             Written:   3 Dec. 1866               # 335
                          Died:      3 Dec. 1866     Bk. A, Pg. 168
                          Probate:   18 Feb. 1867
```

Mother:	Ann Rambo, sole heir
Brothers:	Named by Wm. Wilson; A.J., John L. Lewis A., Jas. H.
Sister:	Lovina, wife of Wm. Wilson
Witnesses:	T.J. Alley, Wm. Wilson

RANARD, JAMES H.   Written: 30 Jul. 1886   #2187
                           Died: 24 Jan. 1892   Bk. E, Pg. 557
                           Rec.:   7 Mar. 1892

    Wife: Fanny
    Children: Caroline Railsback, wife of Caleb; Zilpha Fellows,
                 wife of David S.; Mary L. Flewelling, wife of
                 Beverly; Etta M.; John; Irving D.
    Children: Of son, Anderson (deceased): Rofa, Lina, Arthur
    Children: Of son, Thomas (deceased): Maude
    Executors: Caleb Railsback; Irving D. Ranard, son
    Witnesses: W.E. Cox, Wm. B. Haskell both of Petaluma

RANARD, JOHN MONROE   Written: 9 Feb. 1892   #2263
Petaluma   Died: 17 Apr. 1892   Bk. F, Pg. 34
                           Rec.:   21 Nov. 1892

    Wife: Henrietta Ella
    Executors: Wife, Sam'l. Martin
    Witnesses: E.L. Lippitt, W.R. Veale

RANGE, CHARLES   Written: 8 Mar. 1898   #3439
RANGE, ELIZABETH E   Died: 18 Jul. 1898   Bk. H, Pg. 116
                           Charles
                           Filed: 24 Mar. 1898

    Daughter: Louisa J.W. Reid
    Sons: John M. Range, Columbus Range
    Executor: Louisa J.W. Reid
    Witnesses: W.W. Peatross, Hester Ann Peatross both of Santa
                 Rosa

RANKIN, ADAM LOWRY   Written: 3 Jun. 1893   #2526
Petaluma   Died: 20 Apr. 1895   Bk. F, Pg. 360
                           Rec.:   11 Jun. 1895

    Wife: Margaret Do--nell Rankin
                 Holographic

RAY, JAMES FLETCHER   Written: 19 Apr. 1887   #1653
         Age 69   Died: 9 Jun. 1887   Bk. D, Pg. 486
                           Filed: 13 Jul. 1887

                 Mexican War Veteran

    Wife: Julia Ray
    Daughters: Mrs. America Fuller of Chico, Ca.; Mrs. Sarah
                 Ellen Mitchell of Elco Co., Nev.; Mrs. Mildred
                 A. Newcomb of Vallejo, Ca.
    Executor: Wm. H.H. Fuller of Chico, Ca.
    Witnesses: Robert Thompson of 1037½ Market St., San
                 Francisco; Frank W. Yale of 413 Brannan St.,
                 San Francisco

READ, MARY FIDELIN   Filed: 18 Nov. 1879   #1043
                                                            Bk. D, Pg. 290

    Children: William Parsons Read, Harriet Cordelia Read,
                 Mary Fidelia Read
    Executor: Dr. W.S. Read
    Witnesses: Wm. Y. Wilson, Isaac Parsons

RECTOR, WM. H.   Written: 21 Sep. 1887   #2639
                            Died: 23 Feb. 1890   Bk. F, Pg. 510
                            Filed: 20 Sep. 1897

    Wife: Ann Rector
    Son: B.F. Rector

REDMOND, DENNIS AKA   Dated: 24 Dec. 1897   #2816
REDMAN, DENNIS   Died: 25 Dec. 1897   Bk. G, Pg. 95
                            Filed: 17 Jan. 1898

    Friend: William Bourke
    Executor: Bourke
    Witnesses: F.A. Meyer, C. Therkelsen

REED, WILLIAM C.   Written: 5 Apr. 1880   #2062
Santa Rosa   Died: 29 Mar. 1891   Bk. E, Pg. 381
                            Rec.:   13 Apr. 1891

    Wife: Margaret Elizabeth
    Daughter: Mary Jane Campbell
    Executor: John Tyler Campbell
    Witnesses: Wm. E. McConnell, Jas. H. McGee

REICHARDT, OSWALD   Written: 20 Mar. 1863   # 299
Santa Rosa   Died: 19 Aug. 1865
                            Filed: 15 Nov. 1865

    Daughter: Emma
    Executor: Thos. L. Thompson
    Guardian: Thos. L. Thompson (of Emma)
    Witnesses: Chas. P. Wilkins, Wm. E. McConnell

REICHENBACH, ANNA   Written: 7 May 1889   #1955
Petaluma   Age 75   Died: 13 Apr. 1890   Bk. E, Pg. 251
                            Rec.:   23 May 1890

    Husband: Magnus F.
    Children: John Gatteker of Switzerland, Emma Hubert of
                 San Francisco, Ida Schwenk of Paterson, N.J.
    Executor: Husband
    Witnesses: Geo. Griess, F.A. Meyer

REILLY, EDWARD   Dated: 18 Sep. 1865   # 297
Vallejo Tnsp.   Died: 9 Oct. 1865
Naturalized citizen   Filed: 24 Oct. 1865

                  Mary, wife of James Clark
                  Family, if any, is unknown
  Witnesses: Fredric H. Alberding, James S. Singley, Thomas Shone

REIMER, RUDOLPH   Written: 25 Jul. 1901   #3381
Santa Rosa   Died: 18 Oct. 1901   Bk. H, Pg. 74
                            Filed: 4 Nov. 1901

  Children: Jessie Reimer, Fred Reimer
  Executor: Fred Reimer, son
  Witnesses: Holographic
            Mentions property on Lincoln Street

REMMEL, CHARLES   Written: 7 Nov. 1890   #2035
Geyserville   Died: 19 Nov. 1890   Bk. E, Pg. 340
                            Rec.:   5 Jan. 1891

  Wife: Mary S.
  Daughters: Ada E.
  Son: Geo. E.
  Executor: Wife
  Witnesses: J.J. Wood, C.A. Parrott, Henry Crocker

RESPINI, JOHN   Written: 28 Nov. 1896   #3393
                            Died: 24 Nov. 1901   Bk. H, Pg. 89
                            Filed: 30 Dec. 1901

  Wife: Mary Ann
  Son: Henry
  Children: Attillo, Leodina, Americo, Florencia, Ricardo,
            Allido
  Executor: Wife
  Witnesses: F.A. Meyer, Wm. B. Haskell both of Petaluma

RICHARDS, GRANT O.   Written: 17 Jan. 1898   #2936
                            Died: 22 Oct. 1898   Bk. G, Pg. 226
                            Filed: 14 Nov. 1898

  Wife: Dollie Francis
  Father: O.M. Richards (deceased) of Elk Grove, Lafayette
            Co., Wisconsin
            Smeker (?) of Grant Co.
  Executor: Wife
  Witnesses: Holographic
            Stock in Santa Rosa Press Democrat Publishing Co.

```
RICHARDS, WM. E.            Written:  23 Jun. 1873              # 622
                            Filed:    28 Jul. 1873

   Wife:       Mary A.
   Children:   Un-named
               Sarah Baronetta Barnes
   Executor:   Wife
   Witnesses:  F.J. Pullee, Nelson R. Norton, W.H. Moss


RICHARDSON, MARIA           Written:  20 Aug. 1873              #1814
                            Filed:    28 Dec. 1888

   Mother:     Catherine O Rourke
   Husband:    W. Nathan
   Executor:   Husband
   Witnesses:  R.A. Thompson, E.W. Maslin


RICHELEAU, CATHERINE N.     Written:  10 Jun. 1886              #1621
Formerly MRS. C.N. TRUE     Died:     28 Feb. 1887    Bk. D, Pg. 406
Santa Rosa                  Rec.:     28 Mar. 1887

   Husband:    James V.
   Son:        Thos. Jenness True
   Daughter:   Edith Richeleau
   Executors:  Husband, son
   Witnesses:  L.W. Burris, Wm. E. McConnell


RIDGWAY, JEREMIAH           Written:  14 Jun. 1878              #1467
Santa Rosa      Age 75      Died:     19 Feb. 1885    Bk. D, Pg.  55
                            LaPorte, Ind.
                            Rec.:      4 May  1885

   Children:   Judith A. Todd, Jeremiah Ridgway, Joseph W.
               Ridgway
   Executors:  All children
   Witnesses:  A. Thomas, Isaac Parsons, A.L. Justice, George
               Jeffers


RINGSTROM, P. R.            Written:   1 Nov. 1875              #1127
                            Died:      2 Dec. 1880    Bk. C, Pg. 116
                            Filed:    20 Dec. 1880

   Wife:      Cornelia, in Sweden
   Executor:  Rev. John Doughty of San Francisco
   Witness:   Peter Anderlini
```

RISK, JAMES CALDWELL   Written: 15 Feb. 1888   #1851
                           Filed: 25 Apr. 1889

   Wife: Sarah
   Daughters: Mary Motherwell White, Elizabeth Rankin, Jane
                 Henderson, Nancy Caldwell Moiles, Josephine Boyd,
                 Martha Motherwell
   Sons: David Rankin, James Caldwell Jr., William Bond
   Executor: James B. Roberts
   Witnesses: Daniel L. Bishop of San Francisco, Waldo M. York
                 of San Luis Obispo

ROBERTS, JAMES L.   Dated: 2 Apr. 1896   #2738
          Age 80   Died: 2 Apr. 1897   Bk. G, Pg. 18
                          Filed: 14 Apr. 1897

   Wife: Elizabeth Roberts
   Children: Jonathan Roberts, James W. Roberts, Joseph C.
                 Roberts, Charles A. Roberts, Amanda Jane Johnson,
                 Ann Eliza White, John C. Roberts, Ephriam W.
                 Roberts (deceased), Mary Ann Bass (deceased),
                 Nancy "Nannie" Roberts
   Executors: Jonathan Roberts, T.A. White, son-in-law
   Witnesses: F.M. Cooper, D.R. Gale

ROBERTS, WILLIAM R.   Written: 2 Mar. 1881   #1152
                           Died: 1 May 1881
                           Filed: 9 Aug. 1881

   Wife: Mary Jane Roberts
   Daughter: Henrietta Roberts
   Son: William Roberts
                 Other children mentioned
   Executor: Mary Jane Roberts
   Witnesses: James H. McGee, H. Moore

ROBERTSON, WM. R.   Written: 16 Sep. 1866   # 324
          Age 47   Died: 17 Sep. 1866
                           Probate: 22 Oct. 1866

   Wife: Artilla
   Daughters: Lavina, Mary Jane, Sarah Ann
   Sons: Chris. Columbus, John W.
   Friend: Milas Laton
   Executors: Artilla & A.L. Purrine
   Witnesses: Sam'l Potter, Lorenzo Gale of Bodega Town

```
ROBINSON, MARY ANN        Written:  25 Sep. 1901              #3386
         Age over  Died:     -- Oct. 1901      Bk. H, Pg. 83
         45        Alameda Co.
                   Filed:     9 Dec. 1901
```

Daughter:	Mary Emma Turner
Sons:	James Wm. Robinson, Arthur Robinson
Executor:	Geo. P. McNear
Witnesses:	F.A. Meyer , A.L. Tibbetts both of Petaluma

```
ROBINSON, MARY            Written:  10 Oct. 1882              #2092
Albany, N.Y.              Died:     26 Apr. 1883    Bk. E, Pg. 418
                          Rec.:     28 Spe. 1891
```

Husband:	Henry (deceased)
Brothers:	John J. VanAlen of Healdsburg, Egbert VanAlen of Cloverdale
Nephews:	William VanAlen, John VanAlen both sons of John
Nieces:	Harriet Van Alen, daughter of Egbert; Sarah
Friends:	Henry Robinson Benkard; Patrick Dorrnan or wife Margaret; Sarah Starkweather; Margaret G. Meldrum, wife of James, of Washington D.C.; Anna R. Hewitt, daughter of Sam'l (deceased), of Newburgh, N.Y.
Executors:	Nephew, John VanAlen; Henry R. Benkhard; Eugene A. Brewster
Witnesses:	Chas. M. Jenkins, Theo. V. VanHensen, Fred. W. Brown

```
ROBUSON, GEORG            Written:  11 Sep. 1883              #1364
Petaluma Tnsp.            Died:     17 Oct. 1883    Bk. C, Pg. 464
                          Rec.:     26 Nov. 1883
```

Wife:	Carolina
Children:	William, Sophia, Lizzie, Georgia, Katy, Julia
Executor:	Wife
Witnesses:	A. Morstadt, C. Temple

```
ROCHFORD, SEBINA          Dated:     8 Aug. 1891              #3140
                          Died:      7 Mar. 1900    Bk. G, Pg. 408
                          Filed:     2 Apr. 1900
```

	Widow of Thomas Rochford
Daughter:	Josephine Morrow Rochford (minor) (adopted), daughter of John Morrow
	Mrs. G.P. Hall, Nettie Brown, Josephine Brown, Emma Brown, Alice Brown, all daughters of Daniel Brown
Executor:	Daniel E. Brown, nephew, of Fresno
Witnesses:	Wm. B. Haskell, J.S. Blackburn

```
ROCHFORD, THOMAS          Written:  17 Aug. 1890              #2001
Petaluma      Age over    Died:     18 Aug. 1890         Bk. E, Pg. 306
              50          Rec.:     10 Sep. 1890

    Wife:        Sebina
    Daughter:    Josephine Morrow Rochford (adopted), daughter of
                    John & Virginia Morrow
    Bequest to:  James Rochford of Dixon, Solano Co., Ca.
    Executors:   Daniel Brown, J.L. Dinwiddie
    Witnesses:   F.M. Daly of San Francisco, Wm. B. Haskell


RODGERS, ALEX. W.         Written:  17 May 1873                # 629
                          Died:     15 Jul. 1873
                          Filed:     4 Aug. 1873

    Wife:        Mary Ann
    Children:    Un-named
    Executor:    Wife
    Witnesses:   Frank W. Shattuck, J.H. Crane


RODGERS, SILAS            Written:  12 Feb. 1892               #2422
Healdsburg    Age 71      Died:      2 Jun. 1894          Bk. F, Pg. 264
                          Rec.:     25 Jun. 1894

    Wife:        Lucinda
    Sons:        John, Warren, Robert
    Grand-
    Daughter:    Mamie Hudson
    Daughters:   Mary Ingram, Leymiza Vesser, Sarah Stevens,
                    Elizabeth Haigh, Jane Cantrell, Ruth Faught, Julia
                    Lambert
    Executor:    Wife
    Witnesses:   C.W. Weaver, J.T. Coffman


ROGERS, E. A.             Written:   9 Apr. 1882               #2080
                          Died:     20 Apr. 1891          Bk. E, Pg. 391
                          Rec.:      1 Jun. 1891

    Wife:        L.M.
    Executor:    Wife
                 Holographic


ROGERS, JOHN              Dated:     3 Aug. 1866                # 319
                          Died:     23 Aug. 1866          Bk. A, Pg. 157
                          Filed:     1 Oct. 1866

    Wife:        Ann Rogers
    Executor:    Ann Rogers
    Witnesses:   G.W. Burrows, Wm. McPherson Hill
```

```
RONEY, JAMES M.            Written: 26 Nov. 1892              #2304
Santa Rosa                 Died:    12 Mar. 1893   Bk. F, Pg. 85
                           Filed:   10 Apr. 1893

    Wife:         Mary A. Roney
    Daughters:    Margaret May, Edith Alleen
    Mentioned:    Dora Spencer, Youngsville, Warren Co., Pa.
    Executor:     Wife
    Trustee:      Wife
    Witnesses:    Oscar Morrison, C.S. Farquar


ROOD, WILLIAM W.           Written: 22 Sep. 1862              #  22
Petaluma                   Filed:   14 Jan. 1863

    Father:       Un-named
    Mother:       Un-named
    Admin:        Jas. Whittaker of Tomales
    Witnesses:    Edw. A. Everett, Wm. Spencer


ROSE, MARY                 Written: 24 Jan. 1884              #1531
Petaluma                   Died:    24 Feb. 1886   Bk. D, Pg. 163
                           Rec.:    22 Mar. 1886

    Husband:      Joseph
    Sons:         Manuel Coreia of San Francisco, Joseph, Jr.,
                  Frank, Willie
    Grandson:     Peter Roque of Nevada Co., Ca.
    Daughters:    Mary Enos, Rosaline Roque (evidently mother of
                  Peter)
    Executor:     John King
    Witnesses:    Frank Shattuck, Thomas Kyle


ROSS, ELIZABETH GRACE      Written:  9 Aug. 1888              #1792
                           Filed:   20 Mar. 1889

    Son:          James Edwin
    Trustees:     Patrick Hyde, (two others are unreadable)
    Bequests to:  Rev. Father Geo. Montgomery of San Francisco;
                  Alice & Frank T---an; Rev. Father Conway of
                  Santa Rosa; Mary Redmond Ogive, daughter of
                  Patrick Hyde; Mrs. Welch of Santa Rosa
    Executors:    Same as three trustees
    Witnesses:    Annie H. Stevenson of San Francisco, Francisco
                  Cassin of St. Mary's Hospital, San Francisco
```

ROSS, GEORGE   Written: 8 Feb. 1884   #2288
Petaluma   Age 52   Died: 23 Jan. 1893   Bk. F, Pg. 70
                            Rec.:   20 Feb. 1893

   Brothers: Thomas, Alexander of Australia
   Bequests to: Mrs. Eliza A. Rowlson, E.E. Rowlson, A.R. Millett,
                  Mrs. Louis H. Molte of San Francisco, J.Q. Reed,
                  Mrs. & Mrs. A. Chambers, Nettie Millett
   Executors: Wm. B. Haskell, E.E. Rowlson
   Witnesses: Pater torn off

ROSS, WILLIAM   Written: 14 Feb. 1874   # 680
                            Died: 10 Apr. 1874
                            Filed: 18 May 1874

   Wife: Eliz. G.
   Son: Jas. E. (darling little son)
   Executor: Wife
   Witnesses: J. Beam, Wm. J. Hardy

ROYCE, RACHEL   Written: 14 Aug. 1889   #2050
Santa Rosa   Age 68   Died: 20 Dec. 1890   Bk. E, Pg. 346
                            Rec.:   9 Feb. 1891

   Husband: Spaulding A. (deceased)
   Son: George A.
   Daughter: Mary F. Gamble (deceased)
   Sister: Mrs. Sarah McWillimas of Lewiston, Montana
   Grand-
   Daughter: Dora Virginia Gamble
   Executors: O.A. Hoag, Abram Gamble
   Witnesses: Terry Driscoll, Cushing E. Hoag

RULE, ELIZABETH   Dated: 21 Feb. 1890   #3171
Widow   Age 69   Codicil: 21 Mar. 1900   Bk. H, Pg. 8
                            Died: 19 Jun. 1900
                            Filed: 9 Jul. 1900

   Sons: Charles H.S. Rule, Wm. J. Rule, Edward J. Rule,
                  John Richard Rule
   Daughters: Josephine Rule (deceased when codicil written),
                  Nannie A. Hebbard
   Executor: Charles H.S. Rule
   Witnesses: James W. Oates of Santa Rosa, Thos. M. O'Brien of
                  San Francisco
   Codicil: James W. Oates, Sadie R. Morrill, Oscar Charles

RUNYON, JULIA ANN		Written: 26 Jun. 1886	#1577
Santa Rosa	Age 62	Died: 24 Sep. 1886	Bk. D, Pg. 306
		Rec.: 1 Oct. 1886	

- Sons: Oliver Perry Runyon, George of The Dalles, Ore.
- Daughters: Sarah Ann Teague of Pomona, Ca.; Mary Jane Britton
- Grand-Daughter: Ada Skinner, child of daughter, Martha Washington Skinner (deceased)
- Executor: Oliver Perry, son
- Witnesses: John T. Campbell, M.M. Shearer

RUNYON, MARY		Written: 18 Sep. 1888	#2674
	Age 63	Died: 25 Sep. 1896	Bk. F, Pg. 562
		Filed: 26 Oct. 1896	

- Daughters: Victoria A. Brown, Emma M. Earl
- Sons: Henry A. Runyon (deceased), Albert J. Runyon, William N. Runyon, Charles E. Runyon, Frederick M. Runyon
- Grandson: Harry LeGrande Runyon
- Grand-Daughter: Grace Runyon
- Executors: Wm. N. Runyon, A.B. Ware
- Witnesses: R.M. Swain, H.G. Hahman, A.B. Ware

RUTHERFORD, THOS.		Written: 19 Dec. 1885	#1524
Petaluma	Age 22	Died: 22 Dec. 1885	Bk. D, Pg. 156
		Filed: 8 Mar. 1886	

- Brothers: Wm. S., James Adam
- Sister: Sadie J. Lightner
- Executor: Adam Davidson
- Witnesses: John Loranger, J.W. Davidson

RUTHERFORD, MARY JANE		Written: 8 Jan. 1880	#1115
	Age 50	Filed: 4 Oct. 1880	Bk. C, Pg. 108

- Children: William Spencer, Sarah Jane, Thomas, James Adam
- Executor: John & Adam Davidson, brothers
- Witnesses: J.S. Rutherford, G.L. Miller

SABINE, JOSEPH FRATES		Written: 9 Feb. 1887	#1617
Petaluma Tnsp.	Age 60	Died: 11 Feb. 1887	Bk. D, Pg. 382
		Rec.: 7 Mar. 1887	

- Wife: Mary
- Children: Ralphine, Mary, Joseph, Frank, Flamina, Antonio, Louisa, John, Carmen
- Executor: Wife
- Witnesses: John King, F.F. Marks

```
ST. CLAIR, FRANK C.           Written:   24 Apr. 1883              #1373
Healdsburg      Age 46        Died:      10 Dec. 1883     Bk. C, Pg. 470
                              Rec.:       7 Jan. 1884
```

Wife:	Nancy E. (36)
Step-Daughter:	Addie Godfrey (15)
Children:	Frank C. (11), Mary E. (7), Freddie (4), Richardson (2)
Executor:	Wife
Witnesses:	H.K. Braun (Brown), R. Powell

```
SALMON, SIDNEY                Written:   24 Nov. 1874              # 718
                              Died:      26 Nov. 1874     Bk. B, Pg. 130
                              Filed:      3 Dec. 1874
```

Father:	John Salmon of Osyth, Essex Co., England
Mother:	Harriett Salmon of Osyth, Essex Co., England
Executors:	Albert Downs, copartner in business; McHugh Russell
Witnesses:	H.A. Russell, Mrs. J.D. Bailiff

```
SAMUELS, JAMES                Written:   20 Mar. 1886              #1790
Healdsburg                    Died:      30 Oct. 1888     Bk. E, Pg.   8
                              Filed:     26 Nov. 1888
```

Daughter:	Isabella
Step-Daughter:	Luella A. Sibbold (Myers), wife of John Of Golconda, Nev.
Executors:	John Sibbold, Wilson Brown
Witnesses:	T.J. Riley, A.E. Cochran

```
SAWTELL, ELNATHAN             Written:   29 Jun. 1893              #2413
PRESCOTT                      Died:      10 May  1894     Bk. F, Pg. 250
Sebastopol                    Rec.:       4 Jun. 1894
```

Cousin:	Columbus Sawtell of Healdsburg
Executor:	Geo. P. Baxter
Witnesses:	P.H. Atkinson, Fred. W. Searby

```
SCANLON, MARGARET             Written:   10 Sep. 1885              #1498
Petaluma        Age 65        Died:      14 Sep. 1885     Bk. D, Pg. 101
                              Filed:     19 Oct. 1885
```

Cousin:	Mrs. Mary Scully of Adair, Ire.
Friend:	Mrs. W.P. Meadows
Executor:	Philip Dunn
Witnesses:	Frank Shattuck, John Perry

```
SCHENCK, AUGUST          Written:  13 Jan. 1881              #2158
Eureka, Ca.              Died:      3 Jan. 1892    Bk. E, Pg. 591
                         Sonoma Co.
                         Rec.:      6 Apr. 1892

    Wife:        Annce Emilie
    Executor:    Wife
    Witnesses:   J.D.H. Chamberlin, S.S. Laveren both of Eureka


SCHIECK, JOHANN          Written:  27 Jun. 1899              #3282
GOTTFRIED                Died:     19 Feb. 1901    Bk. H, Pg.  49
Glen Ellen    Age 76     Rec.:     15 Apr. 1901

    Wife:        Margaretha Agnes
    Sons:        Frederick, David, Hermann
    Daughter:    Agnes Brockmann
    Executor:    David Schieck
    Witnesses:   Robt. A. Poppe, Jas. M. Cowan


SCHLAKE, HEINRICH        Dated:    19 Dec. 1896              #2824
(HENRY)       Age over   Died:     27 Dec. 1897    Bk. G, Pg. 107
              60         Filed:     7 Jan. 1898

    Sons:        Heinrich T. Schlake, William Schlake
    Children:    Sophie Buckrig (?), Margaret Bose (?), Lizzie
                 Light, Annie Schlake, Frederick A. Schlake
                 Mamie Green (minor) of Mary Green (deceased)
                 and Fred Green
    Executor:    William Schlake
    Witnesses:   F.A. Meyer, H.J. Poehlman


SCHLOSSER, THOMAS C.     Written:  27 Mar. 1889              #2144
Petaluma                 Died:     21 Dec. 1891    Bk. E, Pg. 495
                         Rec.:     11 Jan. 1892

    Brothers:    Columbus Oliver, Hazard Zebulon
    Daughter:    Eugenia Frances McCarthy
    Sister:      Mary Ann Norris
    Sister-in-
    Law:         Maria P. Schlosser
    Executor:    Thomas Hopper
    Witnesses:   E.L. Lippitt, Thos. Roach


SCHNEIDER, MARIA C.      Written:   5 May  1894              #2701
Petaluma                 Died:      6 Jan. 1897    Bk. F, Pg. 589
                         Filed:     1 Feb. 1897

    Brother:     Charles J. Peterson
    Sister:      Anna Core Peterson
    Niece:       Hannah Klinge
    Executor:    H.P. Brainerd
    Witnesses:   A.B. Hill, L.A. Wick both of Petaluma
```

SCHULT, MARTHA A.   Died: 21 Aug. 1875   # 764
                           Filed: 6 Sep. 1875

    Heirs: Evalena V. Hammond (20) of San Franicsco;
                  Caroline S. Brown (18) of Healdsburg; Marietta
                  Brown (16) of Healdsburg; Daniel Brown (14) of
                  Healdsburg; Martha E. Brown (12) of Healdsburg;
                  James W. Brown (9) of Healdsburg
    Executor: Aaron Hassett
                  No will available

SCHULTZ, WILLIAM HENRY   Written: 1 Feb. 1890   #1944
Healdsburg   Age 56   Died: 25 Mar. 1890   Bk. E, Pg. 233
                         Rec.:   28 Apr. 1890

    Bequests to: Children of wife, Martha A. (deceased): Samantha
                 C. Fitch of Healdsburg, Eveline Richardson of
                 San Francisco, Mariette Allen of San Francisco,
                 David Brown of San Francisco, Martha E. Phillips
                 of San Francisco, James H. Brown of San Francisco
    Executor: R.K. Truitt
    Witnesses: J.W. Rose, F.J. Schwab

SCHWOBEDA, JOHN B.   Written: 15 Sep. 1884   #1431
Two Rock Valley   Died: 7 Oct. 1884   Bk. C, Pg. 616
                          Rec.:   17 Nov. 1884

    Wife: Medea (Merttea)
    Sons: Henry J., John L (minor)
    Executor: Wife
    Witnesses: S.Q. Barlow, T.C. Keegan

SCHWOBEDA, MEDEA   Written: 13 Sep. 1902   #3552
                          Codicil: 13 Sep. 1902
                          Died: 30 Dec. 1902
                          Rec.:   19 Jan. 1903

    Sons: John, Henry
    Executor: Frank K. Lippitt
    Witnesses: E.L. Lippitt, L.E. Rankin
    Codicil: D.B. Fairbanks

SCIAPACASA, ANTONIO   Dated: 23 Jun. 1871   # 493
                          Died: 24 Jun. 1871   Bk. A, Pg. 233
                          Filed: 7 Aug. 1871

    Brother: Nicholas Sciapacasa
    Sister: Mary
    Niece: Lasaunta
    Daughters: Clara Shivo and her six children all un-named,
                  Antonio Flora Barbieri
    Executor: Joseph Barbieri, son-in-law
    Witnesses: Frank Shattuck, Fred Frasier, Julius Bloom

SCOTT, THOMAS				Written:	29 Oct. 1874			# 757
					Codicil:	---			Bk. B, Pg. 171
					Died:		3 Aug. 1875
					Filed:		16 Aug. 1875

   Daughter:	Anna Maria Scott (6)
   Heirs:		Living in Italy
   Codicil:	Names Mary O'Grady, mother-in-law
			Born on Island of Madalini, Province of Sardinia,
			Italy, known there as Antonio Scottie
   Executor:	H.H. Atwater, resident priest of St. Vincent
			Parish, Petaluma
   Witnesses:	I.G. Wickersham, J. VanderWort

SCOTT, WILLIAM W.			Written:	16 Apr. 1849			# 5
									Bk. C, Pg. 119

   Wife:		Ann
   Daughter:	Mary M.
   Executor:	Mariano G. Vallejo
   Witnesses:	J.E. Bracket, M.G. Vallejo of the District of
			Sonoma

SCUDELLATTI, JAMES			Dated:		7 Jan. 1898			#2831
Valley Ford		Age 26		Died:		10 Jan. 1898		Bk. G, Pg. 121
					Filed:		14 Feb. 1898

   Mother:		Teresa Scudellatti
   Sisters:	Angiolina Scudellatti, Ceserina Masotti
   Executors:	M.J. Pellascio, A. Giacomini
   Witnesses:	Peter Pellascio, Steve Pellascio

SEAVY, ROBERT				Written:	10 Oct. 1884			#2430
Petaluma				Died:		3 Jun. 1894		Bk. F, Pg. 271
					Rec.:		2 Jul. 1894

   Wife:		Anna (present wife)
   Daughters:	Hattie M. (18), Minnie A. (14) both children
			by deceased wife; Laura (infant) by present
			wife
   Executor:	Lee Ellsworth
   Witnesses:	Wm. B. Haskell, M.H. Falkner

SHADDUCK, PHOEBE W.			Written:	7 Feb. 1887			#1648
Santa Rosa				Died:		17 Jun. 1887		Bk. D, Pg. 454
					Rec.:		5 Jul. 1887

   Sister:		Maria Watson
   Next of Kin:	Pauline Moore of New York, Emilie Thompkins
			of Pa., Amanda Bascom of Mo., Philip Wells
			Abroth (?) of N.Y.
   Executor:	Sister
   Witnesses:	John T. Campbell, W.D. Reynolds

```
SHAFER, IGNATZ            Written:  13 Nov. 1888            #2660
Cloverdale     Age 50     Died:     16 Aug. 1896     Bk. F, Pg. 544
                          Rec.:     21 Sep. 1896

    Wife:       Sarah Cecelia
    Executor:   Wife
    Witnesses:  D.F. Spurr, J.F. Handley


SHAFER, JOHN S.           Written:  19 Jan. 1880            #1063
Healdsburg                Filed:     3 Feb. 1880     Bk. C, Pg.  84

    Wife:       Elizabeth G. Shafer
    Sons:       William Terry Shafer, Frank Shafer, Eloen Shafer
    Daughter:   Dora Jamison
    Executor:   Elizabeth G. Shafer
    Witnesses:  Jno. N. Bail---, J.D. Hassett, D.G. Jewett


SHEARER, JOHN             Written:  13 Jan. 1879            #1769
Petaluma       Age 53     Died:     28 Jul. 1888     Bk. D, Pg. 624
                          Filed:     3 Sep. 1888

    Wife:       Harriet Amelia
    Executor:   Wife
    Witnesses:  B.F. Tuttle, Wm. B. Haskell


SHELDON, CHARLES LA BAR   Written:  16 Jul. 1889            #2606
Sebastopol     Age 54     Died:      8 Dec. 1889     Bk. F, Pg. 458
                          San Francisco
                          Rec.:     18 Feb. 1896

    Wife:       M. Alice
    Executor:   Wife
    Witnesses:  Jno. S. Schenck, H.M. Beall both of The Dalles,
                Oregon


SHEPHERD, REVE. DR. J.    Written:  29 Sep. 1893            #2682
AVERY                     Died:     30 Mar. 1898     Bk. G, Pg. 159
                          Filed:    25 Mar. 1898

    Bequests to: Elizabeth D. Porter; D. Porter, husband of Hon.
                 Judge W.W. Porter
    Executor:    Elizabeth D. Porter


SHEPHERD, REBECCA         Written:  20 Oct. 1896            #3292
Petaluma       Age over   Died:     21 Mar. 1901     Bk. H, Pg.  51
Widow          60

    Daughters:  Emily M. Jenke, Clara Annie Hutchins
    Son:        Charles James
    Executor:   Daughter, Clara
    Witnesses:  Wm. B. Haskell, Mrs. H.L. Weston
```

```
SHERIDAN, FLAN              Written:    9 Jul. 1875              # 760
                            Filed:      4 Sep. 1875   Bk. B, Pg. 183

    Wife:        Ellen Sheridan
    Brother:     James Sheridan
    Sister:      Mary Ann Orr
    Executor:    James Sheridan
    Witnesses:   John Dougherty, B.G. Dougherty


SHERIDAN, JOHN              Written:   22 Apr. 1872             #1542
Sacramento Co. Age 51       Died:       7 Apr. 1886   Bk. D, Pg. 275
                            Santa Rosa
                            Rec.:      27 Sep. 1886

    Wife:        Phebe
    Executors:   Wife; Edward Christy, friend, of Folsom
    Witnesses:   C.G.M. French, Jas. L. English both of Sacramento
                 City


SHOEMAKER, WILLIAM          Written:   17 May   1881             #1159
Mendocino Co.               Filed:     23 Jun.  1881

    Bequests to: Wm. Kitchen, John Kitchen
    Brothers:    John, Drewry, Daniel, Luther
    Wife:        Susan Shoemaker
    Grand-
    Daughters:   Mary Oliver, Pauline Shoemaker
    Executor:    Susan Shoemaker
    Witnesses:   F.M. Cummins, E.W. King both of Ukiah


SHUSTER, JOHN               Written:   19 Jul. 1883              #1339
Freestone      Age 65

    Wife:        Emmaline
    Children:    Mentioned
    Executors:   Wife, A.S. Purrine
    Witnesses:   Nelson R. Shaw, R.B. Campbell


SICOTT, FERDINAND           Written:   11 Oct. 1893              #2356
Guerneville    Age 60       Died:      12 Oct. 1893   Bk. F, Pg. 169
                            Rec.:       6 Nov. 1893

    Wife:        Angeline
    Son:         Freddie (14)
    Children:    Others un-named
    Executor:    H.W. Ungewitter
    Witnesses:   H.L. Bagley, J.A. Banks both of Guerneville
```

```
SILVA, MARTHA              Written:   7 Jan. 1894           #2919
AKA SILVIE, MARTHA         Died:     30 May  1894       Bk. G, Pg. 212
                           Filed:    19 Sep. 1898

    Husband:     Anton E. Silva
    Sons:        Joseph Silva, Edward Silva, Felix Silva, Bernard
                 Silva
    Daughters:   Pauline Cuadro, Mary Martin, Veronica Parks, Ada
                 Silva, Rose Silva
    Executor:    Anton E. Silva
    Witnesses:   F.J. Cope, F.A. Meyer both of Petaluma


SINGMASTER, EDWIN          Written:  16 Nov. 1895           #2591
Green Valley    Age 52     Died:     28 Nov. 1895       Bk. F, Pg. 441
                           Rec.:      2 Jan. 1896

    Children:    Annie Scott, Charles Edwin, Owen Sylvester, Jacob
                 Earl (minor), Henry LaHeist (minor)
    Executor:    Annie Scott
    Witnesses:   Simon Graham, Joseph Dixon


SINK PHOEBE                Dated:    22 Jul. 1899           #3208
                           Died:     26 Aug. 1900       Bk. G, Pg. 463
                           Filed:    15 Oct. 1900

    Son:         William D. Sink
    Grand-
    Daughter:    Mrs. McCray
    Others:      Addie, Gene---, Bess, Daniel, Berl (Barb?) Currie,
                 Marretta, Stella Meryl, Edward Connolly, Hattie
                 A note states Phoebe was wife of Walter S.;
                 mentions Bess Sink of St. Helena and Edward
                 Connolly as a cousin
                 Holographic


SIOLI, PAOLO ANDREA        Written:   8 Aug. 1894           #3051
San Francisco   Age 56     Died:     11 Aug. 1899       Bk. G, Pg. 329
Single                     Filed:    18 Sep. 1899

    Brothers:    Victor Sioli of Healdsburg and others un-named
    Executor:    Victor Sioli
    Witnesses:   Holographic
```

SISSINGOOD, CHRISTINA   Written: 9 Aug. 1889   #1885
AKA JOHN   Died: 3 Sep. 1889   Bk. E, Pg. 155
Cloverdale
Livery Stable

   Children: Of brother John of Germany
   Step-sister: Mary of Germany
   Bequests to: John Purcell, employee; Cornelia Sutten, wife of
              Aaron; Wm. Sacray, employee
   Executors: Frank Spencer, Wm. Sacray
   Witnesses: Michael Menihan of Cloverdale, Edw. J. Livernash
              of Ukiah

SKINNER, HUGH R.   Written: 20 Jan. 1890   #3337
Santa Rosa   Died: 7 Jul. 1901   Bk. H, Pg. 62
                         Rec.:   12 Aug. 1901

   Wife: Rebecca T.
   Children: Mrs. Lucretia Brown, George, Fidelia, Milton,
              Mrs. Julia Henry
   Witnesses: E.B. Woodward, W.D. Reynolds

SKINNER, LAVINA T.   Written: 21 Nov. 1888   #1799
Santa Rosa   Died: 26 Nov. 1888   Bk. F, Pg. 30
                         Filed: 17 Dec. 1888

   Sons: Oliver C. of Blue Lake, Humboldt Co., Ca.;
              Martin B.; George A.; W.G.
   Daughters: Matilda A. Ostrom, Lavina T. Harrison
   Executor: W.G.
   Witnesses: John Goss, L.J. Benton

SLATTERY, CATHERINE   Written: 18 Apr. 1901   #3511
Analy Tnsp.   Age 71   Rec.:   23 Sep. 1902

   Children: Catherine Taber, wife of John S.; Mary; Wm. H.;
              Michael; John J.; Patrick; Jas. Francis (deceased)
   Executors: Son, Wm.; daughter, Catherine
   Witnesses: Emmet Seawell, Ben S. Wood, Jr.

SMITH, DAVID A.   Written: 5 Aug. 1892   #2952
Petaluma   Age 53   Died: 19 Dec. 1898   Bk. G, Pg. 238
                         Santa Clara Co.
                         Filed: 16 Jan. 1899

   Wife: Cecelia
   Daughter: Nellie May Barber Smith (adopted)
   Nephew: David Allen Smith
   Brother: Shelden H. Smith
   Executor: Wife
   Witnesses: J.L. Dinwiddie, H.P. Brainerd both of Petaluma

SMITH, GEORGE THOMAS	Written:	14 Aug. 1880	#1334
Coquimbo, Chili &	Rec.:	1 Oct. 1883	Bk. C, Pg. 400
26 Great St. Helens, London, England			

- Wife: Anita Page Smith
- Sisters: Rosa, Ana Marie, Sara, Esabel DeWard
- Executors: Brother, Benito Forbes Smith of London; or brother-in-law, Henry Page of San Francisco
- Witnesses: C.M.M. Rawlins, Wm. Stubbs

SMITH, GEORGE W.	Written:	6 Aug. 1899	#3055
	Died:	27 Aug. 1899	Bk. G, Pg. 334
	Filed:	18 Sep. 1899	

- Daughter: Sarah A. Peery
- Sons: Abraham B., George W. Jr., Lucas D.
- Grandson: Alonzo T. Peery
- Executor: Grandson
- Witnesses: Chas. E. Gamble of Santa Rosa, Chas. S. Peery of 820 Gun St., San Francisco

SMITH, HENRY P.	Written:	21 Oct. 1901	#3389
Cloverdale	Died:	8 Nov. 1901	Bk. H, Pg. 82
	Filed:	2 Dec. 1901	

- Brother: William Smith
- Executor: Brother
- Witnesses: George Watson, Carl C. Coker both of Cloverdale

SMITH, ISAAC PARSONS	Written:	-- Jul. 1874	#1011
	Died:	2 Apr. 1879	
	Filed:	26 May 1879	

- Wife: Lucinda Jane
- Daughter: Mary Ann Frances
- Bequest to: John Britton Crisp (minor)
- Executor: Wife; or brother, Thos. U. Smith
- Witnesses: C.C. Farmer, A. Thomas

SMITH, JACOB	Written:	26 Jul. 1873	# 661
	Died:	24 Oct. 1873	
	Filed:	8 Dec. 1873	

- Wife: Margaret Ann
- Daughters: Eliza Elliott Smith; Caroline Hood, wife of Thos. B.; Oliva Jane Smith
- Sons: Geo. W., Wm. R., John K., Thos. J., James M., Robt. E. (deceased) and his children: Wm. Adolphus; Birdenia A. Hand, wife of Milton; Lucia Adelia; Cora Ann; Florence Eliz.
- Grandchild: Mary Ann Linn, daughter of Mary Ann (deceased) and Wm. S. Linn
- Executors: John K. Smith, Thos. B. Hood
- Witnesses: W.S. McWright, C.S. Ames

```
SMITH, JOHN B.              Written:  29 Jun. 1889              #2056
Petaluma                    Died:     23 Feb. 1891   Bk. F, Pg. 158
                            Rec.:     18 Sep. 1893
```

- Wife: Octavia Susie
- Son: Henry Rhodes
- Daughter: Allie Plumb
- Executor: H.H. Atwater
- Witnesses: Fred A. Wickersham, J.E. Johnson

```
SMITH, LUCINDA J.           Written:  17 Dec. 1884              #1595
Santa Rosa                  Died:     24 Nov. 1886   Bk. D, Pg. 340
                                      San Francisco
                            Rec.:     20 Dec. 1886
```

- Daughter: Mary Frances Downing of San Francisco
- Executors: Chas. S. Smythe, Henry White
- Witnesses: A.H. Smith, Maggie Smith

```
SMITH, MARGARET A.          Written:   1 Mar. 1889              #2551
Santa Rosa    Age 71        Died:     18 Jul. 1895   Bk. F, Pg. 401
                            Rec.:      5 Aug. 1895
```

- Step-Daughters: Eliza E. Smith; Mrs. Caroline E. Hood; Mary Ann Linn (and her heirs); Melvina Jane, wife of Jas. Smith; Ellen, wife of Thos. Smith
- Stepsons: Wm. R., Geo. W., Rob't. E. (and his heirs), J.K. Smith of Washington Terr.
- Executor: Caroline Hood
- Witnesses: J.H. Dyson, A.G. Bennett

```
SMITH, MARGARET H.          Written:   4 Sep. 1884              #2556
Santa Rosa    Age 51        Died:      7 Aug. 1895   Bk. F, Pg. 405
                            Rec.:     26 Aug. 1895
```

- Husband: John F.
- Executor: Husband
- Witnesses: Chas. W. Otis, Geo. Bew

```
SMITH, MARIA C.             Written:  30 Jan. 1893              #2293
Healdsburg                  Died:      7 Feb. 1893   Bk. F, Pg.  82
                            Rec.:     10 Apr. 1893
```

- Husband: John (1st husband, James Kruse)
- Children: John Kruse (34), F.A. Kruse (27), Chas. G. Kruse (24), Jas. H. (22), Henry A. (19), August (17), Mrs. C. Voss (32)
- Executor: Son, F.A.
- Witnesses: C.W. Weaver, E.M. Norton

```
SMITH, OLIVER P.          Written:  25 Mar. 1889              #1857
Santa Rosa    Age 54      Died:     15 Apr. 1889    Bk. E, Pg. 132
                          Rec.:     24 Jun. 1889
```

- Daughter: Harriet Moone, wife of Harry, of N.Y.
- Son: Edmund of N.Y.
- Executor: Father, Abraham P.
- Witnesses: R.G. Temple, Silas Weller

```
SMITH, PRESTON B.         Written:  7 Oct. 1873               # 656
                          Died:     7 Oct. 1873
                          Filed:    8 Dec. 1873
```

- Wife: Gabrella Augustino
- Son: Geo. Taylor
- Executor: Wife
- Witnesses: N.A. Bailey, E.T. Farmer

```
SMITH, RALPH              Written:  6 May 1886                #1547
Sea View      Age 65      Died:     7 May 1886     Bk. D, Pg. 203
                          Rec.:     1 Jun. 1886
```

- Wife: Catherine
- Daughters: Caroline Boothby, Honora Smith (32) both of Sea View
- Executor: Caroline Boothby
- Witnesses: Joe Coburn, Thomas Herbert both of Austin, Sonoma Co.

```
SMITH, ROBERT PRESS       Written:  3 Feb. 1896               #3073
              Age 56      Died:     19 Oct. 1899   Bk. G, Pg. 243
                          Filed:    13 Nov. 1899
```

- Wife: Nellie M. Smith
- Sons: Edwin D. Smith, Temple Smith, Daniel Lesesne, Press Smith
- Daughters: Nellie Temple Smith, Mary Gaillard Smith, Harriet Porcher Smith
- Executor: Nellie M. Smith

```
SMITH, SARAH A.           Written:  21 Dec. 1899              #3100
Santa Rosa    Age 52      Died:     21 Dec. 1899   Bk. G, Pg. 375
                          Rec.:     8 Jan. 1900
```

- Husband: Daniel
- Executor: Husband
- Witnesses: Jas. C. Sims, Geo. E. Dohn

SMITH, SIMON P.   Dated: 4 Mar. 1898   #2900
Alexander Valley   Died: 3 Apr. 1898   Bk. G, Pg. 203
           Age 55   Filed: 14 Jun. 1898

   Wife: Martha E. Smith (45)
   Children: Mary J. Stovall, Jesse W. Smith, Luther N. Smith,
                 Charles A. Smith, Albert L. Smith, Alice R.
                 Smith, Andrew S. Smith, Simon L. Smith, Annie
                 E. Smith
   Executors: Martha E. Smith
   Witnesses: J.W. Rose, Henry S. Gird, Florence A. Rose all
                 of Healdsburg

SMITH, STEPHEN (CAPT.)   Dated: 7 Aug. 1854   # 74
           Age 68   Filed: 21 Jan. 1856

   Wife: Manuella T. Smith of Bodega
   Sons: Stephen Smith, James Smith
   Daughter: Manulla Smith
   Children: Of former wife: S. Henry Smith, Giles Smith,
                 Ellen Morison, Elvira Pond
   Executors: Capt. William A. Richardson of Sauselito,
                 James Wilson of San Francisco
   Witnesses: Sam'l Merritt, H.P. Hoyt, Henry Baker

SMITH, THOMAS   Written: 14 Feb. 1896   #3541
Valley Ford   Age 67   Died: 28 Nov. 1902   Bk. G, Pg. 532
                         Rec.:   29 Dec. 1902

   Wife: Mary E.
   Sisters: Annie Salina Short of Whiterock, New So. Wales;
                 Jane Blackburn of Home Rule, New So. Wales;
                 Bathsheba Sloggett of Bathurst, New So Wales
   Niece: Eliz. Blackburn of Home Rule, New So. Wales
   Executor: John Henry Fowler
   Witnesses: M.J. Striening, Frank B. Cornue (?)

SNEED, RICHARD   Written: 9 May 1877   #1961
                         Died: ------ 1890   Bk. E, Pg. 245
                         Rec.:   19 May 1890

   Wife: Nancy M.
   Daughter: Mary Helen Hartford (adopted)
   Executor: Wife
   Witnesses: Jacob G. Mayer, Jacob F. Mayer

SNODDY, BENJAMIN A.   Dated: 23 Jan. 1872   # 527
                         Died: 12 Feb. 1872   Bk. A, Pg. 262
                         Filed: 18 Mar. 1872

    Children: Sarah Ann Snoddy, Susanah Snoddy, Virginia Snoddy,
                 John Wesley Snoddy, Mariah Turner Snoddy, Mary
                 Elizabeth Snoddy all of Missouri
    Executors: R.B. Lyons, John Tivnen(?), W.A. Berry
    Witnesses: Wm. E. McConnell, A.J. VanEvery

SOUZA, A. C.   Written: 10 Nov. 1895   #2644
                         Died: 11 Dec. 1896   Bk. F, Pg. 528
                         Filed: 29 Jun. 1896

    Brothers: J.C. Souza, F.C. Souza

SPENCE (?), GEORGE   Written: 14 Jun. 1855   # 79
                         Probate: 3 Jul. 1855   Bk. A, Pg.   3

    Wife: Elizabeth
    Executor: Wife
    Witnesses: Nicholas Carriger, E.J. Schellhous, Wm. Bradley,
                 J.H. Kelley

SPENCER, MARY E. (C.)   Written: 29 Sep. 1884   #1705
CHAMBERS   Died: 14 Jan. 1888   Bk. E, Pg. 56
                         Filed: 18 Jan. 1888

    Daughter: Ida Spencer McDaniel
    Son: Homer Spencer
    Grand-
    Daughter: Mary Arabella McDaniel
    Daughter-in
    Law: Ella Murphy
    Executor: Ida Spencer McDaniel
    Witnesses: John Tyler Campbell, James H. McGee

SPRAGUE, JANE   Written: 1 Dec. 1900   #3249
                         Died: 24 Dec. 1900   Bk. G, Pg. 482
                         Filed: 4 Feb. 1901

    Bequests to: Ladies Aid Society of the Methodist Church north
                 of Petaluma, Maude Wiseman, Anti Cruelty Society
                 of Petaluma, Mrs. Eliza A. Rowlson (Bowlson) of
                 Petaluma
                 Holographic

SPRIDGENS, WALTER	Dated:	30 Sep. 1897	#2822
Age 29	Died:	31 Dec. 1897	Bk. G, Pg. 100
	Filed:	5 Jan. 1898	

- Brother: William J. Spridgens
- Sister-in-Law: Jennie L. Spridgens
- Nephews: James Harold Spridgens and Leland B. Spridgens both of Santa Rosa; William Austen Spridgens (minor) of Petaluma
- Executor: Jennie L. Spridgens
- Witnesses: Miles H. Peerman, E.E. Shields

SPRINGER, JAMES LEMONT   Filed: 13 Sep. 1879   #1026
Bodega Corners

- Wife: Mary Boylan Springer
- Executors: Wife, Leopold Soloman Goodman
- Witnesses: A.S. Patterson, Wiley Frazier

SPRINGER, MARY BOYLAN	Written:	7 Oct. 1892	#2285
Bodega	Died:	8 Jan. 1893	Bk. F, Pg. 54
Widow	Filed:	6 Feb. 1893	

- Bequests to: David Goodman, S.J. Goodman, Mrs. Mary Springer Carrillo
- Executor: L.S. Goodman, friend
- Witnesses: J.R. Gallagher, James Furlong

SPOSITO, PETER	Dated:	28 Feb. 1900	#3134
	Died:	5 Mar. 1900	Bk. G, Pg. 411
	Filed:	14 Mar. 1900	

- Wife: Rose Sposito
- Daughter: Annie Enos, wife of Morris S. Enos, of San Francisco
- Executor: Rose Sposito
- Witnesses: Oscar A. Shlarn, Frank ---

SPROUL, JAMES	Written:	8 Feb. 1887	#1612
Age 75	Died:	11 Feb. 1887	Bk. D, Pg. 375
	Rec.:	7 Mar. 1887	

- Bequest to: D.D. Philips
- Sister: Margaret Ross
- James S.
- John & Mary of Wisconsin
- Executor: D.D. Philips
- Witnesses: A.E. Cochran, J.G. Stone

STAB, CLEMENT   Written: 31 Oct. 1870   # 463
                 Age 58   Died: 8 Nov. 1870 Bk. Wills Pg. 199

                 No family
    Bequests to: Children of Eugene Robin
    Executors: C.F. Leiding, John C. Seipp both of Sonoma
    Witnesses: E. Rufus, Chas. VanGeldern

STAEDLER, JOHN G.   Written: 8 Feb. 1887   #1620
Petaluma Tnsp.   Died: 16 Feb. 1887   Bk. D, Pg. 396
                             Rec.:   28 Mar. 1887

    Wife: Elisabeth
    Sons: Charles, Rudolph, Harry
    Daughters: Lizzie, Julia B., Mrs. J.M. Walters, Susie B.,
                 Mary B.
    Executor: Son, Charles
    Witnesses: E.S. Lippitt, Wm. Frohlking

STAPLETON, JOHANNA Dated: 20 Apr. 1897   #2756
         Age Over   Died: 6 Jun. 1897
         65   Filed: 28 Jun. 1897

    Husband: Patrick Stapleton
    Brother: Michael Ryan of Kilkenny, Ire.
                 Ellen Crilly, relationship not named
    Executors: D.J. Healey, B.J. Conolly
    Witnesses: F.A. Meyer, Diedrich Jungclaus

STAPP, MARTHA A.   Written: 2 Oct. 1896   #2702
                             Died: 11 Jan. 1897   Bk. F, Pg. 597
                             Filed: 18 Jan. 1897

    Daughters: Susan M. Smith, Mary E. Nicholson, Dovey Likens
    Sons: M.D. Stapp, John L. Dillingham, Wm. K. Dillingham
    Executor: Wm. K. Dillingham of Ukiah, Ca.
    Witnesses: J.W. Rose, M.V. Hooten both of Healdsburg

STARKE, FREDERICK   Written: 15 Apr. 1882   #1436
Petaluma   Died: 17 Nov. 1884   Bk. D, Pg.   6
Farmer   Rec.:   5 Jan. 1885

    Brother: Augustus
    Sister: Sophie Myerling
    Children: Of sister, Wilhelmina Dahlmann (deceased): Augusta,
                 Martha, Henry, Frederick
    Executor: Niece, Augusta Starke
    Witnesses: Wm. B. Haskell, C.S. Farquar

STARR, ELMON G.	Written:	5 Oct. 1881	#1199
Vallejo Tnsp.	Died:	26 Nov. 1881	Bk. C, Pg. 175
	Filed:	9 Jan. 1882	

- Wife: Ann
- Daughter: Sarah E. Daniels
- Executor: Daughter
- Witnesses: C.A. Bodwell, J. Snow

STARR, THEODORE C.	Written:	24 Dec. 1883	#1923
San Bernardino, Ca.	Died:	15 Jan. 1890	Bk. E, Pg. 202
	Sonoma Co.		
	Rec.:	24 Feb. 1890	

- Wife: Mary E.
- Children: Nellie L., Lewis L., Martha M., Harriet L.
- Executor: Wife
- Holographic

STEADMAN, MARY A.	Dated:	10 Jan. 1900	#3168
Widow	Died:	4 Jun. 1900	Bk. H, Pg. 4
	Filed:	2 Jul. 1900	

- Son: Ernest G. Eagelson
- Daughters: Mrs. Jennie Luke, Mrs. Ella F. Combs
- Executor: Mrs. Ella F. Combs
- Witnesses: D.W. Juillard, B.S. Combs

STEGEMAN, WILLIAM	Written:	13 Apr. 1887	#1649
Cloverdale Age 59	Died:	17 Jun. 1887	Bk. D, Pg. 459
	Rec.:	27 Jul. 1887	

- Children: Mary Ann Bohlin (17), wife of Frank Anton, Anna Catherine (15), Wm. Bernard (14), Anna Margaretha (12), Juliana Clara (10), Margaretha Bru--- (8), Godfred Anton (6)
- Executors: Frank A. Bohlin, Anthony Schute
- Witnesses: N. Rowe, Geo. Bond

STEELE, JOHN	Written:	3 Oct. 1864	# 531
	Died:	6 Dec. 1871	Bk. A, Pg. 273

- Wife: Belleniah (?)
- Sons: Marshall (eldest), A.T. (second), J.H. (third), T.H.B. (youngest)
- Son-in-law: J.C. Russell
- Daughters: Elizabeth Russell, Rachael Rundelman, Martha Peterson, Palina (?) Peterson
- Executor: A.T. Steele
- Witnesses: S.W. Helm, John Braun (Brown)

```
STEPHENSON, JOHN          Written:  14 Aug. 1882              #1258
Healdsburg     Age 48     Died:     16 Aug. 1882     Bk. C, Pg. 271
                          Filed:    11 Sep. 1882
                          Rec.:     17 Apr. 1883
```

- Son: Edward (8), Orphans Asylum, Oakland, Ca.
- Sister: Catherine Stephenson of Scotland
  Ladies Relief Society
- Executor: W.W. Moreland of Healdsburg
- Witnesses: James R. Swisher, John King both of Healdsburg

```
STEWART, ABEL             Written   4 Feb. 1863               # 226
               Age about  Died:     18 Feb. 1863 (about)
               70         Filed:    17 Mar. 1863
```

- Wife: Eliz. (deceased)
- Children: John (deceased); Eliz. (deceased); Charles of Nevada Terr.; Lucinda Greening of Sonoma Co.; Jane Mecham of Sonoma Co.; Mary, wife of E.A. Harris, of Colusa Co.; Lorany, wife of Elam Chapins, of Colusa Co.; Frances, wife of Jas. Faught, of Colusa Co.
- Sons-in-law: Wm. M. Greening, Harrison Mecham
  Probate papers mention Katy, wife of Jas. Stewart of Indiana
- Executors: Greening, Mecham
- Witnesses: A.W. Thompson, J.W. Myers

```
STEWART, JAMES W.         Written:  22 Jun. 1873              # 703
San Antonio, Minn Co.     Died:     16 Aug. 1874     Bk. B, Pg. 106
                          Filed:    21 Sep. 1874
```

- Wife: Hannah Mary Stewart
- Children: William Allen Stewart, Frank Lester Stewart, Robert Henry Stewart
- Executors: Abram Ward, father-in-law; Hannah Mary Stewart
- Witnesses: A.J. Pierce, A. Johnson, Wm. H. Ward

```
STEWART, JOHN             Written:  25 Aug. 1882              #1279
Guerneville               Died:      6 Dec. 1882     Bk. C, Pg. 327
```

- Wife: Sarah
- Grandsons: James Wm. Stewart, Franklin L. Stewart, Robert H. Stewart
- Executor: Wife
- Witnesses: N.E. Manning, S.N. Hudson

```
STEWART, JULIA             Written:  26 Mar. 1883              #1363
Bodega Corners             Died:     27 Oct. 1883    Bk. C, Pg. 459
                           Filed:    12 Nov. 1883

    Husband:     Deceased
    Nephew:      John Thompson of San Francisco
    Executors:   James McGaughy, L.S. Goodman
    Witnesses:   James Stump, W.M. Doran, Henry Owens


STEWART, SARAH             Written:  14 Mar. 1887              #1710
Petaluma                   Died:     27 Jan. 1888    Bk. D, Pg. 572
                           Filed:     5 Mar. 1888

    Grand-
    Children:    Wm. A. Stewart, Frank L. Stewart, Robert H.
                 Stewart
    Daughter-in
    Law:         Mrs. Hannah M. Smith (former)
    Executor:    Joseph Campbell
    Witnesses:   Hubert Naughton, Frank W. Shattuck


STOCKDALE, HUGH            Written:   4 Feb. 1888              #2025
Petaluma       Age 63      Died:     12 Nov. 1890    Bk. E, Pg. 333
                           Rec.:     29 Dec. 1890

    Wife:        Carrie
    Children:    Alice O., Sherman G., Addie, Morton W., Lena
    Executors:   Wife; son, Sherman
    Witnesses:   Josiah H. Benson, J. Campbell


STOLKER, ERNESTINE         Written:  14 Jan. 1891              #2853
                           Died:      7 Mar. 1898    Bk. G, Pg. 143
                           Filed:    12 Mar. 1898

    Sons:        C.W. Stolker, W.D. Stolker, George Stolker, Otto
                 Stolker
    Daughters:   Rosie Stolker, Dora Brunner
    Executor:    C.W. Stolker
    Witnesses:   F.A. Meyer, C.O. Schuler both of Petaluma


STONE, PETER               Written:  29 Aug. 1879              #1846
Santa Rosa     Age 79      Died:     18 Mar. 1889    Bk. E, Pg. 105
                           Rec.:     15 Apr. 1889

    Wife:        Ruth C.
    Sons:        Silas C. of W. Roxbury, Mass.; Frederick P. of
                 San Francisco; Nathan J. of Santa Rosa
    Daughters:   Mary J. Heath of Webster, N.H.; Lottie A.
                 Sargent of Santa Rosa; Emma R. Swett of Santa Rosa
    Executors:   Sons, Frederick P. and Nathan J.
    Witnesses:   Geo. L. Kenny, Joseph Leggett both of San
                 Francisco
```

STONEMAN, GEORGE   Written: 20 Oct. 1886   #1587
Cloverdale   Age 40   Died: 4 Nov. 1886   Bk. D, Pg. 474
                           Rec.:   28 Aug. 1887

   Bequests to: Mrs. C. Worth, Jos. Bowen of Marysville, Yuba Co.
   Executor: Frank Spencer
   Witnesses: Isadore Abraham, Frank Spencer

STOWE, MARTIN D.   Written: 7 Apr. 1888   #2184
Bloomfield   Age 81   Died: -- Jan. 1892   Bk. E, Pg. 548
                           Rec.:   7 Mar. 1892

   Son: Hiram
   Daughters: Isabella Farnsworth; Charlotta Stowe; Mrs. Camilla
                Edwards of Suisun, Ca.; Mrs. Angeline Martin of
                Los Angeles; Mary E. Hewitt of Oakland, Ca.
   Children: Of daughter, F. J. Edwards (deceased)
   Children: Of daughter, Julia A. Connor
   Step-
   Daughters: Mrs. Katie George of Sacramento, Mrs. Lizzie
                McReynolds of Oregon
   Stepsons: Geo. W. Gregory of San Rafael, Thos J. Gregory
   Executors: Wm. Jones, Edw. Henshaw
   Witnesses: F.A. Meyer, Wm. B. Haskell

STRAUB, JOHN N.   Died: 21 May 1889   #1858
Santa Rosa   Filed: 10 Jun. 1889   Bk. E, Pg. 426

   Wife: Anna (second wife)
   Son: John (first child by first wife, deceased)
   Daughter: Lottie (second child by first wife, deceased)
   Executor: Wife
   Witnesses: Theodore O. Yerger, William Smidt

STREETER, ALLEN C.   Written: 31 Aug. 1866   # 366
                           Died: 13 Dec. 1867 (about)
                           Filed: 14 Sep. 1868

   Son: Robert M., property in Berlin, Rensselaer Co., N.Y.
                (listed in codicil)
   Executor: William H. Perry
   Codicil: Robert Streeter
   Witnesses: Wm. McPherson Hill, A.G. Wheelock

STRIENING, M. J.   Written: 8 Aug. 1896   #3391
                           Died: 23 Nov. 1901   Bk. H, Pg. 87
                           Filed: 16 Dec. 1901

   Wife: Caroline A.
   Executor: Wife
   Witnesses: A.B. Ware, Jno. T. Campbell both of Santa Rosa

STROTHER, REBECCA	Written:	22 Jan. 1880	#1311
Santa Rosa	Died:	14 Apr. 1883	Bk. C, Pg. 369
	Rec.:	9 Jul. 1883	

- Daughters: Cora (over 18); Johnnie (over 18); Mary Shipp, wife of Wm., of Fresno Co., Ca.; Martha Bayley, wife of Thos. S., of Butte Co.; Laura Glenn, wife of G.R., of Fresno Co.; Medora Patterson, wife of Elisha, of Fresno Co.; Claramon Heflin, wife of Frank, of Galveston, Tex.
- Executor: Daughter, Cora
- Witnesses: Wm. W. Porter, J.M. White

STUART, ABSALOM BOYLES	Written	3 Jun. 1886	#1672
Winona, Minn.	Died:	30 Jul. 1887	Reg. #2 Pg. 227
	Filed:	30 Aug. 1887	

- Wife: Anabel McGauphey Stuart
- Daughter: Mary Stuart (deceased), Rural Cemetery Lot 231
- Brothers-in Law: Dr. James Brown McGauphey of Winona, Minn.; Dr. John Alexander McGauphey of Chicago, Ill.
- Executor: Anabel McGauphey Stuart
- Witnesses: Geo. Alexander Hocker, Chas. Hamilton Bane

STUART, CHARLES V.	Written:	13 Jul. 1880	#1106
	Filed:	6 Sep. 1880	Bk. C, Pg. 104

- Wife: Ellen Mary Stuart
- Son: Charles Duff Stuart
- Daughters: Mary Ellen Pickett; Emily Stayroom (Stansroom); Antoinette Randall Stuart, Ida Sessions, wife of Geo. W.; Isabel Stuart
- Executors: Ellen Mary Stuart, Charles Duff Stuart
- Witnesses: W. McPherson Hill, Alfred V. LaMotte

STUSSY, DAVID	Dated:	18 Oct. 1880	#1153
Healdsburg	Died:	27 Apr. 1881	
	Rec.:	16 Jul. 1883	

- Wife: Margaretta Stussy
- Sons(?): David Stussy (13), Jacob Stussy (12) Henry Stussy (9)
- Guardians: In event of Margaretta's death: Carl Muller, brewer; John Grater, hotel-keeper
- Executor: Margaretta Stussy
- Witnesses: W.G. Swan, Joseph Luedke

STUKEY, DAVID   Dated: 1 May 1865   # 323
                             Filed: 6 May 1865

  Father: David Stukey of Switzerland
  Mother: Elsbeth Stukey
  Brothers: Henry, Peter, Casper, Gabriel
  Sister: Anna
  Executor: David Stukey
  Witnesses: R. Hettie (?), George Miller, John O. Darrow

SUHLING, ELIZABETH   Written: 15 Dec. 1892   #2388
Petaluma   Died: 7 Jan. 1894   Bk. F, Pg. 215
                             Rec.:   19 Mar. 1894

  Husband: H.H.
  Children: Catherina -sickert, Anna Flower, Bertha -eulein,
              Elizabeth Urbais, Jacob, Sophia, Chas.
  Executor: Husband
  Witnesses: Wm. Gilbert of San Francisco, Geo. V. Metzgar of
              Oakland

SULLIVAN, ISAAC WILSON   Written: 24 Mar. 1883   #2104
Anally Tnsp.   Died: 25 Aug. 1891   Bk. E, Pg. 447
                             Rec.:   28 Sep. 1891

  Wife: Mary
  Children: James Mitchell, John Wesley, Cornelius, Manurva
              Ann Smell (?), Nancy Ellen, Sophronia Clementine,
              Charles Cravens, Lillie Jamima (?), Asa Isaac,
              Amanda Jane, Jabez Benjamin
  Executors: Wife; son, James
  Witnesses: Geo. Y. Kugle, B.B. Allen

SURRYHNE, EDWARD   Written: 13 Apr. 1878   #2783
Alameda Co.   Age 38   Died: 4 Oct. 1897   Bk. G, Pg. 68
                             Filed: 25 Oct. 1897

  Wife: Elizabeth Malina Surryhne
  Son: Charles Edward Surryhne
              Other children un-named
  Executors: Wife; son, Charles Eward Surryhne
  Witnesses: M.B. Smith of 1101 Pine St., Oakland, Ca.; T.M.
              Nicholson of Oakland, Ca.

```
SWEENEY, JEREMIAH          Written:  10 Feb. 1892              #2700
Petaluma       Age over    Died:      7 Jan. 1897   Bk. F, Pg. 593
               60          Filed:     1 Feb. 1897
```

- Wife: Mary Sweeney (deceased)
- Daughters: Ellen Hannan, Mary J. Sweeney, Cornelius P. Sweeney, Annie A. Sweeney, Elizabeth M. Sweeney, Ettie A. Sweeney
- Sons: David W. Sweeney, Edward P. Sweeney
- Executors: David W. Sweeney, Edward P. Sweeney
- Witnesses: Wm. B. Haskell, F.A. Meyer

```
SWETLAND, ALMIRA           Written:   1 Oct. 1872              # 583
                           Died:     22 Nov. 1872
```

- Sisters: Mary B. Swetland; Eliza E. Swetland of Chicopee Falls; Chloe Ferry, wife of Thos. M. Ferry, of Belchertown, Mass.
- Mother: Pasthema Swetland
- Executor: I.G. Wickersham or, if he is unable to serve, Joseph Campbell
- Witnesses: Alex McCune, Henry H. Atwater

```
SWETLAND, NANCY L.         Written:  16 Jan. 1871              #1194
Petaluma                   Filed:    28 Nov. 1881   Bk. C, Pg. 163
```

- Nephew: Edward O. Bragdon of N.Y. City
- Sisters: Martha Bragdon, Anna M. Tirell of Boston
- Bequest to: Simon C. Bragdon of Brooklyn, N.Y.
- Codicil: Adds nephew, Henry F. Allen
- Executor: Edw. O. Bragdon or I.G. Wickersham
- Witnesses: Wm. P. Haskell, Andervil G. Medley
- Codicil: C.W. Burgtorf

```
SWETLAND, ORSEN            Written:  10 Feb. 1868              # 407
                           Died:      6 Feb. 1869
                           Rec.:      5 Apr. 1869
```

- Wife: Nancy T. Swetland
- Mother: Posthuma Swetland
- Sisters: Almira, Mary B., Chloe, Eliza
- Executor: Almira Swetland
- Witnesses: I.G. Wickersham, A.P. Whitney

SZARVASH, SAMUEL T. Healdsburg	Dated: Codicil: Died: Filed:	5 Apr. 1900 14 Apr. 1900 21 Apr. 1900 22 Aug. 1900	#3163 Bk. G, Pg. 442

                --- Bompers; his mother, Dolores Bompers
                D.W. Wessenberg of 709 Tilbert St.; his son,
                Mervin Wessenberg
- **Neighbor:** T.M. Hughes and wife
- **Children:** And widow of brother; Willhelm Kirsch (deceased) of Viena
- **Executors:** California Safe Deposit Co., D.W. Wessenberg
- **Witnesses:** Daniel W. Wessenberg, Herman Kuhn

TABER, ISABELLA Blucher Valley	Written: Died: Rec.:	17 Feb. 1889 19 Feb. 1889 18 Mar. 1889	#1832 Bk. E, Pg. 86

- **Husband:** John S.
- **Friend:** Mrs. Ann Lyman
- **Executor:** Husband
- **Witnesses:** Rena Shattuck, Frank W. Shattuck

TAMMEYER, CAROLINE San Francisco Age 27	Dated: Filed:	1 May 1871 24 Jan. 1872	# 518

- **Husband:** Julius Tammeyer
- **Husband:** Olef Larsen (late)
- **Children:** Edwin, Olef Larsen (8), Charles, Emil Larson (5), Magnus Larsen (3)
- **Executor:** Julius Tammeyer
- **Witnesses:** Martin Tracy, Louis Tammeyer both of San Francisco

TANN, CATHERINE Petaluma	Written: Died: Filed:	5 Apr. 1895 17 Dec. 1895 13 Jan. 1896	#2598 Bk. F, Pg. 445

- **Daughters:** Mary A. Guinn, Catherine Amelia Harris
- **Sons:** Charles Tann, James Tann, Frederick Tann, Thomas Tann
- **Executors:** James Tann, Catherine A. Harris
- **Witnesses:** Nathaniel King, Minnie A. Connolly both of Petaluma

TAYLOR, ELENOR	Written: Died: Probate:	25 Jun. 1866 15 Oct. 1866 Petaluma 23 Oct. 1866	# 326 Bk. A, Pg. 165

    Jeremiah Sweeney; Mary Sweeney; Mrs. Robert Swain; Amelia Chon (?); Eliz. Edwards, daughter of Thos.; Mrs. Hanah Edwards, wife of Edward; Mrs. Eliz. Edwards, wife of Thos.
- **Executors:** Thos. Morison, Thos. Edwards
- **Witnesses:** L.C. Reyburn, Thos. Morison

```
TAYLOR, JAMES A.           Written:   4 May 1856              #  82
Monroe Co., Ohio           Filed:    21 May 1856      Bk. A, Pg. 20

   Father:      Hampton H. Taylor
   Executor:    John White
   Witnesses:   Ephram D. Harris of Bodega, Jos. Knowles of
                Santa Rosa, Warham Easley of Bodega


TAYLOR, SIMPSON P.         Written:  29 Oct. 1889             #1913
Poultry Business           Died:     10 Dec. 1889     Bk. E, Pg. 187
                           Rec.:     24 Dec. 1889

   Wife:             Alice B.
   Step-
   Daughter:         Maud M. Berghstrom (minor)
   Sister-in-
   Law:              Mrs. C.C. Taylor
   Children:         Of brother, B.W. Taylor
   Executor:         Stephan A. Holmes
   Witnesses:        Jas. H. McGee, Harrisin White both of Santa Rosa


TEEVIN, EDWARD ALBERT      Written:  11 Jan. 1890             #1931
Santa Rosa         Age about Died:   28 Jan. 1890     Bk. E, Pg. 206
                   27        Rec.:   10 Mar. 1890

   Brother-
   In-Law:      Thomas Taylor
   Father:      James Teevin of Canada
   Executors:   Thomas Taylor; Wm. F. Teevin, brother
   Witnesses:   J.S. Sargent, M.D.; Margaret Jane Taylor

   Per court information: A British subject born near Lindsay,
   Ontario, Canada


TEMPLE, JACKSON            Written:  20 Nov. 1902             #3549
                 Age about  Died:    25 Dec. 1902
                 75         Filed:   12 Jan. 1903

   Daughter:    Mary H--- Temple
   Son:         Jackson Temple, Jr.
   Executors:   Mary H---Temple, Jackson Temple, Jr.


TEMPLE, JACOB WYTHE        Written:  27 Jul. 1885             #1500
Seaview                    Died:     26 Aug. 1885    Bk. D, Pg. 107
                           Filed:     9 Nov. 1885

   Sister:      Mary Meade Price of Sea View
   Daughters:   Of sister; Sarah Booth, Francis Morget, Mary
                Bates, Virginia Shato all of Sea View
   Sister:      Francis Whitmore Walker
   Daughters:   Of sister; Martha Moyer, Francis McConnell,
                Margaret McClintock
   Executor:    David Carson of Ukiah
   Witnesses:   Joseph Luttenger, A.R. Schweitzer both of Fisk's
                Mill
```

TENNETT, ARCHIBALD   Dated: 18 Jun. 1857   # 109
         Age 37   Filed: 18 Mar. 1858

  Wife: Elizabeth
  Son: Archibald P. Tennent
  Daughter: Isabel Eva (?)
  Brothers: John Tennent of Martinez, Samuel J. Tennent of
              Rancho de Pinole, Contra Costa Co.
  Executor: Samuel T. Tennent
  Witnesses: Lewis Seller, Sam H. Rupe

THACKER, DANIEL   Written: 23 Mar. 1871   # 484
                          Filed: 5 Jun. 1871   Bk. A, Pg. 239

  Brother: Jahn Thacker
  Friend: Mrs. Mary A. Mathews
  Executor: Ira Bedwell
  Witnesses: Robt. Cooke, Wm. K. Brooks, Mary Jane Brooks

THOMPSON, JOHN D.   Written: 20 Apr. 1875   #1576
Healdsburg   Died: 22 Aug. 1886   Bk. D, Pg. 303
                          Rec.:   25 Oct. 1887

  Wife: Eliza A.
  Daughter: Mary M. Barnes, wife of Edward H.
  Son: John M.
  Executor: Edw. H. Barnes
  Witnesses: Wm. E. Cocke, A. Thomas

THOMPSON, ZELIA A.   Written: 13 Sep. 1880   #1608
Santa Rosa   Age 34   Died: 11 Jan. 1887   Bk. D, Pg. 372
                          Rec.:   21 Feb. 1887

  Husband: Dr. Charles H. (45)
  Daughter: Carrie A. (15)
  Executor: Husband
  Witnesses: Thos. B. Hood, Carrie E. Hood

THURGOOD, MARGARET G.   Written: 9 Aug. 1873   # 632
                          Died: 10 Aug. 1873
                          Filed: 8 Spe. 1873

  Children: William Q., Eliz. Margaret, Mary Ann
  Executors: Peter O. Connor, John Ward
  Witnesses: John Mulligan, Rodger Gilbride

TIVNEN, JOHN		Written: 2 Jun. 1885	#2028
Sonoma	Age 52	Died: 19 Nov. 1890	Bk. E, Pg. 323
		Rec.: 15 Dec. 1890	

- Daughter: Mary Clara Tivnen
- Step-Daughters: Roberta Sydnor, Eva Sydnor, Addie Sydnor
- Executors: Roberta Sydnor, David Calloway
- Witnesses: John A. Brewster
- Holographic

TOMASINI, LOUIS	Written: 23 May 1889	#3057
Petaluma	Died: 30 Aug. 1899	Bk. G, Pg. 335
	Filed: 25 Sep. 1899	

- Daughters: Juliet Tomasini, Lila Tomasini
- Son: Waldo A. Tomasini
- Executor/Guardian: Mateo Tomasini, brother, of Nicasio, Marin Co., Ca.; or Luca Bonetti, cousin, of Marin Co., Ca.
- Witnesses: C.S. Farquar, Thos. J. Geary both of Santa Rosa

TOMBS, ANN P.	Written: 30 Oct. 1883	#2688
	Died: 8 Sep. 1896	Bk. F, Pg. 585
	Filed: 1 Feb. 1897	

- Sons: Henry C. Tombs, William L. Tombs, John F. Tombs
- Daughter: Sarena H. Mason
- Bequests to: Taylor Tombs (colored), Sarah Tombs (colored)
- Executors: Henry C. Tombs, William L. Tombs, Sarena H. Mason, John F. Tombs
- Witnesses: J.D. Hassett, R.A. Mason both of Healdsburg

TOMLIN, RICHARD E.		Written: 12 Aug. 1897	#3489
	Age 52	Died: 18 Jul. 1902	Bk. G, Pg. 514
		Filed: 13 Aug. 1902	

- Wife: Harriet C. Tomlin
- Son: Harry D. Tomlin
- Executor: Harriet C. Tomlin
- Witnesses: Thos. W. Nowlin of 210 Fillmore St., San Francisco, Ca.; J. DeTeller, Jr. of Alameda, Ca.

TORONI, BARTOLOMEO	Written: 12 Apr. 1893	#2452
Sonoma City	Died: 26 Aug. 1894	Bk. F, Pg. 302
	Rec.: 24 Sep. 1894	

- Wife: Margherita
- Children: Mary Ricci, Caterina Toroni, Giuseppe Toroni, Ida Toroni
- Executor: Wife
- Witnesses: Lorenzo Modini, Robt. A. Poppe

TORRANCE, SHUBEAL H.	Written:	24 Jul. 1888	#2079
Age 56	Died:	30 Apr. 1891	Bk. E, Pg. 395
	Rec.:	8 Jun. 1891	

- Wife: Elizabeth
- Grand-Daughter: Nellie Torrance
- Sons: Joseph Lane, John
- Executor: Son, Joseph Lane Torrance of Guerneville
- Witnesses: Jno. Brown, Michael Rutlidge both of Santa Rosa

TOWNE, SMITH D.	Written:	19 Oct. 1886	#2113
Petaluma	Died:	6 Oct. 1891	Bk. E, Pg. 461
Drug Store	Rec.:	26 Oct. 1891	

- Sister: Mary A. Dixon (deceased)
- Daughters: Florence, Clarice
- Sons: Walter, Beverly Munday
- Executors: Thomas Munday, Frank M. Towne
- Witnesses: M.E.C. Munday, J.P. Rogers

TREADWAY, AMELIA	Written:	30 Apr. 1866	# 314
	Died:	25 Jul. 1866	Bk. A. Pg. 162

Unmarried
- Brother: Richard M. Treadway
- Niece: Lilly Treadway, daughter of brother John (deceased)
- Nephews: Edward Bamford, J.A. Woodson of San Francisco
- Executors: Wm. Churchman, Jackson Temple
- Witnesses: Clark King, Wm. L. Anderson

TRINQUE, MARGARET	Written:	7 Mar. 1896	#2707
Petaluma	Died:	27 Jan. 1897	Bk. F, Pg. 604
	Filed:	3 Feb. 1897	

- Friends: Mary E. Lewis, daughter of Barbara A. Lewis of Petaluma; Mrs. Linnie Ryder of 513½ Fell St., San Francisco
- Executor: H.H. Atwater of Petaluma
- Witnesses: Wm. B. Haskell, Thos. C. Denny both of Petaluma

TRUITT, PAULINA	Written:	20 Jun. 1883	#1385
Healdsburg	Died:	7 Dec. 1883	Bk. C, Pg. 502
	Rec.:	19 Dec. 1884	

- Daughters: Martha Ann Shoultz, Leoma Dodge, Ellen Truitt, Dora Truitt
- Sons: John R., Rowland K., William, Harrison, Harvey, Solomon, Oliver
- Executor: Wm. Melton
- Witnesses: John G. McManus, Jas. L. Wells
  Much litigation

TRUMPY, FREDRICK		Dated: 23 May 1898		#2883
		Died: 24 May 1898	Bk. G, Pg. 188	
		Filed: 26 May 1898		

Brother: Henry Trumpy of Prairie City, Ill.
Friend: Alfred Johnson
Executor: Alfred Johnson
Witnesses: O.O. Weber, J.W. Jesse

TUNLEY, BRYAN   Written: 19 Nov. 1883   #3494
    Age 33   Died: 23 Nov. 1883
       Brighton, Macoupin Co., Ill.
       Filed: 7 Aug. 1902

Brother: Vincent Tunley
Sister: Sarah Ann Drew, wife of Thomas Drew
Executors: Vincent Tunley, Thomas Drew
Witnesses: Thomas Drew, Henry Yarkam both of Brighton, Macoupin Co., Ill.

TUTTLE, SARAH E.   Written: 7 Nov. 1881   #1195
       Died: 30 Nov. 1881   Bk. C, Pg. 166
       Filed: 27 Dec. 1881

Husband: Jeremiah Tuttle
Daughters: Clara Palmer, Sarah Bryant, Anne Dunsmore, Ella Tuttle
Sons: Cyrus Tuttle, Lawson Tuttle, Edwin Tuttle
Executor: Jeremiah Tuttle
Witnesses: A. Goatley, Daisy Tuttle

VALLEGGIA, GIOV. BATT.   Written: 23 Nov. 1896   #3241
       Died: 23 Nov. 1896   Bk. H, Pg. 14
       San Francisco
       Filed: 24 Dec. 1900

Brother: Guglielmo Valleggia of Geneva, Switzerland
Father: Peter Valleggia of Brione above Minusio (county not named)
Executor: Victor Piezzi of Santa Rosa
          Holographic

VALLEJO, BENECIA F.   Written: 23 Feb. 1890   #2058
Sonoma   Age 74   Died: 30 Jan. 1891   Bk. E, Pg. 369
       Rec.: 9 Mar. 1891

Daughters: Louisa DeEmparon, wife of R.; Maria Cutter, wife of J.H.; Edifania, wife of Gen. Frisbie; Adela, wife of Dr. Frisbie; Natalia, widow of A.F. Harazthy
Sons: Andronico Antonio, Platen, Uladislas (?), Napoleon
Executor: Son, Andronico Antonio
Witnesses: Henry N. Clement of San Francisco; Adele Frisbie A.A. Vallejo both of Vallejo

VALLEJO, MARIANO G.   Written: 26 Jun. 1889   #1964
Sonoma   Age 81 Died: 18 Jan. 1890   Bk. E, Pg. 248
                         Rec.:   2 May 1890

  Wife: Benecia F.
  Sons: Andronico, Platon, Uladulao, Napoleon
  Daughters: Epifania, wife of Gen. Frisbie; Adela, wife of Dr.
               Frisbie; Natalia, widow of A.F. Harazthy; Louisa,
               wife of R. DeEmparon; Maria, wife of Mr. Cutter
  Executor: Wife
               Holographic

VALLEY, RACHEL   Written: 10 Aug. 1883   #1800
Santa Rosa   Died: 17 Oct. 1888   Bk. F, Pg. 40
                         Decatur, Ind.
                         Filed: 14 Jan. 1889

  Niece: Mollie E. Harper of Sardinia, Indiana
  Executor: John T. Campbell
  Witnesses: Jas. H. McGee, W.F. Russell

VAN EPS, JOHN SANFORD   Written: 4 Feb. 1895   #2685
                 Age 66 Died: 24 Nov. 1896   Bk. F, Pg. 580
                         Filed: 10 Dec. 1896

  Wife: Amelia VanEps
  Daughter: Hattie Asken, wife of John, of Maderia Co., Ca.
  Executor: Amelia VanEps
  Witnesses: J.W. Ragsdale of 803 Third St., Santa Rosa; W.D.
               Reynolds of 531 College Ave., Santa Rosa

VAN GELDERN, CHARLES   Dated: 19 Apr. 1864   #1162
                         Filed: 11 Jul. 1881   Bk. C, Pg. 145

  Wife: Eliza
  Executor: Eliza
  Witnesses: G.(J.)S. Wratten (?), C.F. Living (?)

VASCONI, LUIGI   Dated: 20 Jan. 1898   #3135
                         Died: 31 Jan. 1900   Bk. G, Pg. 402
                         Filed: 16 Mar. 1900

  Wife: Luigia Vasconia
  Children: Names and number not mentioned
  Admin.:   Luigia Vasconia

VEAL, WILLIAM   Written: 26 Dec. 1870   # 470
                             Died: 1 Jan. 1871
                             Filed: 30 Jan. 1871

    Children: Mrs. Mary Benson (deceased), Mrs. Sarah Anne
                 Barnes, Mrs. Jane Chamberlain (deceased) of
                 Illinois, Mrs. Zarilda Woods (deceased) of
                 Illinois, Richard R. Veal of Contra Costa Co.,
                 Thomas F. Veal, William R. Veal, Mrs. Martha
                 Hardin
    Executor: Thos. Hopper
    Witnesses: W.R. Veal, Temperance F. Dehaven

VERON, PROSPERO   Dated: 11 Jul. 1888   #1778
ALEXANDRE   Filed: 27 Aug. 1888
Bennett Valley

                 Theobald Scheibel, Marie Therese Scheibel,
                 Marie Therese Hofstetter
    Executor: Theobald Scheibel
    Translator: Jos. E. O'Donnell
    Witnesses: E. Peterson, D.M. Hedrick

WADDELL, ALEXANDER JAMES Dated: -- Mar. 1888   #2724
Salt Point Tnsp.   Died: 7 Jan. 1897   Bk. G, Pg. 1
                          Filed: 24 Apr. 1897

    Wife: Mary Elizabeth Dernot Waddell
    Executors: Hugh Montague of Salt Point, Loui Fairbanks of
                 Pt. Arena
    Witnesses: J. Hope (?) Waddell, A. McCracken

WADE, ELLA C.   Dated: 24 Dec. 1897   #2990
                             Filed: 27 Mar. 1899

    Sister: Jennie

WADE, W. F.   Written: 9 Apr. 1898   #2865
San Francisco   Age 51   Filed: 6 Jun. 1898   Bk. G, Pg. 190

    Nephew: A.F. Wade of San Francisco
    Niece: Stella Wade of San Francisco
    Executor: Robert Poppe of Sonoma, Sonoma Co., Ca.
    Witnesses: Othello C. Pratt, Walter T. Robinson both of
                 San Francisco

WALDEN, EDWARD   Dated: 17 Apr. 1899   #3262
Delaware Co., Pa.,   Filed: 26 Jan. 1901   Bk. H, Pg. 30
Upper Darby Tnsp.

   Wife: Myra S. Walden
   Daughters: Wmily Walden, Ruth
   Sons: Lienan Walden; Edward Walden, Jr.; Franklin
   Friend: James Hay of Philadelphia, Pa.
   Niece: Adele Rockwell
   Executors: Lienan Walden; Edward Walden, Jr.; Emily Walden
   Witnesses: Adeline E. DeDamp of New York City, Walter C.
                  Timm of Morton, Pa.

WALKER, ELEANOR   Written: 29 May 1895   #2549
                              Died: 11 Jul. 1895   Bk. F, Pg. 393
                              Rec.:   5 Aug. 1895

   Husband: John (deceased)
   Sons: John L., Joel, Edward Lee, Wm. V.
   Daughter: Harriet Jane
   Grand-
   Children: Alena, Lawrence, Walter
   Executors: Joel & Edward Lee Walker
   Witnesses: John T. Campbell of Santa Rosa, Mrs. Addie F.
                  Thomson of Sebastopol

WALKER, JOHN KING   Written: 20 Aug. 1881   #1456
Guerneville   Age 80   Died: 8 Jan. 1885   Bk. D, Pg. 23
                              Rec.:   2 Mar. 1885

   Wife: Polina
   Next of Kin: Per court document; Lysander Walker of Dixon,
                  Solano Co.; Leander Walker of Dixon; Leonodas
                  Walker of Guerneville; Eliza Reed of Petaluma
   Executor: Wife
   Witnesses: Lewis C. Lewis, A.C. Bradford

WALKER, LOUISE CAROLINE   Written: 2 Jul. 1888   #2624
(HASSETT)   Died: 1 Nov. 1895   Bk. F, Pg. 494
Healdsburg   Age 24   Rec.:   4 May 1896

   Husband: John Lawrence Walker
   Daughter: Nellena (minor)
   Mother: Sarah E. Hassett
   Executor: Mother
                  Holographic

WALLACE, HIRAM		Written:	24 Mar. 1896	#3084
Healdsburg	Age 57	Died:	12 Sep. 1899	Bk. G, Pg. 362
		Hants Co.		
		Rec.:	11 Dec. 1899	

- Wife: Harriet
- Brothers: Josiah, Michael, Dr. Walter B., Dr. Ira J. all of West Gore, Hants Co., N.S.; Minard of Clements, San Joaquin Co., Ca.
- Step-Mother: Rebekah
- Sister-in-Law: Frances, widow of John B., and her children
- Nephews: W.W., Freeman M. both of Healdsburg
- Sister: Maggie Preston of Bishop Creek, Inyo Co., Ca.
- Executor: Minard Wallace
- Witnesses: H.O. Ferguson, J.T. Coffman

WALLMAN, CATHERINA	Written:	20 Jan. 1900	#3296
Sonoma	Died:	11 Mar. 1901	Bk. H, Pg. 53
	Rec.:	3 Jun. 1901	

- Husband: George
- Children: Three, un-named
- Executor: Husband
- Witnesses: G.D. Rich, M.D.; Georgieanna Wallman; Geo. Wallman

WALTON, SARAH JANE		Written:	21 Jan. 1891	#2118
Healdsburg	Age 36	Died:	22 Jan. 1891	Bk. E, Pg. 469
		Rec.:	9 Nov. 1891	

- Brother-in-Law: Rev. Jas. Hulme
- Sister: Annie Hulme
- Niece: Annie Claire Hulme
- Nephews: Fred. Wm. Walton Hulme, Gerald Coulthard James Hulme
- Father: Jonathon Hulme (deceased) of Cumberland, Eng.
- Executor: Rev. Hulme
- Witnesses: Robert Dudley, Matilda Eyre

WARD, ABRAHAM		Written:	17 Oct. 1899	#3095
Petaluma	Age over 60	Died:	4 Dec. 1899	Bk. G, Pg. 370
		Rec.:	2 Jan. 1900	

- Sons: John H., James, Abraham P.
- Daughter: Hannah Mary Smith
- Daughter-in-Law: Belle Hemmenway (former), widow of Frank Ward
- Children: Of daughter Annie Seavy (deceased): Albert Porter, Laura V., Robt. T.
- Children: Of son Frank (deceased): Franklin Arthur, Bertha May, Ada Lucinda
- Executor: James A. Ward
- Witnesses: Wm. B. Haskell, Thos. C. Denny

WARFIELD, KATE F. Glen Ellen Vineyard	Written: Died: Rec.:	2 Sep. 1889 23 Jan. 1892 14 Mar. 1892	#2188 Bk. E, Pg. 562

- Mother: Mary Overton
- Sister: Hattie L. Cavanaugh, wife of Wm. M., of New York
- Brother: Wm. F. Overton of Tucson, Ariz.
- Son: Charles Basil
- Daughter: Nina Elizabeth
- Executors: Charles B. Warfield, Wm. F. Overton, Wm. M. Cavanaugh, J.H. Drummond
- Witnesses: E.H. Rexford, F.D. Brandon both of San Francisco

WARNER, A. L. Age about 70	Written: Died: Filed:	21 Nov. 1896 12 Feb. 1897 16 Feb. 1897	#2709 Bk. F, Pg. 611

- Wife: Susan I. Warner
- Sons: John E. Warner, Elon L. Warner
- Daughters: Mary E. Maloon, Cora E. Frost
- Executors: John E. Warner, Elon L. Warner
- Witnesses: George A. Storey, Tunis W. Storey both of Healdsburg

WARNER, MARY SOPHIA Santa Rosa (10 Miles So.	Written: Died: Rec.:	16 Nov. 1889 22 Nov. 1889 23 Jun. 1890	#1975 Bk. E, Pg. 288

- Children: Alma, Henrietta, William (minor)
- Executors: Brother, Wm. H. Silsby; daughter, Alma
- Witnesses: Jonas Wescott, Melissa Button

WARREN, WILLIAM P. Age 53	Dated: Died: Filed:	21 Feb. 1889 24 Jun. 1897 29 Jun. 1897	#2760 Bk. G, Pg. 54

- Wife: Mary Jane Warren
- Children: Sarah B. Warren, Olief A. Warren, Hiram P. Warren, George F. Warren, Hattie J. Warren, Clarence A. Warren
- Daughter: Of wife, Mary Lampson
- Executor: Mary Jane Warren
- Witnesses: John N. Bailache, N.B. Coffman both of Healdsburg

WATRISS, EMMA Aqua Caliente	Dated: Died: Filed:	10 Mar. 1897 11 Mar. 1897 14 May 1900	#3151 Bk. G, Pg. 412

- Brothers: George Cabot Watriss, Franklin Watriss
  Holographic

```
WATRISS, MARTHA CABOT      Written:  12 Oct. 1890              #2199
Agua Caliente              Died:      6 Mar. 1892   Bk. E, Pg. 587
                           Rec.:      5 Apr. 1892

    Daughters:   Emma, Charlotte
    Sons:        George, Franklin
    Executors:   Both sons
    Witnesses:   Geo. C. Watriss, Frankling Watriss, Emma Watriss


WATT, RICHARD L.           Written:  10 Jan. 1888              #1720
Sonoma Co.    Age 43       Died:     10 Jan. 1888   Bk. D, Pg. 588
                           Filed:    19 Mar. 1888

    Wife:        Sarah Ellen
    Nephew:      Richard L. Watt
    Brothers:    John Watt (46) of Sonoma, Mathew Watt (37) of
                 Sonoma
    Sisters:     Margaret M. Watt (41) of Sonoma, Helen M.
                 Wainwright (41) of Sonora, Tuolomne Co., Ca.
    Executor:    Wife
    Witnesses:   Robert A. Poppe, L.B. Lawrence


WATTLES, MARY C.           Dated:     7 Sep. 1898              #3227
                           Died:     28 Sep. 1900
                           Filed:    12 Nov. 1900

    Husband:     J.B. Wattles
    Son:         L.L. Wattles


WATTS, RICHARD             Written:  21 Mar. 1884              #2182
Santa Rosa                 Died:     25 Jan. 1892   Bk. E, Pg. 544
                           Rec.:     23 Feb. 1892

    Wife:        Jennett A.
    Daughters:   Mrs. Catherine Jane Fraser, Mrs. Elizabeth Hayden
                 Horne
    Executor:    Wife
    Witnesses:   J.P. Overton, Geo. P. Noonan


WEGNER, EDWARD             Written:  22 Dec. 1900              #3247
Sonoma, Ca.   Age 63       Died:     24 Dec. 1900   Bk. H, Pg.  22
                           Filed:    14 Jan. 1901

    Wife:        Julia
    Daughters:   Lydia, Freda, Isabelle
    Executor:    Wife
    Witnesses:   Carl Walliser, Charles Seehuber, Robert A. Poppe
                 all of Sonoma, Ca.
```

WEIGAND, CHARLES	Dated:	19 Mar. 1898	#3224
	Died:	1 Oct. 1900	Bk. G, Pg. 473
	Filed:	5 Nov. 1900	

Wife: Christina Weigand
Children: Frank, Winifred, Edna, Mary, Charles, George Washington Weigand
Executors: Christina Weigand; Winifred, oldest daughter
Witnesses: F.A. Meyer, Otto Wohlers, Merrick Freeman

WEISE, CHRISTIAN	Written:	23 Mar. 1893	#2318
Age 69	Died:	30 Apr. 1893	Bk. F, Pg. 123
	Rec.:	15 May 1893	

Wife: Rosetta (second)
Children: By first wife; Fred W. Weise (about 34), Hattie M. Suttrell (about 32), John H. Weise (about 30), Chas. C. Weise (about 29)
Daughter: By second wife; Lucy N. Weise (about 10)
Executor: John H. Weise
Witnesses: Wm. F. Cowan, G.W. Pearce both of Santa Rosa

WELLS, JAS. L.	Written:	3 Feb. 1873	# 676
	Died:	8 Mar. 1874	
	Filed:	28 Apr. 1874	

Wife: Hellen E.
Executor: Wife
Witnesses: E.K. Jenner, Chas. K. Jenner

WESCOATT, NELSON	Written:	1 Apr. 1893	#2664
Age 21	Died:	7 Sep. 1896	Bk. F, Pg. 548
	Filed:	29 Sep. 1896	

Wife: Jennie R. Wescoatt (Webber) of Maine
Sons: Oscar King Wescoatt; Wallace Wren Wescoatt of Salt Lake, Utah; Edward Wescoatt of Salt Lake, Utah; W.H. Wescoatt; Jonas W. Wescoatt
Brother: Jonas Wescoatt
Executors: Jonas Wescoatt, Oscar King Wescoatt
Witnesses: Geo. C. Parsons, H.L. Tripp

| WEST, WM. MARK | Dated: | 22 Apr. 1840 | # 62 |
| | Probate: | 10 Oct. 1851 | Bk. F, Pg. 1 |

Wife: Guadalupe (Vasquez)
Executor: Wife
Witnesses: Thos. Farnham, Jeremiah Jones

WHEATON, JOHN	Dated:	14 Nov. 1897		#2818
Dry Creek Valley	Died:	14 Nov. 1897	Bk. G, Pg. 47	
Age 83	Filed:	25 Jan. 1898		

- Sons: David Wheaton, John Thomas Wheaton, George W. Wheaton
- Daughters: Ruth Vernon, Mary Ann Vernon
- Grandsons: Ira Vernon, William Vernon both children of daughter Isabel Vernon (deceased)
- Executor: David Wheaton
- Witnesses: D.M. Howard, J.T. Collman both of Healdsburg

WHEELER, JAMIMA J.	Written:	28 Jun. 1875		#1098
Age 44	Codicil:	14 Jun. 1878	Bk. B, Pg. 99	
	Died:	-- Aug. 1880		
	Filed:	25 Oct. 1881		

- Husband: Jacob Wheeler
- Daughters: Mary Ann Walker, Martha Ann Wheeler, Sarah Jane Wheeler
- Sons: William Andrew Wheeler, George W. Wheeler, David R. Wheeler, Jacob F. Wheeler, Ira E. Wheeler
- Guardian: R.P. Wills, brother
- Executors: Husband, Lewis Lemay (Codicil revokes Lemay)
- Witnesses: Robert Crane, John G. Pressley
- Codicil: Thomas L. Rea, George P. Gammon

WHELDEN, ALEXANDER	Written:	14 Jul. 1884		#1486
Dartmouth, Mass.	Died:	11 Jun. 1885	Bk. D, Pg. 121	
Age 65		Napa, Ca.		
	Rec.:	9 Nov. 1885		

- Wife: Alice M.
- Daughter: Laura W. (26) of Grand Rapids, Mich.
- Father: Isaac
- Executor: Wife
- Witnesses: Mary F. Davis, Jennie L. Poole (Howland, at time of probate), Harry (Henry) G. Jenkins

WHITCOMB, HIRAM M.	Dated:	18 Jul. 1894	#3172
Age 29	Filed:	27 Jun. 1900	

- Mother: Nancy Adolini Whitcomb
- Executor: Nancy Adolini Whitcomb
- Witnesses: W.M. Peery, J.R. Thomas both of Ukiah City

WHITE, ALBERT F.	Dated:	27 Jul. 1884		#2985
Los Angeles	Died:	17 Jan. 1899	Bk. G, Pg. 273	
	Filed:	14 Feb. 1899		

- Wife: Caroline L. White
- Children: Three adopted children un-named
- Executor: Caroline L. White
- Witnesses: Stephen G. Nye, Emma M. Nye both of San Leandro

WHITE, CHARLES L.   Written: 30 Jan. 1872   # 771
                           Died: 29 Aug. 1875   Bk. B, Pg. 197
                           Filed: 1 Nov. 1875

  Wife: Bridget
  Executor: Bridget
  Witnesses: William P. White, Charles K. Jenner

WHITE, WILSON   Dated: 27 Jun. 1863   # 265
Windsor   Died: 7 Dec. 1864
                           Filed: 16 Jan. 1864 or
                                     4 Jan. 1865

  Niece: Melvina White of Summer Co., Tenn.
               Robert T. Mitchell, Henry White, William Carter
  Executor: Robert T. Mitchell
  Witnesses: A.B. Aull, A.T. Hembree

WHITNEY, A. P.   Written: 17 Sep. 1883   #1387
Petaluma   Died: 10 Feb. 1884   Bk. C, Pg. 511
Merchant   Rec.:   20 Dec. 1884

  Wife: Susan D.
  Sons: Calvin E., Arthur L., Albion H. (?)
  Daughters: Cleora M. Hewlett, Nancy J. Morrow, Marcella,
               Clara
  Executors: Wife; son, Calvin; Sons-in-law, Frederick Hewlett
               and Geo. P. Morrow
  Witnesses: E.L. Lippitt, David S. Dickson

WICKERSHAM, FREDERICK A. Written: 4 Mar. 1901   #3331
Petaluma   Died: 22 Jun. 1901   Bk. G, Pg. 500
                           Maracopa Co., Arizona Terr.

  Wife: Mary Catherine
  Children: Jane Elizabeth, Frederick Augustus
  Executor: Wife
  Witnesses: J.C. Campbell of 2619 Buchanan St., San Francisco;
               Milton Bernard of 1427 Folsom St., San Francisco

WICKERSHAM, I. G.   Written: 12 Nov. 1896   #3033
Petaluma   Age over   Died: 20 Jun. 1899   Bk. G, Pg. 325
             70   Filed: 5 Sep. 1899

  Wife: Lydia C. Wickersham
  Sons: Frank Wickersham, Fred A. Wickersham
  Daughter: Lizzie Wickersham
  Grandson: Frank Wickersham
  Bequest to: Katie Bower
  Executors: Lydia C. Wickersham, Fred A. Wickersham, Lizzie E.
               Wickersham, H.H. Atwater (deceased)

```
WICKERSHAM, JESSE C.        Written:  16 Mar. 1870              #1522
Petaluma        Age 35      Died:     18 Jan. 1886   Bk. D, Pg. 151
                            Mendocino Tnsp.
                            Rec.:      1 Mar. 1886
```

Wife:	Sarah A.
Brothers:	E.H. Wickersham (about 55) of Keokuk, Ia.; Lewis (about 40)
Sisters:	Mrs. Eliza Mary McKinney (50) of Keokuk, Ia.; Adeline Pyle (45) of Calif.; Harriet (40) of Calif.
Executor:	Wife
Witnesses:	H.H. Atwater, J.A. Wiswell

```
WICKERSHAM, LYDIA C.   Dated:    2 Sep. 1899              #3120
                       Died:    10 Feb. 1900   Bk. G, Pg. 397
                       Filed:   27 Mar. 1900
```

	Miss Catherine Bowers (relationship unknown)
Son:	Frank Wickersham
Children:	Fred A. Wickersham, Lizzie C. Wickersham, May Bergevin (Wickersham)
	St. John's Episcopal Church of Petaluma
Executor:	Fred A. Wickersham
Witnesses:	E.S. Lippitt, Frank K. Lippitt

```
WILBER, REBECCA A. OR   Dated:   16 Feb. 1878              #1227
REBEKAH                 Died:    14 Feb. 1882   Bk. C, Pg. 212
                        Rec.:    19 Mar. 1883
```

Children:	Mrs. Kate Tull, Mrs. Sarah E. Savage, Henry A. Hampson, Mrs. Lillian V. Bosworth
Husband:	J.W. Wilber
	May and Emma Carle of San Francisco (relationship unknown)
Executors:	G.W. Savage, son-in-law; Henry A. Hampson
Witnesses:	R.B. Allen, L.B. Gardner, J. Burckholter

```
WILEY, HARRIET          Written:  6 Jun. 1893              #2326
                        Died:    14 Jun. 1893   Bk. F, Pg. 134
                        Rec.:    17 Jul. 1893
```

Husband:	Alexander (deceased)
Wife & Children:	Of brother-in-law James Wiley (deceased) of St. Clair, Mich.
Brother-in-Law:	Samuel Wiley of Southbridge, Mass.
Sisters-in-Law:	Mary Allen of Webster, Mass.; Margaret France of Providence, R.I.; mother of Addie Earnes Stanley
Executors:	James Johnson, Mendocino Co. Sheriff; John M. Soggan of Sonoma Co.
Witnesses:	John T. Campbell, Rosanna Gascard both of Santa Rosa

```
WILFLEY, SAMUEL          Written:  28 Feb. 1895                #2531
Healdsburg     Age 88    Died:      5 May  1895    Bk. F, Pg. 364
                         Rec.:     27 May  1895
```

- Wife: Ruth (present)
- Children: Mary Jane Kise, Angeline Kise, Eliza Gale, Cordelia Gale, Thomas J. Wilfley, Sarah Merritt
- Executors: First name cut off document; daughter, Sarah Merritt
- Witnesses: E.H. Barnes, J.T. Coffman

```
WILLIAMS, GEO. B.        Written:  23 Jul. 1893                #3076
Petaluma                 Died:     19 Oct. 1899    Bk. G, Pg. 349
                         Filed:    21 Nov. 1899
```

- Wife: Mehetabel Williams
- Son: Geo. R. Williams, Trustee
- Grandson: Geo. P. McNear, Trustee
- Daughters: Rosetta L. Weeks (oldest), Laura J. Barstow (youngest)
- Grand-Daughters: Grace L. Williams, Claribel Williams
- Executors: Geo. R. Williams, Geo. P. McNear
- Witnesses: Emsley Fine, Emily Fine both of Petaluma

```
WILLIAMS, GEO. C.        Written:   2 Oct. 1885                #1991
Sprechelsville, Maui     Died:      5 Mar. 1890    Bk. E, Pg. 257
          Age 51         San Francisco
                         Rec.:     21 Jul. 1890
```

- Wife: Sarah Elizabeth
- Bequests to: Eldest son of friend, Jos. P. Cooke (deceased) of Honolulu; eldest son of friend, Jos. B. Atherton of Honolulu; Maggie L. Hopper, second daughter of friend, James A. Hopper, of Honolulu
- Executors: W.R. Castle, Chas. M. Cook
- Witnesses: W.F. Mossman, A.F. Hopke both of Kahalui, Maui

```
WILLIAMS, JOHN ENOS      Written:  30 Jun. 1895                #3035
Petaluma Tnsp.           Died:      8 Jun. 1899    Bk. G, Pg. 307
                         Filed:    24 Jul. 1899
```

- Wife: Mary E. Williams
- Son: Manuel E. Williams (20)
- Daughters: Mary E. Williams (18), Jane E. Williams (16)
- Executor: Mary E. Williams
- Witnesses: A.W. Thompson of 913 Twentieth St., San Francisco, Ca.; William Osemal of Petaluma Tnsp., Sonoma Co., Ca.

```
WILLIAMS, JOHN L.            Written:    7 Feb. 1881              #1254
            Age 82           Codicil:    6 Aug. 1882    Bk. C, Pg. 260
                             Died:       9 Aug. 1882
                             Filed:      3 Mar. 1883

     Son:              Thomas Didymus
     Daughters:        Elizabeth Walker (Mrs. Alexander L.) of Oregon;
                       Ellen Ann
     Daughter-in-
     Law:              Margaret Emma Williams
     Executor:         Son
     Witnesses:        Thos. B. Miller, Thomas Kyle
     Codicil:          Thos. B. Miller, Eleanor Plunkett


WILLIAMS, JOSEPH ANTON    Written:   20 Feb. 1882              #1435
Glen Ellen                Died:       3 Nov. 1885 (?)
                          Rec.:      30 Mar. 1885    Bk. D, Pg. 18

     Wife:             Bridget Kirby
     Children:         Sophia, Albert
     Executor:         Wife
     Witnesses:        Robt. A. Poppe, Georg Hermann Heinderich Cornelius


WILLIGAS, EHLER HEINRICH Written:  22 Feb. 1878              #1320
Petaluma Tnsp.           Died:     17 Apr. 1883    Bk. C, Pg. 384
                         Rec.:     11 Jul. 1883

     Wife:             Eliza K. (signs name Elise)
     Executor:         Wife
     Witnesses:        August Henry Dreer (Duer), Frank W. Shattuck


WILLSON, H. M.               Dated:     16 May 1898              #3021
            Age 84           Died:      21 Apr. 1899    Bk. G, Pg. 292
                             Filed:     19 Jun. 1899

     Grand-
     Children:         Henry W. Coffman, Gertrude Coffman
     Executors:        N.B. Coffman, W.S. Coffman
     Witnesses:        John Favour, J.F. Coffman of Healdsburg


WILSEY, HENRY                Written:    1 Jul. 1881              #2786
                             Codicil:   14 Jul. 1896    Bk. G, Pg. 71
                             Died:      14 Oct. 1897
                             Filed:     20 Oct. 1897

     Wife:             Louisa Wilsey
     Daughter:         Ida May Davis (Mrs. A.G.W.) aka Ida May Moyer
     Nieces:           Frances Wilsey, Libbie Wilsey
     Nephews:          Martin Henry Wilsey, Mayes Wilsey
     Brother:          Amasa Wilsey
     Father:           Frances Wilsey
     Witnesses:        Wm. B. Haskell, C.S. Farquar both of Petaluma
     Codicil:          Thomas C. Denny, F.A. Meyer both of Petaluma
```

WILSEY, R. G.				Written:	21 Dec. 1898			#2965
					Died:		28 Dec. 1898	Bk. G, Pg. 278
					Filed:		17 Apr. 1899

   Brother:		D.C. Wilsey
				Mortgage to Hollengren
				Holographic

WILSON, JOHN G.			Written:	8 Sep. 1873			# 779
Sonoma					Died:		30 Oct. 1875	Bk. B, Pg. 212
					Filed:		24 Dec. 1875

   Wife:		Mary E.
   Daughter:	Mrs. Charlot Witt
   Grandson:	Wilhelm Witt
   Nephew:		Andras Wrick Polsk of Stockholm, Sweden
   Executor:	John Trivnen
   Witnesses:	Chas. VanGeldern, J.A. Poppe

WILSON, PRISCILLA AKA		Written:	1 Jan. 1898			#2836
PRISCILLA BURTCH AKA		Died:		13 Jan. 1898	Bk. G, Pg. 179
PRISCILLA DUTTON		Filed:		18 May 1898

   Bequests to:	John Blackburn, Mrs. Charles Bowhoer, Mrs. Mary
			Black, Miss Nettie Guple (Tuple?)
   Sister:		Mary Beeson
   Niece:		Ivy ---
   Executor:	Ivy ---
   Witnesses:	A. Anderson, John S. Blackburn

WILSON, WILLIAM Y.			Written:	16 May 1894			#2614
Santa Rosa	Age 75		Died:		14 Feb. 1896	Bk. F, Pg. 497
				Rec.:		2 Mar. 1896

   Wife:		Ellen P. (?)
   Children:	Eliza Ann Churchman of Mendocino Co.; Rebecca
			Bourland of San Francisco; Isaac T. Wilson of
			Dayton, Ore.
   Executor:	Wife
   Witnesses:	D.R. Gale, S.R. Yoho

WINETT, NANCY A.			Written:	15 May 1855			# 47
		Age about	Codicil:	17 May 1855	Bk. Wills Pg. 59
		37		Filed:		22 Oct. 1855

   Sons:		James Irvin Smith, John Lewis Smith, Isaac B. Smith,
			George W. Smith, Nepolian Bonopart (?)
   Daughter:	Mary Jane Smith
   Guardians:	Judge Ross, William A. Hereford
   Witnesses:	--- Sawyer, Frederick Clarke, Ezra B. Tracy
   Codicil:	William Hereford, Frederick Clark

```
WINTERS, LAWRENCE L.        Written:   30 Dec. 1890                  #2160
Petaluma        Age 65      Died:       3 Jan. 1892    Bk. E, Pg. 529
                            Rec.:      25 Jan. 1892
```

Brothers:	Patrick K. of Port Orem, N.J.; Dennis; Thomas; Michael of Oakland, Ca.
Sister:	Maria Anderson, wife of Chris., of San Francisco
Executor:	Wm. Hill
Witnesses:	F.A. Meyer, Wm. B. Haskell

```
WOLFSKILL, JOSEPH           Written:    9 Jul. 1885                  #2254
Livingston Co., Mo.         Died:       ---    1892    Bk. F, Pg.  57
                            Rec.:      27 Dec. 1892
```

Wife:	Catherine A.
Daughter:	Mary J. Kester
Executor:	Wife
Witnesses:	T.C. Wilhite, C.S. Hagaman, Lydia Hagaman

```
WOODS, GEORGE               Written:   27 Feb. 1900                  #3231
Petaluma        Age 59      Codicil:    2 Nov. 1900    Bk. G, Pg. 478
                            Died:       4 Nov. 1900
                            Filed:     26 Nov. 1900
```

Brothers:	Matthew Woods of Maine, Robert Woods, Isaac Woods, Simon Woods
Nephews:	James Woods of Canada; Robert Woods of Petaluma, Ca.; William John Woods of Marin Co., Ca.; George E. Woods of Santa Rosa, Ca.
Nieces:	Mrs. Leila Jordan, Mrs. Lizzie Garrett, Eliza Jane Bennett
Grandniece:	Lillie Woods
Grandnephew:	James Woods
Executors:	A.B. Hill, William Loftus both of Petaluma
Witnesses:	P.H. Atkinson, George HaneKamp both of Petaluma

Description of real property in Petaluma

```
WOODS, JAMES                Written:   13 May  1872                  # 551
                                                       Bk. A. Pg. 297
```

Wife:	Isabella
Executor:	Wife
Witnesses:	Joshua Snow, W.W. Carpenter

```
WOODWORTH, SCOTT J.         Written:   28 Feb. 1866                  #2193
Petaluma                    Died:       3 Feb. 1891    Bk. E, Pg. 580
                            Rec.:      21 Mar. 1892
```

Wife:	Jennette E.
Executor:	Wife
Witnesses:	Frank Smith, A.W. Benjamin

WRIGHT, CHARLES ERNEST	Written:	19 May 1888		#1974
Santa Rosa Age about	Died:	31 Dec. 1889	Bk. E, Pg. 344	
31	Rec.:	13 Jan. 1891		

Wife: Flor--- Fredericka
Children: Un-named
               holographic

WRIGHT, HELEN C.	Written:	2 May 1893		#2873
Santa Rosa	Died:	21 Apr. 1898	Bk. G, Pg. 177	
	Filed:	16 May 1898		

Husband: Augustus S. Wright
Mother: Electa Fay (?)
Bequests to: Helen Rue Wright, Helen C. Nason
Executor: Husband
Witnesses: J.G. Spaulding, Calista Spaulding both of San
               Fransisco

WRIGHT, SAMPSON	Dated:	27 Jun. 1867		# 353
	Died:	13 Aug. 1867	Bk. A, Pg. 184	
	Rec.:	7 Oct. 1867		

Grandson: Peter Wright
               John Wright (a black man)
Executors: Winfield; S.M. Wright, son
Witnesses: Alonzo Thomas, Jackson Temple

WRIGHT, SYLVANUS	Written:	19 Feb. 1881		#1362
Santa Rosa	Died:	24 Oct. 1883	Bk. C, Pg. 452	
	Rec.:	19 Nov. 1883		

Son: Augustus
Daughter: Catherine G. Dimmick
Grand-
Children: Harry L. Wright, Eleanor M. Wright
Executor: Son
Witnesses: R.M. Spencer, S. Armstrong
Codicil: Dated 19 Feb. 1881 names sister, Mrs. Eliz.
               Goodsell of Cold Springs, N.Y.

WRIGHT, WINFIELD S. M.	Written:	17 Aug. 1891		#2227
Santa Rosa Age 67	Died:	27 Jun. 1892	Bk. F, Pg. 1	
	Rec.:	11 Jul. 1892		

Wife: J.D.
Son: Sampson B.
Daughter: Mahala Olive Hall, wife of J.E.
Grand-
Daughters: Jessie Robinson, Janey Robinson
Uncle: Paternal uncle of Jessie & Janey, Wm. Robinson
Executors: Son, Sampson; son-in-law, J.E. Hall
Witnesses: Geo. P. Noonan, Jas. W. Oates

WRIGHTSON, FRANCIS	Written:	29 Aug. 1890	#2429
Kings Norton, Worcester, Eng.	Died: Age about 76	6 Aug. 1893 Worchester	Bk. F, Pg. 276
	Rec.:	2 Jul. 1894 Sonoma Co.	

- Children: Richard (deceased), Albert (deceased), Percy (deceased)
- Daughters: Margaret Laura, Frances Louise, Fanny Charlotte, Alberta Violet, Marie
- Sons: Arthur (inherits farm at Los Guillicos), Harold (inherits Mark West ranch), Robert Baldwin, Richard Edgar
- Bequest to: Dr. George Gore
- Nephew: Chas. James Wrightson
- Niece: Isabella Owen
- Executors: Thos. Hiron Bartleet, Thos. Eberall Cooke
- Witnesses: John Howard Baker, Harry Parish both of Biringham, Eng.
- Codicil: Dated 25 Aug. 1892 states Executor Baker deceased and appoints Royle Shore of Birmingham

WRIGHTSON, HENRY	Written:	27 Apr. 1886	#1901
Age 53	Died:	1 Nov. 1889	Bk. E, Pg. 180
	Rec.:	25 Nov. 1889	

- Bequests to: Geo. R. Skinner; Jane C., wife of Geo.; children of the above
- Executor: Friend, Geo. R. Skinner
- Witnesses: Mrs. Ann Gill, J.P. Rodgers both of Petaluma

YORDI, FRED	Dated:	24 Dec. 1900	#3321
Cloverdale Age 50	Died:	22 Mar. 1901	Bk. H, Pg. 76
	Filed:	11 Nov. 1901	

- Wife: Sarah Jane Yordi
- Children: Alfred H.; Carla; Frank A.; Flora I.; Nellie E. (minor); Alice C. Yordi (minor)
- Executors: B.A. Dunn, Carl A. Yordi
- Witnesses: John S. Drum, Sydney M. Ehrman, William B. Bosley

YORK, CHARLES W.	Written:	8 Sep. 1896	#2683
Healdsburg	Died:	31 Oct. 1896	Bk. F, Pg. 576
	Filed:	7 Dec. 1896	

- Wife: Mary York
- Daughter: Annie M. York
- Son: Charles A. York
- Executor: Annie M. York of Healdsburg
- Witnesses: J.W. Rose, Gus Lind (Lund)

YOUNG, AMELIA	Dated:	13 Feb. 1901	#3278
Alexander Valley	Died:	20 Feb. 1901	Bk. H, Pg. 41
Age 54	Filed:	25 Mar. 1901	

- Sons: George Elwin Young, Nelson Warner Young, Clarence Henry Young
- Daughter: Myrtle Lee Young (Allenden)
  Michael Young (deceased)
- Grand-Daughter: Ruth Allenden
- Executor: George Elwin Young
- Witnesses: J.W. Rose, H.S. Gird

YOUNG, BYRD S.	Written:	12 May 1888	#2229
Santa Rosa	Died:	29 Jun. 1892	Bk. F, Pg. 17
	Rec.:	1 Aug. 1892	

- Wife: Carrie B.
- Daughters: Mrs. Minnie Kolliker (?), Neva Young
- Executor: Wife
  Holographic

YOUNG, HIRAM	Written:	3 Dec. 1873	# 663
Strawberry Ridge	Died:	4 Dec. 1873	
	Filed:	5 Jan. 1874	

- Wife: Sarah
- Son: Henry
- Daughters: Celia Groshong; Rebecca Jane Hershberger (deceased) heirs of; Sarah Ann McCracken (deceased) heirs of
- Executor: Henry Young of Bennet Valley
- Witnesses: John Hughes, Aaron Lacque, Daniel E. Miller

ZAMBELICH, NICHOLAS	Written:	13 Dec. 1889	#1917
Santa Rosa Age 70	Died:	20 Dec. 1889	Bk. E, Pg. 197
	Rec.:	20 Jan. 1890	

- Wife: Nettie
- Executor: Wife
- Witnesses: J.A. Barham, Chas. A. Barham

ZANE, WILLIS	Written:	4 Jun. 1877	#1074
Healdsburg	Died:	18 Mar. 1880	Bk. C, Pg. 90
	Filed:	29 Mar. 1880	

- Wife: Martha Alice Zane
- Children: Willis, Joel, Della, Evelena
- Brother: Joel Zane
- Sister: Mary Gale
- Executors: Albert Zane, Isaac Gum
- Witnesses: J.W. Rose, Thos. Riley

ZIMMERMANN, GEORGE		Written:	1 May 1891	#2084
Petaluma	Age over	Died:	14 May 1891	Bk. E, Pg. 398
	50	Rec.:	8 Jun. 1891	

Wife: Louisa
Sons: Geo. H., Charles
Daughters: Hattie, wife of L.L. Gross; Caroline Goldeggar; Hannah Doehring; Julia Karev
Bequest to: Louisa Corrick
Executors: D.B. Fairbanks, Geo. H. Zimmerman
Witnesses: Conrad Poehlmann, J.L. Gerckous

Name	Page	Name	Page
Abendroth, Josephine K.	114	Anderlini, Peter	163
Ables, Mary E.	121	Anderson, A.	4
Thomas J.	121	"	26
Abraham, Isadore	188	"	210
Abroth(?), Philip Wells	173	Mrs. Alexander	41
Ackerman, Charles L.	109	Chris	211
Acuff, Luella	91	J.P.	34
Adams, Tabitha F.	136	James	64
Adamson, W.H.	53	Maria	211
Adcock, Polly Ann	70	William L.	46
Agnew, Emma Linda	26	"	75
Aherns, Jacob	149	"	196
Aiken, Wm. H.	106	Andree, Wm. Herman	74
Aikin, Mat	108	Andrews, Lyman P.	33
Akers, M.T.	158	Angwin, Wm.	120
Alamany, I.L.	139	Anker, Catherine	74
Alberding, Fredric	113	Kate	102
Albert, M.	64	Appleton, W.	29
T.B.	64	Wellington	70
Alderson, Ann Eliza		Armeda, Isabel	3
(McCann)	128	Juoquina	3
Aling, Joseph	129	Lauriana	3
Allen, B.B.	46	Marie	3
"	190	Armeida see Almeida	
Caroline	107	Armes, Cha. W.	81
Carrie E.	44	Armstrong, Albert	45
Charles H.	107	Belle	27
Cornelia L.	64	Fannie	120
Darwin C.	100	Margaret	47
George	14	Martin	31
James W.	119	S.	212
Lavica Jane	14	Sheldon	158
Mariette	172	Arnold, Foster	76
Mary	207	Arrants, Joseph	117
Mary E.	119	Asher, Hardin	50
O.L.	130	Asken, Hattie	198
R.B.	207	John	198
Robert Bruce	5	Atherton, Joseph B.	208
S.L.	82	Atkinson, Eleanor	68
Samuel J.	158	H.L.	11
William T.	119	Joseph	73
Allenberg, L.	141	Mary	77
Therese	141	P.H.	11
Allenden, Myrtle Lee		"	52
(Young)	214	"	68
Ruth	214	"	170
Alley, T.J.	159	"	211
Almeda see Almeida		Atwater, Addie A.	85
Alvord, Wm.	69	H.H.	79
Ames, C.G.	96	"	92
C.S.	178	"	105
Dot	96	"	131
Lee	96	"	173
T.M.	47	"	179

Name	Page	Name	Page
Atwater, H.H. cont.	206	Barnes, Alice Electa	63
"	207	Anna	63
Henry H.	191	Charles	63
Aull, A.B.	206	E.H.	12
Avella, Frank	3	"	13
Avery, James	56	"	208
Aylsworth, George W.	65	Edward C.	63
Sarah F.	65	Edward H.	194
		Frank	63
		J.T.	12
Babb, Sarah Frances	88	James	63
Baechtel, S.D.	146	John	56
Baer, Geo. B.	35	John T.	143
"	90	Mary M.	194
"	124	Oscar	63
Reuben E.	4	Richard O.	61
Baesi, Amadeo	156	Ruth	61
Bagley, H.L.	175	Sarah Anne	199
Bailache, John N.	174	Sarah Baronetta	163
"	202	Sarah J.	67
Bailey, James D.	50	Sophia A.	59
M.C.	1	William	63
Michael C.	130	Barstow, Laura J.	208
N.A.	180	Bartleet, Thos. Hiron	213
R.F.	1	Bartlett, Columbus	68
Bailiff, Mrs. J.D.	170	"	75
Baker, Hattie	17	George A.	105
Henry	181	Barton, Ella	69
J.T.	29	Robert	69
"	73	William H.	69
John Howard	213	Bascom, Amanda	173
L.H.	19	Bass, Mary Ann	164
Louisa Ennice	19	Bates, Addie C.	50
Baldwin, Abraham	69	J.L.	12
Elizabeth	69	Jane	120
Bamford, Edward	196	Laura	130
Bane, Chas. Hamilton	189	Mary	193
Banks, J.A.	175	Nealy	130
Banneyburg, Bell Sorey	96	Batten, Sam'l	80
Jourdan	96	Bauer, John	83
Banta, John	11	"	94
Mary Ann	11	Mary	94
Barbieri, Antonio Flora	172	Baugh, Joseph F.	72
Joseph	172	Baxter, George P.	58
Barbour, Clitus	120	"	77
Barham, Aubrey	13	"	102
J.A.	23	"	170
"	118	Harriet	77
"	214	Sutcliffe	77
Barlow, Emma E.	53	Bayley, Belle	129
Mary Ann	158	Martha	189
Nancy	152	Thomas S.	189
S.Q.	172	Baylis, Thomas Fulcher	58

Name	Page	Name	Page
Bayliss, Theodore	139	Bidwell, Selina	128
Beach, Chester	56	Billett, Addie M.	27
Elizabeth	56	Birch, Thomas E.	133
Beall, H.M.	174	Bishop, Daniel L.	164
Beam, J.	168	Thomas B.	69
Jeremiah	32	Bissordi, Terrisa	63
Beatty, Wm. F.	66	"	66
Beaumont, Chas.	46	Bjorkman, August	99
Beaver, Henry	156	Black, Agnes	71
Beckers, Louis	155	John	71
Bedwell, Ira	194	"	126
Beeson, J.B.	133	Mary	210
"	135	Blackburn, Eliz.	181
Mary	210	J.S.	165
Behler, William J.	99	Jane	181
Bejarano, Joan	154	John	210
Bell, Bradford	101	John S.	66
John W.	125	"	210
Bells, Maria	106	Blackwell, Andrew J.	95
Benedict, Anna	69	Elizabeth	95
Edwin	69	Blair, Susan	61
Benjamin, A.W.	211	Blakeley, Elizabeth	130
Maria	49	Blanckenburg, Theo	47
Benkard, Henry R.	165	Blatchley, Mary Esther	98
Bennett, A.G.	179	Bledsoe, A.C.	116
Eliza Jane	211	Blinn(?), Alice	29
William	150	Grace	29
Benson, Josiah H.	89	Blip, Wm. D.	1
"	187	"	6
Mary	199	"	24
William	35	"	62
"	89	Bliss, Wm. D.	140
Bentley, Horatio	36	Blood, J.H.	106
Pauline	36	Bloom, David	128
Reuben	36	Jonas	71
Rodney	36	Julius	172
Willie	36	Bodwell, C.A.	185
Benton, L.J.	177	Bogan, C.L.	136
Bergers, Eliz. Ann	28	Bogle, George	133
Bergevin, May	207	Bohlin, Frank Anton	185
Berghstrom, Maud	193	Mary Ann	185
Berglund, Alfred	112	Bojorquez, Joaquin	154
Bernard, Milton	206	Pedro	154
Bernhard, Isaac	9	Bolder, Mrs. Wm.	155
Berry, B.B.	24	Bolles, Alice	71
"	159	W.A.	71
W.A.	182	Bolza, Annie E.	16
Bertolani, P.	44	William	16
Bethel, C.	133	Bompers, Dolores	192
Bever, Ruth	150	Bond, Geo.	185
Bew, Geo.	179	William H.	116
Biagi, Jenny	44	Bondshu, Bertha	148
Bice, Cornelius	136	Bonetti, Luca	195
Mary	104	Bonjour, Leo Paul	151
Bickford, Mrs.	29	Bonnel, B.F.	98

Name	Page	Name	Page
Bonter, Hannah Aryelia	114	Brainerd, Henry P.	50
William D.	114	Jessie E.	50
Boon, Eva	65	Braint, Sina(?)	102
Helen T.	65	Brammer, May	14
Jessie	65	Branch, Louisa	153
Maud	65	Brandon, F.D.	202
May	65	Braun, H.K.	170
Booth, Emilie	63	John	185
James Rogers	136	Braunsfield, Priscilla	71
Jesse	104	William Hudson	71
Sarah	193	Breitenbach, F.	10
William F.	63	"	32
Boothby, Caroline	180	Franz	132
Bose(?), Margaret	171	George	10
Bosley, William B.	213	"	72
Bostwick, Addie L.	114	Brewster, Eugene A.	165
"	115	John A.	14
Boswell, J.H.	103	"	195
Bosworth, Lillian V.	207	Brickwell, John	115
Sarah A.	45	Briggs, Frank	108
Bourke, William	161	Henry H.	11
Bourland, Rebecca	210	Sarah Eliza	11
Bowbeer, Anne	10	Briol, Pierre Philippe	72
Bowen, Jos.	188	Bristol, Joseph D.	70
Bower, Katie	206	Bristow, Larina L.	114
Bowers, Catharine	207	Britenbach, F.	32
Hazel G.	70	Britton, Mary Jane	169
Bowhoer, Mrs. Charles	210	Broback, C.W.	116
Bowles, Bourbon	16	Charles	75
Jesse M.	16	Frances	75
Octavia P.	16	Brockman, Israel	20
Scott	16	Brockmann, Agnes	171
Bowman, Rachel	66	Brons, H.	88
Boyce, J.F.	103	Brooks, Henry	12
"	120	Henry Clay	28
John F.	98	J.L.	155
"	104	John L.	155
Boyes, Henry E.	22	Laura	77
Boyse, J.B.	143	Mary Jane	194
Brackett, J.E.	173	Polly	12
Bradford, A.C.	200	Rachel	49
Bradley, Julia A.	78	Thomas	3
William	182	Wm.	54
William E.	78	William K.	194
Bradshaw, Arthur	28	Brotherton, Margaret	
Brainerd, Mrs. G.L.	40	Elvira	28
H.P.	40	Brown, Alice	165
"	44	Antoine	53
"	51	Caroline	12
"	84	Caroline S.	172
"	124	Charlotte	110
"	151	Daniel	143
"	171	"	148
"	177	"	165

Name	Page	Name	Page
Brown, Daniel cont.	166	Bryant, Julia	134
"	172	Malvina	77
Daniel E.	165	Sarah	197
David	172	Thomas	134
Emma	165	Buckle, Regina M.T.	126
Eugene	124	Buckrig(?), Sophie	171
Frances	53	Budd, James H.	130
Fred W.	165	Buettner, Clara	14
H.	146	Buhlmann, Anton	68
H.K.	84	Bull, Henry R.	104
"	99	Burbank, David	124
James H.	172	George W.	124
James W.	172	Burchalter, J.	40
John P.	5	Burgess, Mary Jane	113
"	18	Burhard, Gustavus	14
"	61	Maria Ignacia	
"	68	Valenzuela	14
"	87	May	14
"	96	Minnie	14
"	104	Burgtorf, C.W.	191
"	108	Burke, James	59
"	128	Burnett, Matt	15
"	155	"	61
"	196	Burns, William	35
John George	101	Burr, E.W.	119
Josephine	165	Frank	111
Lizzie	153	Burrel, D.W.	87
Lucretia	177	Burris, Elizabeth	42
Mareitta	172	Jesse	47
Martha	41	L.W.	42
Martha E.	172	"	44
Nettie	165	"	116
Ralph	140	"	125
Susan J.	49	"	147
Victoria A.	169	"	163
W.E.	50	T.W.	61
William	128	Burrows, G.W.	166
Wilson	135	William	157
"	170	Bush, Cordelia	63
Browning, Ada E.	57	Delila Jane	58
Broyles, Beulah	155	Dora Story	82
Brunner, Dora	187	Butler, James	116
Bruns, C.	123	Button, Melisss	202
Brush, Frank A.	145	Butts, T.J.	70
Fred W.	113	Byrns, James W.	13
G.W.	45	Byron, Alice	127
George E.	113		
George M.	4		
William T.	35	Cain, Margaret	67
Bryant, Angelina	119	Calder, John	39
Ann	134	Caldwell, F.M.	158
C.G.	85	Call, C.C.	70
John	134	William E.	73

Name	Page	Name	Page
Calloway, David	146	Carithers, D.N.	82
"	195	Mary Ellen	28
Cameron, John	70	Carle, Emma	207
Campbell, B.F.	79	May	207
Barbara	79	Carmony, Cyrus W.	119
C.	37	Carnes, Caroline H.	3
Eugene	110	Caroet(?), H.E.	11
George	79	Carothers, Thomas L.	4
J.C.	206	Carpenter, L.F.	63
J.P.	79	Llewellyn E.	154
"	100	W.W.	211
"	187	Carpy, Chas.(?)	109
Jennie L.	145	Carr, Edward	2
John T.	17	Hannah	106
"	22	Nelson	106
"	23	Carriger, Nicholas	182
"	37	Carrillo, Delorez	115
"	49	Felicidad	115
"	50	Francisco	115
"	151	Joaquin	115
"	161	Josepha	115
"	173	Juan	115
"	182	Julio	60
"	188	"	115
"	198	"	154
"	207	Maria de la Lus	115
Joseph	56	Marta Inana	115
"	79	Mary Springer	115
"	86	Ramon	115
"	187	Carson, David	193
"	191	Carstens, Samuel	71
Mary Jane	161	Carter, C.W.	62
Peter	70	Clemmie P.	62
R.B.	175	Lou J.	86
W.R.	83	William	206
Canan, W.S.	109	Cary, Clarry	90
"	141	Hattie	110
Cannon, Eda J.	31	James C.	110
L.L.	31	James H.	110
Cantel, Henrietta	90	Ladema	90
Louis	90	Walter M.	110
Cantrel, Jane	166	Case, Addie	36
Cantrell, Jane	166	Adelaide	36
Capell, Susan F.	45	George	36
Carberry, Peter	142	Georgie	36
Carder, D.D.	9	Letta	36
"	12	P.M.	57
"	13	Walter	36
"	88	Cashdollar, Alzia B.	60
"	133	Cass, Sarah Catharine	113
"	134	Cassenbaum, William	20
"	156	Cassidy, Fanny	44
Cardoza, Anton	3	Cassin, Francisco	167
Carey, Annie J.	101	J.M.	55
Rosey	101	"	129

Name	Page	Name	Page
Castle, John	113	Church, A.M.	80
Margaret	113	Annie M.	101
W.R.	208	Douglas	54
Casto, Louisa	156	Margaret Ann	101
Catran, Elizabeth	87	Churchill, H.H.	134
Cavalli, Geo. S.	154	Churchman, Eliza Ann	210
Cavan, JOhn	38	William	116
Cavanagh, J.	139	"	196
John	139	Clack, J.W.	19
Cavanaugh, Hattie L.	202	"	100
John	22	John	136
"	49	Claner, Frankie M.	118
"	51	Susie M.	118
"	73	Clark, Benjamin	38
"	92	Cadwell	72
"	110	"	88
"	138	E.B.	93
T.J.	73	Edward	73
William M.	202	F.T.	24
Cazswell, D.A.	51	Frederick	210
Cereghino, Antonio	56	George C.	22
Chadbourne, Mary		George W.	49
Josephine	10	"	143
Chamberlain, David	35	"	156
"	36	James	162
Jane	199	Louisa E.	141
Martha	35	Mary	162
Martha A.	36	Mary F.	102
Chamberlin, J.D.H.	171	Clarke, Frederick	210
Chambers, Mr. A.	168	William	93
Mrs. A.	168	Cleary, Anne	117
Chapins, Elam	186	I.	9
Lorany	186	J.F.	3
Chapman, A.P.	154	"	139
Adeline	79	James	100
M.C.	145	James F.	92
W.W.	121	Thomas J.	117
William A.	107	Clement, Henry N.	197
"	154	Coburn, Joe	180
Charb, Obed	101	Cochran, A.E.	11
Chardin, Joseph B.	107	"	170
Charles, James M.	134	"	183
Oscar	168	J.P.	137
Cheberle(?), Illeg.	146	Cocke, Wm. E.	194
Cheney, Lillie	114	Cockrill, Bruce T.	26
Thos. H.	115	Codding, G.R.	10
Chenoweth, Miles H.	30	"	32
Chon(?), Amelia	192	"	88
Christian, Niels	5	M.M.	145
Christie, John B.	15	Codman, Robt.	3
Christmas, William	13	Coffer, Nancy	150
Christofani, Arcangelo	156	Coffman, A.B.	81
Christy, Edward	175	Gertrude	209

Name	Page	Name	Page
Coffman, Henry W.	209	Connelly, Ellen	117
J.F.	209	Francis	9
J.G.	3	James	117
J.T.	4	Theodore	9
"	47	Thomas	9
"	111	Connolly, Annie A.	128
"	138	Edward	176
"	166	Minnie A.	192
"	208	Connoly, Arthur Henry	139
N.B.	69	Minnie	139
"	202	Connor, Julia A.	188
"	209	Peter O.	194
W.S.	209	Conolly, B.J.	184
Coggins, Catherine	55	Converse, Allen A.	146
Coker, Carl C.	178	Conway, Mrs.	4
Colburn, Clara W.	126	William	4
Frank S.	126	Cook, C.H.	103
James	126	Carrie S.	86
Samuel S.	126	Charles H.	86
Colby, George	154	Charles M.	208
Mary	154	Frances M.	152
Phebe	79	George A.	152
Phoebe	154	Isaac	152
Cole, Hiram	90	Israel	71
Coleman, Jas.	155	James C.	88
W.T.	149	Mary Jane	71
Colgan, E.P.	100	Minnie	49
Collins, Allie	53	Polly M.	152
F.M.	121	Cooke, Joseph P.	208
Frederick H.	121	Martin E.	70
Germain A.	32	Robert	194
Gertrude	121	Thomas Eberall	213
James D.	40	William E.	25
Jennie	93	Cooney, M.	144
John M.	121	Coons, John M.	57
Martha A.	121	Cooper, F.M.	164
Nancy E.	121	John D.	138
Thomas	93	John R.	79
Zillah E.	121	"	115
Zittah G.	121	Malinda	148
Collman, J.T.	205	Martin E.	14
Colton, F.D.	32	Thomas S.	79
"	51	Thomas Spriggs	115
Filena	85	Cope, F.J.	176
Colvin, C.L.	157	Corbett, John	73
Coman, Iolena	11	Coreia, Manuel	167
T.	111	Corey, Hattie May	36
Combs, B.S.	185	Wm. F.	36
Ella F.	185	Corley, M.V.	48
Mariah	17	Cornelius, Geo. H.H.	44
Comegys, Sarah Jane	68	"	209
Comelines, Emily	52	Cornue, Frank B.	28
Geo. H.H.	52	"	40
Comfort, Charles B.	144	"	54

Name	Page	Name	Page
Cornue, Frank B. cont.	181	Crisp, John Britton	178
Corrick, Louisa	215	Sarah J.	12
Corum, James	10	Crist, Martha C.	96
Lena	10	Roseann	96
Costello, Bridget M.	99	William	96
Coughran, W.	25	Critchfiled, Geo. W.	72
Coulter, Nellie J.	67	Crocker, Henry	162
County, Nora	93	Cromwell, F.A.	105
Cowan, Jas. M.	171	Cronche(?), Rob	107
William F.	40	Cronien, Ann S.	91
"	82	Michael	91
"	204	Crook, James	139
Coward, H.A.F.	155	Cross, C.W.	89
Cowdery, G.F.	110	Cynthia Jemima	92
Cowles, Louis	147	Crow, Eliz. Ann	66
Cox, Ann Eliza	78	Crum(?), Hettie Forest	37
Elzann	147	Cuadro, Pauline	176
W.E.	160	Cummins, F.M.	175
William E.	15	Cunningham, John J.	124
William J.	78	Mary	89
Cozzens, Abigail W.	30	Robert	89
Craig, John Rice	98	William J.	151
Mary E.	98	Cunninghame, W.J.	43
Mary Ellen	8	Curran, Thos. E.	127
O.W.	80	Currey, Edward	129
"	156	Nellie	129
Cramer, Albert A.	65	Margaret	129
Charles Walter	65	Thomas	129
David Fleet	65	Currie, Berl (Barb?)	176
David R.	65	Curtis, Charles P.	3
Elizabeth	65	Mary	127
Crandall, O.L.	6	Richard V.	144
Crane, J.H.	166	Cushing, Ben F.	78
Jane E.	41	Cutter, J.H.	197
Joel	60	Maria	197
R.H.	113	"	198
Richard H.	148	Cyriax, Albert	59
Robert	133		
"	205	Dabla, Rosie	3
Susan C.	41	Dahlmann, Augusta	184
Crawford, Alice H.	2	Frederick	184
E.H.	55	Henry	184
Maggie M.	21	Martha	184
"	137	Wilhelmina	184
R.F.	11	Daly, F.M.	166
"	21	Dandel, Mrs. M.	26
"	55	Daniels, Sarah E.	185
"	117	Darden, W.H.	73
"	123	Darrow, John O.	135
"	129	"	190
"	137	D'Avellar, Manuel J.	159
Thomas	48	Davidson, Adam	169
Crilly, Ellen	184	Clara E.	66
Cripps, Emma	65	J.W.	169

Name	Page	Name	Page
Davidson, John	169	Denny, Thomas C. cont.	80
S.E.	36	"	97
Davis, A.G.W.	209	"	114
B.J.	76	"	196
Climena	76	"	209
"	94	Densmore, George	118
Edward W.	96	Derby, A.B.	51
George A.	81	"	134
George W.	82	Desilets, Charles	50
"	96	Deteller, J. Jr.	195
H.H.	79	DeWard, Esabel	178
"	103	Dickenson, A.C.	25
Ida May	209	Dickerson, Hannah M.	82
J.W.	84	Dickey, S.R.	62
Joseas	93	Dickson, David S.	92
Julius A.	76	"	206
"	94	Difrintoz, Feliciana	
L.F.	119	Arbaez	115
Mary F.	205	Dinsmore, Fred. A.	36
Mary M.	57	Dignan, M.H.	56
Milo S.	76	Dillingham, Martha	104
Rose	81	William K.	184
Sallie I.	87	Dimmick, Catherine G.	212
W.	34	Dinwiddie, J.L.	26
W.K.	34	"	40
Walter S.	30	"	84
Davisson, D.D.	118	"	166
Dawes, George	3	"	177
Mary E.	3	Dittamore, Theodore	135
Dean, James O.	119	Ditty, Sarah	50
Dearin, Louisa	50	Dixon, John	62
DeBendeleben, O.	125	Joseph	176
DeCamp, Adeline E.	200	Mary A.	196
DeCoe, Rettie	8	Dobkins, Jacob S.	152
Thomas	8	Dodge, Leoma	196
DeEmparon, Louisa	197	Doe, Chas. F.	103
"	198	Doehring, Hannah	215
R.	197	Doescher, Charles	45
"	198	Dogget, W.J.	71
Dehaven, Temperance F.C.	199	W.J. Jr.	71
Deig, Frank P.	21	Doh, John	16
DelaRosa, Jose	155	Dohn, Geo. E.	180
DeMattos, William H.	93	Dolan, Annie L.	25
DeMott, Minnie	17	James F.	25
Dempsey, Annie	55	Katie A.	25
Catherine	55	Donahue, Peter	153
Denike, Emma Jane	50	Donner, Eliza	20
Denison, Abel	126	Georgianna	20
Denmark, Chas.	19	Donohue, J.M.	46
Denning, Margaret	59	Peter	46
Mary A.	59	Doran, W.M.	187
Denny, Thomas C.	4	Dorchester, H.R.	49
"	8	Dorrnan, Margaret	165
"	60	Patrick	165

Name	Page	Name	Page
Dortmund, Thomas	101	Dunsmore, Anne	197
Doty, Albert	115	Dupuy, Aline Berthe	89
Vera	114	Jean Baptiste	89
"	115	Durie, Pauline	12
Dougherty, B.G.	132	Dwyer, Jerry	143
John	66	Dyer, C.	108
"	127	Frances F.	65
"	132	Dyson, J.H.	179
"	175		
Doughty, John	163	Eagan, Ellen	32
Douglas, Robt.	38	Eagleson, Ernest G.	185
William	58	Earl, Emma M.	169
Douglass, Mary L.	35	Easley, Warham	90
"	36	"	193
Wm. A.	35	Eberhard, Charley E.	29
"	36	Edelman, J.J.	118
Dow, J.G.	116	"	132
Dowal, Leo	9	Eden(?), Chas.	101
Richard	9	Edmunds, Joseph	46
Theodore	9	Mary	46
Downing, Mary Frances	179	Rueben	46
Downs, Albert	170	Edwards, Camilla	188
Doyle, Ellen	32	Edward	192
Frank P.	42	Elizabeth	192
"	63	F.J.	188
M.	144	Hannah	192
Drahms, A.	71	J.G.	135
Drennan, Mary A.	30	Thomas	192
Dressel, Bertha	155	William P.	115
Carl	52	Eggleton, Geo.	12
"	155	Ehlert, Chas. O.	59
Emil	155	Ehlinger, Peter	39
Gustave	155	Ehr, Frank	18
Helene	155	Ehrman, Sydney M.	213
Johanna	155	Eidleman, G.W.	39
Julius	155	Elledge, Ethel	152
Drew, Sarah Ann	197	Martha J.	152
Thomas	197	Elliott, James	50
Driscoll, Terry	168	R.W.	66
Drum, John S.	213	Ellis, Leander	136
Drumgold, F.	139	Nancy E.	136
Drummond, J.A.	202	Ellison, Nicena	151
Ducker, Benjamin	141	Rachel N.	152
Ducon, Alexandrine	4	Ellsworth, L.	133
Dudley, Robt.	201	Lee	173
Duer (Dreer) August		Engler, Geo.	47
Henry	209	English, Jas. L.	175
Dumlin, Daniel	26	Enos, Annie	183
Duncan, J. Allan	101	Mary	167
Dunlap, Frank E.	130	Morris S.	183
Dunn, Alexander	131	Eppinger, Jesse I.	59
B.A.	213	Erland, Anna Thora Zelle	5
John W.	113	Peter Christian	5
Philip	170	Ervin, Polly A.	152

Name	Page	Name	Page
Escalle, Ellen	37	Favre, Louise	151
Estes, George	83	Faxen(?), Elisha	107
Mary	83	Sarah A.	107
Eugley, Emma Elizabeth		Fay(?), electa	212
(Engley)	140	Mary E.	11
Evans, Henry	25	Faylor, Minnie	155
Nancy	25	Orson	155
Everett, Edw. A.	167	Feddersen, Heinrich M.	151
Eyre, Matilda	201	Feige, C.	120
		Fellows, David S.	160
Facey, Richard	25	Zilpha	160
Fairbanks, D.B.	16	Fenkhausen, Louisa V.	104
"	26	Walter	104
"	44	Fensier, Louisa G.	72
"	105	Ferguson, E.C.	40
"	114	H.O.	201
"	172	John N.	66
"	215	Russell	122
Eva	124	Fernands, Antonie	159
H.T.	135	August	159
Hiram	34	Joseph	159
"	51	Marie	159
Hiram T.	154	Ferry, Chloe	191
J.F.	124	Thomas M.	191
Loui	199	Fetz, Joseph	75
Lucinta	135	Fichtner, Charles	140
Falkner, M.H.	51	Friederike	140
"	173	Field, C.E.	43
Fare, L.	14	Filitz, Mary	18
Farmer, C.C.	61	Finck, Zorah, A.	135
"	178	Fine, Emily	208
E.T.	31	Emsley	208
"	75	F.F.	88
"	180	Fink, Luis	132
Farnham, Thos.	204	Finlaw, Col. W.	17
Farnsworth, C.C.	31	"	40
Isabella	188	Finney, Nancy E.	152
Farquar, C.S.	22	Fisher, A.L.	40
"	90	Fisk, Cornelia Ann	94
"	139	Fitch, Samantha C.	172
"	167	Fitton, Edward	77
"	184	Helena	77
"	195	Flack, Racilla	57
"	209	Flega(?), H.	141
Farrar, A.L.	45	Fletcher, Mary Jane	15
M.C.	81	Sarah M.	15
Farris, Louisa	58	Flewelling, Beverly	160
Faught, Frances	186	Mary L.	160
James	186	Flint, Caroline L.	1
Ruth	166	Ella (Jewell)	97
Faulkner, M.H.	65	Eugene	79
"	121	Purdy	79
Faviner(?), George L.	11	Flippen, J.T.	134
Susanna	11	Flohr, Martin H.	151
Favour, John	209	Florence, S.C.	148

Name	Page	Name	Page
Flower, Anna	190	Freeman, John M.	80
Focha, Louisa F.	39	Lillian R.	144
Fohrion, Lillie	67	Merrick	204
Foley, Patrick A.	46	Susan E.	80
Folger, Mrs. S.J.	67	Frei, Andrew	91
Forbes, M.	67	French, C.G.M.	175
Ford, Martha	152	Frey, Lena	118
Forshew, Frank	107	Frick, Geo. W.	96
George	107	Frisbie, Adelia	197
Forsyth, Edward Lee	31	"	198
H.M.	101	Dr.	197
Henry M.	28	"	198
Martha C.	28	Edifania	197
Mary Ellen	31	"	198
Mary M.	31	Gen'l	197
Robert	31	"	198
Sarah F.	31	Fritsch, John	52
William B.	31	"	103
Forsythe, Robt. A.	18	"	117
Fortier, Peter	57	"	136
Fortson, John T.	75	"	137
"	130	Frohlking, Wm.	184
Foss, Alice Maria	68	Frost, Cora E.	202
Foster, Chas.	21	Isabella	95
Robert D.	14	Fugel, Hugo	6
Foushee, Mary C.	76	Fulkerson, John	134
Foutz, Jacob	142	Ruth	61
Fowler, A.F.	110	Fuller, Mrs. America	160
Ada R.	11	William H.H.	160
"	128	Funk, Barbara	69
E.J.	31	William	69
"	95	Furlong, James	183
Eliza A.	110	Rosanna	97
Eliza Ann	110	Furry, Frank P.	65
John H.	127		
John Henry	181	Gadsby, Fred L.	89
William W.	31	Gaffney, Benjamin	144
Fox, C.M.	54	James	144
Joseph	130	Joseph	144
Sarah Angeline	54	Gaines, T.J.	98
France, Margaret	207	Gale, Cordelia	208
Francoeur, N.	73	D.R.	5
Frank, Elizabeth	61	"	35
Franklin, James	91	"	41
Fraser, Catherine Jane	203	"	63
Frasier, Fred	172	"	69
Frates, Antoine	159	"	164
Joseph	159	"	210
Rosa	159	Eliza	208
Frazier, J.A.	39	L.D.	62
Fred	39	Lorenzo	164
N.H.	116	Mary	214
Wiley	183	Gallagher, Bridget	142

Name	Page	Name	Page
Gallagher, J.R.	183	Gilbert, Mrs. Platt	4
Galusha, N.H.	96	Platt B.	27
Gamble, Abram	168	Thomas A.	32
Charles E.	178	William	190
Dora Virginia	168	Gilbride, Rodger	194
John	75	Gile, Daniel	38
"	81	Giles, Lewis R.	53
Mary F.	168	Gill, Ann	213
Gammon, George P.	205	F.W.	77
Gannon, J.P.	77	Harriet	29
Garber, John	149	Gilman, P.E.	23
Garcelon, M.	124	Gilmore, Zachariah	50
Garcia, Facendo	154	Gimbel, Mrs. George	105
Gardner, Clement	87	Greta	105
Jerome T.	105	Girardin, Manuel H.	43
L.B.	207	Gird, H.S.	181
Garrett, Lizzie Mary	211	"	214
Gascard, Rosanna	155	Henry S.	130
"	207	Glenn, G.R.	189
Gason, Mary	153	Laura	189
Gass, George	77	Goatley, A.	197
Minnie	77	Godfrey, Addie	170
Willie	77	Godman, James M.	59
Gatteker, John	161	Goethe, Barbara Emma	139
Gauldin, Benjamin F.	61	Goldeggar, Caroline	215
John V.	61	Goldner, Alfred C.	23
Willis W.	61	Goller, Christine	69
Gay, Hile	144	Henry M.	69
Jane	144	John	69
Gayle, D.R.	151	Good, John	64
Geary, Thos. J.	195	Goodfellow, Thomas C.	76
Geiger, Jane	96	Goodman, David	183
Geiman, Wm. F.	58	L.G.	27
Geiser, John	74	L.S.	187
Gendelg, Emma	114	Leopold Solomon	183
George, Julius	140	S.J.	183
Katie	188	W.C.	71
Mary Jane	158	Goodsell, Eliz.	212
Gerckous, J.L.	215	Goodspeed, Georgie	65
Gerichter, Della D.	134	Goodwin, Benjamin	59
Gericke, Julia	137	James Livingston	59
Getchell, Francis A.	1	Mary Jane	59
Giacomini, A.	173	Mary Lizzie	135
Gianello, Mary D.	75	Wilhelmina	59
Vicenzo	75	Goodyear, Louis P.	147
Gianola Maria Stetler	72	Gordon, A.J.	13
Gibbs, Amanda	18	Daisy M.	69
Henry	37	Elizabeth	89
Joseph	18	Frank W.	69
Gibson, C.S.	25	Marie	69
Emma	106	Robert	89
Silas	106	Gore, Geo.	213
Gilam (Gilliam) W. Wash.	133	Gorum, James	10

Name	Page	Name	Page
Gorum, Lena	10	Grise, Peter	92
Goshen, M.D.	69	Grissom, Eliz. F.	22
Goss, John	75	Groschong, Uriah	133
"	155	Groshong, Celia	214
"	177	Gross, Hattie	215
Gowell, Edith Lucy	7	L.L.	215
Frank Baker	7	Grosse, Guy E.	64
Kate	7	"	103
Gracier, J.E.	112	Grothaus, F.	52
Graff, Alma B.	107	"	149
Milton	107	Grove, Edward	81
Graham, Simon	48	Grover, Aner(?)	79
"	176	Venia	12
Thomas Jefferson	156	Groves, Julia A.	135
Grainger, W.C.	155	Guaca, Juan	154
Grater, John	189	Guernsey. A.A.	90
John F.	111	Guidotti, Florindo	44
Gray, Annie	116	Francisco	44
Ibby	61	Guilfoyle, Bridget	153
James W.	61	Johannah	153
Nancy	129	Michael	153
Thomas	3	Patrick	13
Green, Fred	171	Guinassa, Lucy	44
Jennie	116	Guinn, Ellen	95
John L.	116	Geo. W.	95
L.B.	15	John E.	44
Louis H.	24	Mary A.	192
Lyman	13	Gum, Isaac	12
Mamie	171	"	214
Mary P.	171	Gundlach, Jacob	47
Morgan	15	"	155
Nancy Eliza	116	Gunn, Adam F.	60
P.H.	70	Beatrice J.	105
Greene, James C.(?)	39	Eliza P.	48
Greening, Lucinda	186	Louise	105
William M.	186	Ray	105
Greenleaf, E. Price	3	Guple, Nettie	210
Richard C.	3		
Greenwood, Henry	139	Hacke, Adele	131
Gregoire, Louis	90	Christopher	131
Gregory, Geo. W.	188	Haehl, Amy	102
Thomas J.	188	Conrad	35
Grey, Cyril V.	28	Harry	102
"	123	Hagaman, C.S.	211
Griess, Geo.	52	Lydia	211
"	161	Hahman, F.G.	99
Griffin, Joseph	20	"	105
Lola	20	"	121
Maggie	20	"	149
Margaret	20	H.G.	37
Sarah	55	Paul T.	86
Griffith, A.C.	55	Haigh, Eliz.	166
Griggs, William B.	17	Halbert, Rosa H.	90
Grimes, Christina	95	Haldane, Wm. H.	154

Name	Page	Name	Page
Haley, Patrick	32	Hardin, Nancy	131
Hall, Augusta	36	William	131
Mrs. G.P.	165	William J.	
Hattie	36	Hardy, William J.	168
Henry	32	Harlow, Caroline Ann	31
J.E.	212	Harmen, Henry H.	1
L.T.	114	Harmon, Jno. B.	16
Laura	61	Harper, Mollie E.	198
Lena	36	Theodore	62
Lester	36	Harrington, Mrs. B.	151
Lowry B.	122	J.F.	9
M.G.	23	John F.	9
Mahala Olive	212	Harris, Arthur L.	96
Prudence J.	122	Catherine Amelia	192
Rebecca H.	136	E.A.	186
William	36	E.D.	78
"	61	Ephram	193
William P.	36	G.S.	30
Willie	36	George	135
Hallinan, Catherine	55	Jacob	61
Thomas	55	James McKee	135
Ham, Jennie	29	Jennie	114
Hamilton, James E.	140	John	152
Lottie L.	70	Mary	186
Hammer, Cordelia	91	Mary Ellen	152
Hammill, Grace	69	Phoebe F.	61
Hammond, Evalena V.	172	Sarah Ann	78
Sarah	44	T.M.	61
Hamond, S.L.	62	William H.	18
Hampson, Henry A.	207	"	114
Hand, Birdenia A.	178	Harrison, Lavina T.	177
Milton	178	R.	127
Handley, J.F.	174	Hartford, Mary Helen	181
Hanekamp, George	211	Harting, George	97
Hanger, W.H.	83	Harvey, C.M.	49
Hannah, August	72	Charles M.	115
Hannan, Ellen	191	J.C.	117
Hansen, Emma C.M.	151	Julia	117
Hermann C.	151	Permelia	94
L.V.	5	Harwood, James	93
Thrina	102	John	93
Hanson, Gorge	102	Philip	93
Josie	102	Hasbrouck, H.B.	91
Harazthy, A.F.	197	Haskell, Mrs. B.	15
Natalia	197	Emma A.	127
"	198	William B.	3
Hardegen, August	57	"	4
Hardin, Bridget F.		"	8
Lawler	109	"	26
George W.	131	"	30
H.A.	10	"	50
J.T.	1	"	51
James A.	25	"	52
James T.	99	"	60
Martha	199	"	64

Name	Page	Name	Page
Haskell, William B.	65	Haywood, Albert	115
"	70	Robert	115
"	74	Heald, J.G.	97
"	80	Julia	72
"	86	Robertson	130
"	90	Thomas T.	72
"	95	"	132
"	97	Healey, Agnes O.	139
"	103	D.J.	101
"	105	"	184
"	107	Heath, Emily	60
"	109	Mary J.	187
"	114	Heaton, S.O.	153
"	117	Hebbard, Nannie A.	168
"	119	Hebe(?), John R.	153
"	121	Heberle, C.	146
"	124	Hedges, Nathan M.	59
"	127	Nellie L.	60
"	146	William H.	131
"	154	Hedrick, D.M.	199
"	160	Heflin, Claramon	129
"	162	"	189
"	165	Frank	189
"	166	Hefty, Fred Jr.	94
"	168	Lydia	94
"	173	Heidonn, Hermann	78
"	174	Held, Georgina	122
"	184	Helm, S.W.	185
"	188	Helmke, F.	104
"	211	Hembree, A.T.	206
Hassett, Aaron	172	Hemenway, D.D.	85
J.D.	71	Hemmenway, Belle	201
"	174	Hemphill, Lizzie	89
"	195	Willie	89
Sarah E.	200	Henderson, Mary	61
Hatch, C.T.	31	Hendley, Barclay	96
Hulda Jane	22	Gionette	96
Lucretia A.A.	49	John	14
"	116	"	21
Walter T.	126	Hendricks, Caroline	45
Hawkins, C.W.	82	Elizabeth M.	3
Elizabeth	115	James M.	3
L.J.	8	Hendrickson, A.	119
Mamie	8	Hendry, Amy Fay	53
"	61	Henley, Barclay	24
Mark	8	"	133
"	61	Sanford B.	112
Mariah	8	Henricksen, Louise Marie	
Maud	8	Josephine	5
"	61	Henry, A.	85
Hay, James	200	"	91
Hayden, John Selden	95	James	155
Samuel Richmond	95	Joseph W.	14
Hayes, Ellen	114	Julia	177

Name	Page	Name	Page
Henry, Walter	94	Hoag, Charlie	36
Henshaw, Edw.	188	Cushing E.	168
Hensinger, J.W.	73	Eddie	36
Herbert, Alexander	133	Eldie	36
John	133	Elizabeth	31
Thomas	180	J.C.	36
Hereford, William A.	210	Linda	36
Herman, G.G.	132	Minerva	36
Hershberger, Rebecca		O.H.	26
Jane	214	"	61
Hess, Louisa	133	"	95
Hettie(?), R.	190	"	110
Hewgitt, Janney	98	Hoary, Ann	153
John	98	Hocker, Geo. Alexander	189
Hewitt, Anna R.	165	Hoeffer, Geo. F.	107
Mary E.	165	Hoen, Berthold	34
"	188	Mary	34
Samuel	165	Hoffer, C.A.	110
Hewlett, Cleora M.	206	"	114
Frederick	206	Hoffnagle, Maria L.	84
Heynes, James	28	Hoffstetter, Bernard	100
Hibler, Euphemia L.	135	Jeanne	43
Hickey, J.M.	111	Jeanne Elonore	43
Hickok, J.C.	7	Marie Therese	199
Higbee, H.B.	44	Hogg, Fred.	51
Higgins, Edward	55	Holden, Sarah C.	141
James	55	Holl, S. Solon	82
Patrick	55	Hollengren, ---	210
Thomas	55	Holleran, Catherine	37
Hill, A.B.	11	Holliday, Mamie Montana	119
"	40	Sarah	40
"	171	Hollingshead, Ed	15
"	211	Holloway, Lewis	4
Alexander B.	14	Holmes, Albert	24
Allie	30	Mary Josephine	24
Humphry	91	Sally T.	76
Louise	40	Stephan A.	94
William	18	"	193
"	30	Hood, Caroline E.	178
"	211	"	179
William C.	13	Carrie C.	194
William McPherson	91	Eliza	126
"	166	Thomas B.	178
"	188	"	194
"	189	William	126
Hines, Julia A.	98	Hooper, Catherine	138
Hinkle, J.B.	102	O.C.	107
Hinman, Miles	88	Hooten, M.V.	184
Hinreichsen, R.H.	72	Hopke, A.F.	208
Hittel, Theodore	112	Horne, Eliz. Hayden	203
Hoadley, James F.	62	Horrell, John B.	84
"	78	Johnson	84

Name	Page	Name	Page
Horwege, Henry J.	4	Hussey, U.J.	86
Lilian	4	Hutchins, Clara Annie	174
Hoskins, A.D.	37	Hyde, Patrick	167
Houseworth, Thos.	68		
Howard, Caroline	104	Ingram, Mary	166
D.M.	205	Maud	113
H.A.	155	Irving, Mary D.	16
Horace H.	155	Irwin, Polly	130
Howe, Andrus B.	69	Ivancovich, George	27
Howell, Anna J.	22	Ivins, C.H.	102
Thos. W.	22		
W.M.	97	Jackson, Elizabeth	4
Howes, Edward	75	Jacob A.	124
Jabez	75	Zadock	4
Howland, Jennie L.		"	20
(Poole)	205	Jacobsen, C.F.	5
Hoyle, G.W.	29	James, Ellen	45
"	55	John Paul	45
Hogt, Bertie	17	Jamison, Dora	174
H.P.	181	John C.	16
Hettie	17	Janssen Frederick A.	59
Jessie	17	Jarvis, John F.	102
Hubbard, Henry	29	Morgan	13
"	56	Jeffers, Geo.	163
"	70	O.O.	148
Hubert, Emma	161	Jenke, Emily M.	174
Hudson, Henry W.	30	Jenkins, Chas. M.	165
"	105	Harry G.	205
Mamie	166	Henry	205
S.N.	186	John A.	49
T.W.	132	Mary	126
Hueffner, Wm.	88	Jennent, Archibald	14
Huff, Johannah	129	Jenner, Chas. K.	33
Huffman, Jane	61	"	120
Hughes, Arthur	8	Cornelia E.	33
John	6	E.K.	204
"	214	Jenny, Laura K.	103
Mary Jane	78	Jesse, J.W.	67
Roland	78	"	94
T.M.	192	"	197
Hulme, Annie	201	Jewell, Abram S.	154
Annie Claire	201	J.R.	64
Fred. Wm. W.	201	Jewett, D.G.	174
Gerald C.J.	201	Daniel G.	65
James	201	Donald	53
Jonathan	201	Mary	53
Humbert, Chas. E.	86	Johannsen, Ludwig M.	143
Ida L.	86	Johnson, A.	186
Humphries, Chas.	141	A.T.	15
Hunt, W.J.	159	Alfred	76
Hunter, Jonathon	73	"	197
Huntley, Lucilia	50	Alice	62
Hunziker, Gaspar	74	Amanda Jane	164

Name	Page	Name	Page
Johnson, Arch M.	125	Justice, A.L.	163
Augusta Nathalia	24	Justin, Frank	150
Benj. F.	76	Gertie	150
Bernard H.	13		
Charles	52	Kamp, Harold L.	20
G.A.	125	"	130
George A.	125	Karev, Julia	215
Henry A.	3	Keegan, John W.	93
J.E.	179	T.C.	172
J.G.	132	Keen, R.A.	144
J.K.	144	Keenan, Mary	46
James	207	Keene, Geo. B.	12
Levi	127	Kellenberger, Susana	91
M.	1	Keller, Fred	32
Maggie F.	76	Mary	32
Mary	67	Kelley, J.H.	182
Richard Stephenson	61	Kellogg, Anna N.	19
W.K.	24	Clara	19
William	153	E.N.	86
Johnston, William R.	144	Ella F.	19
Jones, Catherine E.	137	Emma B.	19
Clarissa J.	25	Kelly, Alfred	79
Cornelia	116	Effie	15
Daniel H.	148	Margaret J.	152
George C.	11	Mary E.	15
Hannah Merlin	99	Kelso, Joseph	71
Henry Spencer	54	Kennedy, Ann E.	141
Hobarta Merlin	99	Charles A.	6
Hu	122	James	54
Jeremiah	204	Kenney, John	29
John Joseph	7	Mary Ann	7
John Whitfield	54	Michael	55
Lovinah B.	11	Winnifred	55
Lucinda	46	Kenny, Geo. L.	187
Martha	42	Kent, Maria	25
Mary Rebecca	54	Kernan, George	83
Thomas	124	Kerr, Catherine	17
Thomas J.	25	Kester, Mary J.	211
William	78	Kidd, Alice Almina	30
"	116	Edward Geo.	30
"	188	Frances Agnes	70
Jonzon, Johan	25	Kier, H.	41
Jordan, Eliz. Ann	149	Henry	16
Leila	211	"	97
Jorgensen, Mrs. C.	112	Kilcorse, Aggie M.	118
Carrie	102	Kiles, Abbie E.	119
Christina	102	Kimmerling, Eliz.	12
Joy, Edwin	69	King, A.T.	142
Wm. H.	144	Clark	196
Juilliard, D.W.	185	E.W.	175
Louis W.	67	Fred	138
"	82	John	39
Jungclaus, Diedrich	184	"	53

Name	Page	Name	Page
King, John cont.	120	Laird, Ann	145
"	167	Charles	95
"	169	Lucinda	95
"	186	Lake, Helen	31
Mary E.	111	Prudence	76
N.	4	Lambert, Julia	166
Nathaniel	192	Lamberton, L.	128
Robert A.	140	Lewis	20
Saurin W.	78	Lamereaux, George W.	17
Kirsch, Willhelm	192	"	85
Kise, Angeline	208	"	156
Mary Jane	208	Lamond, John Maria	62
Kitchen, John	175	LaMotte, Alfred V.	64
Wm.	175	"	189
Klein, Minnie	100	Lampson, Mary L.	202
Kline, Minie (Minnie)	100	Lance, J.A.	22
Klinge, Hannah	171	Lizzie	22
Klingel, Caroline	34	Lane, A.W.	63
Kate	34	G.W.	98
Klintworth, Anna M.	132	L.C.	86
Salome Auguste	132	Mary	15
Knecht, Francis	87	Lang, Alice	158
Knight, Emma	45	Langdon, C.W.	122
Joseph	45	"	130
Lucy	45	"	143
Knowles, J.H.	7	Charles W.	107
Joseph	193	Lanham, Patsy	150
S.W.	35	Lanison, James W.	137
Knowlton, Harriet	84	Larsen, Emil	192
Kohler, Geo. F.	117	Magnus	192
Mary E.	69	Olef	192
Kolliker, Minnie	214	Latimer, L.D.	35
Kruse, August	179	Laton, Milas	164
Chas. G.	179	Latture, J.	106
F.A.	179	Laughlin, A.D.	6
Henry A.	179	"	24
James	179	"	42
Jas. H.	179	"	74
John Anton	139	"	115
Kryer, Clara	27	"	157
Kubeck, C.	29	Ada	18
Kugle, Geo. Y.	190	Frances E.	18
Kuhn, Herman	192	James H.	38
Kummer, Edward	105	Laveren, S.S.	171
"	132	Laurence, A.	3
Kyle, Thos.	167	Lauxer, Richard (?)	144
"	209	Lavalley (Lovalla),	
		Daniel T.	45
Lacque, Aaron	214	Henery	45
LaFranchi, Eliza	154	Laveel, Jane	106
Maurizio	154	Lawlor, James	95

Name	Page	Name	Page
Lawlor, P.H.	95	Lippitt, E.L.	29
Peter	95	"	103
Lawrence, Belle	153	"	114
H.E.	146	"	160
Henry E.	86	"	171
James H.	78	"	172
L.B.	32	"	206
"	79	E.S.	32
Lawson, Elizabeth A.	136	"	46
Lawton, Israel	109	"	64
William D.	109	"	94
Leach, Harold	43	"	135
Leaft, Rachel J.	131	"	184
William	131	"	207
Leal, F.A.	150	Frank E.	
Learz, James	68	Frank K.	19
Leavenworth, T.W.	108	"	135
LaBaron, A.J.	63	"	172
H.M.	86	"	207
Lechon, Mary	10	Littlefield, Eddie	36
Lee, David J.	20	Emma	36
William F.	139	Sarah	36
Leemoine, Edward	45	Warren	36
LeFebier, O.M.	14	Litton, Hamilton B.	84
LeFeburg, Eugene Oliver	16	Litzius, L.	132
Leggett, Joseph	187	Livernash, Edw. J.	177
Leichau, Mary	10	Jessie	145
Leiding, C.F.	184	Living(?), C.F.	198
Leithrop, Harry	17	Llonso, Mr.	154
Lemay, Lewis	205	Locke, Lavinia B.	65
Leslie, Jonathan	133	True	65
LeValley, Louisa K.	107	Locknane, Henry	94
Lewes, Geo. Henry	142	Loftus, William	211
Lewis, Barbara A.	196	Loomis, F.C.	67
I.S.	94	Lopez, A.B.	39
Joshua H.	1	Loranger, John	169
Levisa	24	Lovel, Betsy Ann	15
Lewis C.	200	Lavelady, J.A.	59
Loreta	42	Lovett, O.H.	18
Mary E.	196	Low, Mary Jane	113
Lifner(?), Ane	5	Lowery, G.W.	34
Light, Lizzie	171	Lowrey, Mary J.	37
Lightner, Sadie J.	169	Rose	128
Likens, Dovey	184	Loyd, Kate	22
Lind, Gus	213	Lunden, Otto T.	72
Lindhard, N.C.	5	Ludolph, H.	112
Lindsay, Eleanor L.	28	Ludwig, Bergitha	102
Jasper J.	101	Peter H.	102
Linn, Mary Ann	178	T.J.	31
"	179	Luedke, Joseph	189
William S.	178	Luke, Jennie	185

Name	Page	Name	Page
Lumsden, William H.	44	Martin, Angeline	188
Lund, Carrie	71	Elizabeth	158
Marie	5	F. McG.	71
Luth, Fred H.	102	"	92
Luther, W.L.	43	James	45
Luttenger, Joseph	193	Joshua	129
Lyman, Ann	192	J. West	63
Lymones, J.M.	148	Mary	176
Lynch, Charles	143	Milton	12
William	24	Samuel	160
Lynde, John H.	126	William	120
Lyons, R.B.	182	Martinelli, E.B.	106
Lyppo, J.T.	24	Martinoni, Pietro	106
		Maslin, E.W.	32
Maclay, Thomas	105	"	121
MacWhinnie, J. Wallace	145	"	163
Macy, Elizabeth	58	Mason, M.	34
Harry	58	Mary Alice	148
Lizzie R.	58	R.A.	195
Madeira, Geo.	58	Serena H.	195
"	63	Masotti, Ceserina	173
Madler, Anna Clara	134	Massey, Florence	33
Frances	134	H.W.	33
Lizzie Maria	134	Mathers, Martha	95
Margueretta	134	Wm. Francis	95
Stephen	134	Mathews, Frank W.	143
Magrath, John	139	Mary A.	194
Mahl, Emmie	75	Mary Ann	128
Mahler, J---	91	"	129
Main, Wm. W.	38	Morgan	12
Malech, Gustave H.	140	Oscar	149
Maleuvre, Aline Berthe	89	Mathisen, C.T.	108
Fanny	89	Maury, John M.	13
Francoise Aimee	89	Maxwell, Mrs.	17
Maloon, Mary E.	202	May, Amelia H.	2
Manahan, Albertina	61	Mayer, I.G.	47
Mary	61	Jacob F.	181
Mangan, P.J.	120	Jacob G.	181
Manly, Mary	64	Mayfield, Lucy A.	62
Mann, E.E.	52	Maynard, F.F.	10
Manning, N.E.	186	Mazzi, Frank	123
Mannon, Jas. M.	28	McAfee, Wm.	98
Martha Ann	28	McAlister, John A.	78
Mansfield, Walter D.	109	McBain, Nancy (Nina)	11
Mapes, Sarah	76	McCain, Frank	141
Marble, T.	97	McCall, James	46
March, Andrew H.	5	McCann, Ann Eliza	128
James T.	5	McCarthy, E.R.	139
Lilburn W.	5	Eugenia Frances	171
William J.	5	Julia	3
Markell, R.S.	74	McCaughey, Jas. Walter	74
Marks, F.F.	169	McChristian, Jas.	77
Marshall, Isaac M.	1	McCleave, H.P.	80

Name	Page	Name	Page
McCleave, Mary	80	McDaniel, Mary Arabella	108
McClellan, Ella Isabella	38	Oliver	130
Mary Jane	38	McDaniels, Olivia	130
Mary M.	149	McDermott, Wm.	38
Mary Margaret	149	McDill, Allie James	125
Ruth	149	McDonald, Alice	81
McClintock, Margaret	193	Emma	79
McClish, Florence	12	Frank	63
James	12	J.R.	79
John N.	12	McDonnoll, Oliver	1
Nellie	12	McElhany, S.	15
Thomas	104	McElhinney, John W.	57
McConnell, Francis	193	McElroy, Eliza M.	42
W.E.	31	William	42
William	8	McGarvey, Henry	41
"	17	James	41
"	23	John	41
"	42	McGaughey, James Brown	189
"	44	John Alexander	189
"	50	McGaughy, James	187
"	54	McGee, Jas. H.	8
"	61	"	23
"	64	"	29
"	67	"	35
"	88	"	36
"	89	"	76
"	98	"	118
"	116	"	161
"	129	"	164
"	139	"	182
"	141	"	193
"	157	"	198
"	159	McGinley, R.H.	23
"	161	McGlynn, Catherine	117
"	163	Hugh	117
"	182	Wm. John	117
McCornack, W.A.	124	McGrew, Sophia	62
McCracken, A.	199	McGuire, Altemus	51
Jasper	106	C.	143
Sarah Ann	214	McKinney, Eliza Mary	207
McCray, Carrie	35	McKoon, H.H.	74
McCullough, John	83	McLean, Minnie	120
Michael	20	McLeod, J.H.	112
S.M.	32	McMahon, Michael	71
McCune, Alex	112	McMahon, S. Green	45
"	191	McManus, J.G.	114
McCutchan, David Mc.	82	John G.	96
T.B.	82	"	196
McCutchen, E.J.	110	McMenamin, James	125
McDaniel, Hattie C.	71	McMinn, Ada Belle	50
Ida Spencer	182	John	12
L.J.	71	Joseph	12

Name	Page	Name	Page
McNair, John E.	20	Meyer, F.A. cont.	64
McNear, Geo. P.	14	"	70
"	44	"	80
"	86	"	86
"	165	"	101
"	208	"	105
Ida B.	44	"	109
McPeak, Mary Jane	141	"	119
McPear, M.A.	122	"	120
McPherson, Annie	1	"	146
Buell	1	"	148
Erly	1	"	150
French	1	"	159
Joseph Atkinson	73	"	161
Mary E.	1	"	162
Sarah	73	"	165
Stonewall	1	"	171
McReynolds, James	115	"	176
Lizzie	188	"	184
McTerney, H.C.	105	"	187
McWillimas, Sarah	168	"	188
McWright, W.S.	178	"	211
Meacham, P.	139		
Mead, W.H.	15	Michelsen, Mrs.	112
W.R.	17	Edward	112
Mrs. W.R.	69	Middleton, A.W.	41
Meadows, Mrs. W.P.	170	Emilie	72
Meanor, John	125	Z.	46
Mecham, Harrison	186	"	148
Jane	186	Miller, Caroline P.	148
Medan, John P.	72	Daniel E.	214
E.A.	72	Fred H.	31
Medley, Andervil G.	191	G.L.	169
Meeham, Maggie	53	George	53
Meigh, Geo.	49	"	92
Meiler, John	142	"	190
Meldrum, James	165	George E.	31
Margaret G.	165	Greenberry	148
Melton, William	196	James J.	88
Mendez, Salvador	154	Josephine Alice	152
Menefee, H.G.(?)	34	Martin	82
Menihan, Michael	177	Mrs. T. Marshall	39
Merchant, Joel	135	Thomas B.	116
Merriman, Peter	124	"	209
Merritt, John	38	Millet, A.R.	168
M.D.	86	Nettie	168
Samuel	181	Mills, A.J.	44
Sarah	208	Andrew	92
Metzgar, Geo. V.	190	Eva Jane	50
Meyer, Anton	118	Paulina	95
F.A.	3	Milnes, Chas. G.	36
"	30	M.F.	36
"	33	Mims, O.(?)R.	25
"	52	Miner, A.F.	77
		Mary A.	103

Name	Page	Name	Page
Miser, Henry S.	53	Morget, Francis	193
Mitchell, Robert T.	206	Morison, Ellen	181
Sarah Ellen	160	Thomas	192
W.J.	112	Morrow, Geo. P.	206
Mittner(?), J.N.	112	John	165
Mize, Albert	8	"	166
Julia	61	Nancy J.	206
Thompson	8	Virginia	166
Mock, Edward	118	Morrill, Sadie R.	168
Theodore	118	Morris, Abraham	111
Wesley	118	J.H.P.	2
William	118	J.J.	96
Modini, Lorenzo	7	Joseph H.P.	57
"	195	Morrisey, William	76
Moffet, John	79	"	94
Mogan, M.F.	153	Morrison, Ellen	181
Mogensen, Mrs.	112	Oscar	167
Moiles, Nancy Caldwell	164	Morshead, Philip	159
Mollison, H.P.	104	Morstadt, A.	47
Molt, John	133	"	132
Matilda	133	"	165
Molte, Mrs. Louis H.	168	Mortensen, Carl	5
Moltzen, D.F.	104	Morton, A. Jackson	136
Monday, Permelia H.	113	George W.	136
Montague, Hugh	199	Joseph	136
Montgomery, Caroline W.	98	Richard	136
George	167	Wm. G.	136
Moody, R.C.	67	Zachariah T.	136
Moone, Harriet	180	Moss, W.H.	163
Harry	180	Mossman, W.F.	208
Moor, Talitha Jane	5	Mothorn, Wm.	111
Moore, A.P.	139	Mould, C.H.	110
Amanda	8	Moyer, Ida May	209
"	61	Martha	193
George W.	134	Muir, Andrew J.	131
H.	34	Mulgrew, J.F.	5
"	134	"	26
Pauline	173	Muller, Carl	189
T.B.	43	Martin	37
Moral, S.	157	Mulligan, Geo.	100
Moran, Delia A.	137	John	194
Harriet A.	156	Margaret	2
Moreland, W.W.	66	William	2
"	111	"	135
"	112	Munday, Beverly	196
"	158	Fanny	22
"	186	M.E.C.	196
Morely, Jennie G.	115	Thomas	196
Morey, Mary Ann	68	Munro, James L.	134
Morgan, D.B.	22	Murdock, L.A.	8
"	48	Mary	8
"	62	"	61
"	137	Murphey, John	148
John J.	48	Murphy, C.G.	77

Name	Page	Name	Page
Murphy, Ella	182	Norton, E.M.	45
H.C.	58	"	63
John	148	"	152
S.G.	77	"	179
Murray, John	26	L.A.	2
John O.	58	"	45
Mary	9	"	92
Musselman, A.J.	103	Mrs. L.A.	2
Myerling, Sophie	184	Louisa	45
Myers, J.W.	186	Nelson R.	163
Myrick, Kate R.	115	William	81
		Nowlin, Thos. W.	195
Nagasawa, K.	147	Nye, B.M.	125
Nagle, F.G.	9	Emma M.	205
"	23	Stephen G.	205
"	30		
"	41	Oates, G.W.	67
"	56	"	119
"	101	James W.	8
"	125	"	13
Nalley, A.B.	96	"	82
George	96	"	94
Nash, Philana	105	"	98
Nason, Helen C.	212	"	134
Naughton, Hubert	99	"	149
"	117	"	168
"	187	"	212
Nay, Lewis G.	39	O'Brien, Richard	32
Neblett, Edward	131	Thomas M.	168
Neil, Wash.	134	Odell, Cynthia Anne	14
Neller, Leopold	6	David	14
Nelson, Mary	102	Lafayette	14
Nesbit, Maggie	157	Minerva	14
Newcomb, Mildred A.	160	Simpson	14
Newhall, Mrs.	15	O'Donnell, Jos. E.	199
Neyce, J.H.	74	Oette, F.	140
Niblock, James	22	Ogden, Mary	103
Nicholas, Eusardia	147	William M.	3
Nichols, Elizabeth N.	66	Ogive, Mary Redmond	167
John	91	Ogle, J. Oliver	38
Margaret	91	O'Grady, Annie	9
Nicholson, Mary E.	184	"	139
T.M.	190	Bridgett	139
Nicklas, Crist	69	George	23
Nielson, John	129	Honoria	139
Kate	129	Margaret	139
Nins, C.H.	102	Marria	139
Nohl, A.V.	47	Mary	173
Noonan, Geo. P.	105	Michael	139
"	212	Standish	9
Norris, Mary Ann	171	Olwer, Kate	22
Norstadt, A.	97	Mary	175

Name	Page	Name	Page
Orear, W.E.	31	Pattee, Eliz. Greenleaf	3
Ormsby, Glenda	27	Mary E.	3
J.S.	81	William Greenleaf	
Orner, Hannah	44	Appleton	3
Orr, Mary Ann	175	Patterson, A.S.	183
W.T.J.	77	Elisah	189
Ortega, Antonio	155	John A.	40
Osemal, William	208	Josephus L.	93
O'Shea, P.J.	101	Lieu Hattie	66
Ostrom, Matilda A.	177	Martha J.	93
O'Sullivan, Daniel	23	Medora	189
Otis, Chas. W.	179	Millard F.	2
Ovendale, Jas. H.	54	"	16
Overholser, Wm. R.	103	Pattison, Mary Jane	49
Overland, W.P.	110	Wm.	49
Overton, John P.	102	Patton, Charles	113
"	105	Samuel	150
"	114	Sarah Amanda	150
"	203	Patty, L.H.	147
Mary	202	Pauli, Mr.	154
Sarah	10	F.A.	132
William F.	202	F. Albert	123
Overturf, Jane	94	"	140
Owen, Isabella	213	G.T.	108
William D.	45	"	131
Owens, Henry	187	R.J.	123
		Payne, Kate G.	131
		Frank	131
Packer, Mary	31	Payran, S.	113
Page, Henry	178	"	141
Palache, Mrs. ---	15	Pearce, Geo.	45
Palmer, B.H.	29	"	113
Clara	197	"	122
Delia G.	70	"	204
George H.	59	Pease, Edward R.	93
J.M.	85	Peatross, Hester Ann	160
Lucy Ann	85	W.W.	160
Wales L.	133	Peck, C.G.	119
Parena, Rebecca Jane	66	S.S.	114
Parish, Harry	213	Susan	114
Sarah Elizabeth	113	T.A.	76
Parker, Isaac	43	Pedrini, Pietro	73
J.F.	42	Peerman, Miles H.	183
Lucretia	128	Peery, Alonso T.	178
Parkerson, Henry	148	Charles S.	178
Parks, Lavina	95	Sarah A.	178
Veronica	176	W.M.	205
Parr, W.W.	147	Pellascio, M.J.	173
Parrott, C.A.	162	Peter	173
Parsons, George C.	204	Steve	173
Isaac	161	Penington, Caroline	53
"	163	Penwell, J.C.	107
Mary F.	67	Pera, Angelo	122

Name	Page	Name	Page
Perkins, R.E.	115	Poff, Anthony	95
Perrman, M.H.	63	Poggi, Nancy Jane	92
Perry, Henry	48	Sorophina	92
James	146	Pole, Agnes	101
Jeannette B.	146	Thomas Aloysius	101
John	170	Polk, James K.	137
Kate A.	60	Polsk, Andras Erick	210
William H.	188	Pond, C.H.	69
Peter, H.	32	"	152
Martin	139	Elvira	181
Peters, David	46	Pool, Harry	20
David P.	155	Theophilus	38
Peterson, Anna Core	171	Poole, Chester	61
Chas. A.	171	Jennie L.	205
E.	199	Poppe, J.A.	210
Martha	185	Joseph B.	24
Palina	185	Robert A.	2
Petray, H.C.	104	"	7
Pettit, M.L.	94	"	22
Pfister, Millie Lucenda	70	"	27
Phelan, Bridget	21	"	71
Phillips, D.D.	17	"	72
"	183	"	73
Jacob	9	"	99
Martha E.	172	"	103
Mary A.	4	"	115
Polly Ann	4	"	122
T.	111	"	171
Philpott, J.F.	112	"	195
Sarah Ann	17	"	199
Phinny, J.W.	104	"	209
Pickett, Mary Ellen	189	R.A.	158
Pierpont, John	107	Porta, G.E.	154
Robert R.	107	Porter, D.	174
Pierce, A.J.	186	Elizabeth D.	174
J.G.	156	Hon. Judge W.W.	174
Maria	58	Mrs. W.W.	39
Sarah C.	145	William W.	189
Piezzi, Victor	116	Potter, Samuel	57
"	197	"	121
Pimm, Minnie	120	"	164
Pinchower, Simon	86	Powell, Louisa L.	24
"	93	R.	170
Pine, J.B.	73	Power, John	26
Pinelli, Agostino	7	Powers, Mrs. C.	139
Pitkin, Ralph	79	David	81
Sarah	23	Mary	81
"	79	Pratt, Othelo C.	199
Plunkett, Eleanor	209	R. Augusta	136
J.C.	157	Prescott, Hattie	16
Poe, Mary E.	111	Presko, Mathew	89
Poehlmann, Conrad	122	Presho, Mathew	89
H.J.	171	Pressley, J.B.	110

Name	Page	Name	Page
Pressley, John G.	42	Ranard, J.H.	37
"	131	Raney, Henry	98
"	205	Rankin, L.E.	19
L.A.	38	"	33
Preston, Emily	29	"	172
"	93	Rase, J.W.	57
Price, Andrew	138	Rawlins, C.M.M.	178
E.W.	14	Raymond, Helen A.	33
John	17	Rea, Olive	27
John D.	14	Thomas L.	205
Mary Meade	193	Redm, Patrick	129
Prince, Morris	114	Read, Carrie S.	86
Tillie A.	114	Harriet Cordelia	147
Prindle, Wm.	105	Mary Fidelia	147
"	147	Williams Parsons	147
Prowse, Chas.	158	Reed, Eliza	200
Pullee, F.J.	163	Henrietta	22
Purcell, John	177	J.Q.	168
Richard	127	Regand, L.	89
Purrine, A.L.	164	Reichert, John A.	47
A.S.	81	Reid, Louisa J.W.	160
"	175	R.	158
Artilla	164	Reigle, George J.	132
Purvine, Frank C.	121	Rendall, S.A.	87
Orcella	64	Rendenpaker, L.F.	99
Putnam, Harriet	67	Renfrow, Louisa	42
Pyle, Adeline	207	Reniff, Eddie	28
		Mary	28
Quant, Minnie M.	13	Respini, Jeremiah	123
W.E.	13	Reyerson, Addie Ann P.	156
Quartaroli, L.	44	Ann	156
Quinlan, Dan'l	74	James	156
"	97	Rexford, E.H.	202
Lizzie	87	Reyburn, L.C.	192
William H.	104	Reynolds, Bennie	36
		Bertha	36
Raabe, M.	66	Charlie	36
Rafael, A.E.	120	E.E.	53
Rafferty, J. Mary	67	Edwin	110
Michael	67	Melinda	36
Owen	67	P.J.	34
Patrick	67	W.B.	79
Ragsdale, J.W.	17	"	84
"	96	"	105
"	198	"	147
		"	173
Railsback, Caleb	37	W.D.	177
"	160	"	198
Caroline	160	William D.	103
Ralston, Henry C.	128	Riby, Chas. V.	34
Rambo, Jacob	89	Emilie Torgine	34
Katy Ella	30	Ricci, Mary	195
Sarah	89	Rice, Jacob	89
Ramey, Albert Newton	152	John	114
J.	107	Mary	114
Martillus	151		

Name	Page
Rice, Nancy Maria	89
Rich, G.D.	30
"	201
Mary E.	39
Richards, Margaret	138
Richardson, Eveline	172
Julia R.	35
"	36
William A.	36
"	181
Richie, Elizabeth	129
M.G.	128
Rickert, T.M.	2
Ridenhour, Mary Eliz.	81
Riensch, Adelheid	30
Riewerts, John	115
Rigdon, R.L.	144
Riley, T.J.	170
Thomas	150
"	214
Thomas T.	135
Ringstrom, Sigurd	98
Riva, Norman G. Silva	84
Roach, Bridet	137
Thomas	117
"	171
Roberts, Emma	65
Emma Irene	46
James B.	164
Kitty	20
Mary	62
Stephen	79
William R.	60
Robertson, JOhn	36
Robeson, S.B.	107
Robin, Eugene	184
V.G.	106
Robinson, Janey	212
Jessie	212
Julia A.	151
Sarah A.	45
Walter T.	199
William	212
Robuson, Geo. R.	66
Rockwell, Adele	200
Rodda, Annie	149
Rodehaver, J.P.	9
"	18
Rodgers, Irene	78
J.P.	9
"	27
"	56
"	62

Name	Page
Rodgers, J.P. cont.	68
"	196
"	213
John P.	56
"	145
Lucinda	129
William H.	78
Rodoni, Chas.	5
Roe, Wm. S.	74
Rogers, Daniel	136
E.	100
Emma Grace	18
J.P.	27
James	25
Mrs. L.M.	67
Lucy M. Lawler	109
William	62
"	104
Rohrer, Charles F.	129
Romer, Chas.	81
Roney, J.M.	1
"	157
Alice Mary	1
Mary A.	1
Roque, Peter	167
Rosaline	167
Rosa, Dela Jose	154
Rose, Amelia George	36
Emma	72
Florence A.	180
J.W.	11
"	12
"	57
"	58
"	69
"	151
"	152
"	172
"	180
"	184
"	214
John	35
Rosenbaum, F.H.	153
Ross, Allan C.	124
Judge	210
Luann	76
Margaret	183
William	21
"	57
Rourke, Catherine O.	163
Roux, Emily Hannah	95
Mary Lucinda	95

Name	Page	Name	Page
Roveda, Pietro	122	Sargetn, A.A.	141
Rowe, N.	185	Ethel	12
Rowlson, E.E.	168	J.S.	193
Eliza A.	168	Lizzie	12
"	182	Lottie	187
Rowse, Edward S.	34	Satterfield, James	46
Rudolph, Nevada	114	Nancy Ann	47
"	115	Sauders, W.M.	21
Rued, J.C.	91	Saul, George M.	56
Ruffin, Nathaniel	13	Saunders, John S.	57
Rufus, E.	184	"	59
Rundelman, Rachael	185	"	102
Runyon, Chas. E.	26	"	147
Ruoff, John	155	"	152
Rupe, Sam H.	42	Savage, G.W.	207
"	67	Sarah E.	207
"	194	Scarborough, James	125
Russ, Sarah C.	42	Schaefer, Adam	75
Russell, Elizabeth	185	Schaffer, Ellen Virginia	68
H.A.	170	Schardin, Jos. B.	107
Isaac	142	Scheibel, Marie Therese	199
J.C.	185	Theobald	199
McHugh	170	Schellhous, E.J.	133
W.F.	198	"	182
William F.	84	Schenck, Jno. S.	174
"	151	Schenk, Hugo	75
Rutledge, Thomas	8	Schieffer, Annie	
"	38	Elizabeth	102
"	50	William	102
"	53	Schirmer, Emile	87
"	89	Henriette Antoinette	87
"	124	Schloper, T.C.	77
"	145	Schlusser, Thomas	1
Rutlidge, M.	196	Schmidt, Emma	105
Ryan, Edw. P.	48	George	105
Joseph	47	John Kron	105
Michael	184	Lizzie	105
Ryder, Linnie	196	Mary	105
		Mary Delphine Blanche	73
Sacray, Wm.	177	Millie	105
Saere, Maryetta	144	Schocken, Solomon	7
St.Clair, F.C.	1	Schroder, John	56
Frank C.	130	Schroyer, Aaron	124
Sales, Wm. L.	150	Schudy(?), Mrs.	112
Samuels, James	135	Nora	112
Sanborn, Charles	124	Schuler, C.O.	187
G.N.	25	Schuster, Caspe	132
Sanchez, Don Ramon	154	Schute, Anthony	185
Sanders, W.M.	21	Schwab, F.J.	172
Santa Ana, Mr.	154	Schwartz, Jane E.	113
Santellan, Jose	155	John	113
Santos, Gussie	150	Schweitzer, A.R.	193
Mary	150	Barbara	74

Name	Page	Name	Page
Schweitzer, Elizabeth	74	Shattuck, Frank cont.	167
Lizzie	74	"	170
Schwenk, Ida	161	"	172
Scott, J.C.	16	Frank W.	9
"	26	"	10
John C.	16	"	12
John Thomas	85	"	13
Louisa C.	16	"	15
Sarah Ann	95	"	17
William L.	95	"	27
Scully, Mary	170	"	28
Scudder, N.W.	156	"	34
W.W.	39	"	39
Searby, Fred. W.	170	"	42
Searles, Wm. T.	58	"	45
"	102	"	55
Sears, G.C.	7	"	59
Seaton, D.M.W.	68	"	83
"	85	"	85
Dill W.	15	"	91
Seavy, Albert Porter	201	"	92
Annie	201	"	99
Laura V.	201	"	111
Robt. T.	201	"	113
Seawell, Emmett	177	"	126
George	75	"	135
J.B.	42	"	147
Mary Alice	75	"	148
Seegelken, E.	93	"	150
E.A.	131	"	153
Seehuber, Charles	203	"	166
Seipp, John C.	184	"	187
Seites, Calvin	112	"	192
Seitz, Geo. J.	21	"	209
Seller, Lewis	194	Lee	15
Sessions, George W.	189	Mattie	15
Ida	189	Rena	15
Sevensaler, J.G.	28	"	192
Sexton, William	78	Mrs. S.O.	15
Shafer, Mary S.	26	William F.	126
Shamp, H.S.	29	"	153
Shane, Amos M.	138	Willie	15
Sarah	157	Shaver, Mary	119
Shannon, Joseph W.G.	131	Shaw, C.B.	90
Mary E.	131	"	93
Meldrum D.	131	I.E.	64
Sharkey, Mary	142	James A.	64
Shato, Virginia	193	"	140
Shattuck, Arthur E.	150	John George	126
D.O.	42	Mary L.	109
Frank	15	Nelson R.	175
"	39	O.B.	109
"	41	Sarah	81
"	63	Shearer, Helen	63

Name	Page	Name	Page
Shearer, John	41	Skinner, Ada	169
M.M.	169	George R.	65
Shelford, Levi L.	2	"	213
Shelton, Annat.	41	Jane C.	65
Shepherd, J.S.	126	"	213
Sheridan, Jane	77	Martha Washington	169
John S.	77	Slater, Mary E.	67
Thos. J.	77	Slatterns, Wm. J.	10
Shetter, Eliz. J.	24	Slogett, Bathsheba	181
Shields, E.E.	183	Small, Annie	46
Shinn, S.M.	20	Joseph B.	24
Shipman, Sarah	77	"	27
Shipp, Mary	189	Smell, Manurva Ann	190
Wm.	189	Smidt, Wm.	188
Shireman, Mariah	44	Smith, A.H.	13
Shivo, Clara	172	"	31
Shlarn, Oscar A.	183	Alexander	119
Shoemaker, Emeline	47	Ann	127
John W.	137	Annie	127
Shone, Thomas	141	B.F.	102
Shore, Robt. E.	36	Catharine Augusta	127
Royle	213	Charles	21
Short, Annie Salina	181	Frank	211
Shoultz, Martha	196	Frank William	127
Shrimplin, Damras	42	George W.	210
Shriver, Andrew	75	H.J.	24
Shumaker, Emeline	46	"	81
Shuster, John	34	Hannah	39
Sibbold, John	170	Hannah M.	187
Luella A. (Myers)	170	Hannah Mary	201
Silsby, Harriet	54	Henry	127
Irma Winfred	54	Holland	109
William H.	202	Hugh	21
Silva, Mary	14	India	145
Silvas, Juan	154	Isaac B.	210
Silvia, J.D. Jr.	158	J.B.	141
Joseph D.	119	J.M.	127
Simmons, Laura	70	James Francis	127
Sylvester	130	James Irwin	210
Simmour, Eliza Lettitia	114	James M.	127
Simon, Mr. A.	5	Jennie	127
Mrs. A.	5	John B.	83
Sims, J.C.	113	John Lewis	210
"	180	Lois W.	116
Singley, James	141	M.B.	190
Sink, Mariette F.	35	Margaret	13
Sippitt, E.S.	136	Mary	21
Skaggs, C.W.	139	"	127
E. Jr.	80	Mary Ann	58
Skelly, Bernard J.	14	Mary Jane	210
Skelton, Nelly D.	100	Nepolion Bonapart	210
Skiffington, John	9	Norman	81
Skillman, Theodore	10	Oliver	21

Name	Page	Name	Page
Smith, Owen	127	Spoon(?), Josaphine	2
Patrick	21	Sprague, Elija	38
"	127	Spurr, D.F.	22
Perry C.	78	"	142
Richard John	126	"	174
Richard Joseph	126	Stacey, Henry	92
Sophia Louisa	126	Staedler(?), Elizabeth	78
Susan M.	184	Stafford, Amanda Jane H.	78
Thomas	127	Stahl, Wm. G.	65
W. Meath	21	Staley, Jennie	51
W.R.	29	Stanger, A.H.	111
William	3	Elizabeth A.	111
"	127	Stanley, Addie E.	207
Smyth, C.S.	54	Stapp, I.N.	88
J.G.	101	Starkweather, Sarah	165
Smythe, Charlotte Sumner	33	Starvolt, Alice	49
Charles S.	179	Charles	49
S. Katherine	119	Mary Amanda	49
Snider, John D.	72	Statler, Mary	72
Snow, J.	126	Stayroom, Emily	189
"	185	Stebbins, Alfred	117
Joshua	116	Steel, Isabella P.	149
"	211	Steele, Frank	40
Soden, Henriette P.	76	Stefi, Anna Mary Matli	123
James Hailman	76	John	123
Laura Hailman	76	Steggmonn, Frank	51
Pennoek	76	Steiger, Edw.	52
William	76	Stelter, John H.	148
Soggan, John M.	207	Stengel, Barbara	
Soldate, Alice	109	Christian	12
John	109	Stephenson, John Edward	51
Solomon, Chas.	147	Sterling, Belle	41
Somes, Geo. R.	153	Eliza	41
Sonders, Amanda C.	114	Stetler, Mary	72
Soper, C.B.	58	Stevens, John Buchanan	20
Southard, J.B.	32	Louisa Jane	20
"	108	Sarah	166
Sparks, G.W.	149	Stevenson, Annie H.	167
Spaulding Calista	212	John Edward	51
J.G.	212	Stewart, Eliz.	55
Speckter, Hannah King	151	Stice, Laura	27
John	151	Stine, Sarah Jane	89
Speers, D.F.	128	Stirling, J.F.	137
Spencer, Caroline G.	70	Stocking, Anna	36
Dora	167	Charlie	36
Frank	78	Cynthia	36
"	177	Ernest	36
"	188	Flora	36
R.M.	212	Frank	36
William	167	George	36
Spergen, Theressa	45	Minnie	36
Sponogle, Libbie	43	Stockton, Emma G.	50

Name	Page	Name	Page
Stockton, Rachel B.	50	Swain, R.M. cont.	145
Stoddart, Eliza	16	Mrs. Robert	192
Stone, Caroline	115	Swan, W.G.	189
Ida May	10	Sweeney, Jeremiah	192
J.G.	183	Mary	192
Louis S.	5	Patrick	9
Storey, George A.	116	Swett, Emma R.	187
"	202	Swift, Granville, P.	111
Tunis W.	202	Swisher, Dr. J.R.	5
Stovall, Mary J.	181	James R.	186
Stowell, C.A.	36	Sydnor, Addie	195
Strider, Jas. A.	156	Eva	195
Striening, M.J.	6	Roberta	195
"	28	Sylvester, Dulancy	1
"	42	Harry	144
"	44	James	1
"	181	Minnie	144
Strong, Willaim	93	Symmonds, Eva	62
Stroud, Mary A.	94	William	62
Strout, George A.	8		
Jacob	30		
Sophromia	30	Taber, Catherine	177
Struck, Elizabeth	114	James P.	70
Stuart, Anabel McCaughey	33	John S.	177
Stubblefield, Marth---	98	Tabor, Abbie Ellen	119
Nancy	98	Talbot, Courtney	144
Stubbs, Wm.	178	Tallant, Thos. B.	77
Studdert, Mary E. Lawler	109	Tarwater, M.W.	124
Stump, Geo. W.	97	Taylor, Alfred	69
James	187	Charles	114
Lottie E.W.	74	Chester P.	65
S.W.	26	Despard	43
Samuel W.	27	Ernest M.	65
"	74	Frances E.	65
Susan C.	26	Jane	114
"	74	John Francis	65
Walter G.	74	John S.	28
Sturgis, Guy Vans	63	"	37
Walter Harry	63	"	40
Suders, Otto	72	L.S.	82
Sullivan, Delia	62	Margaret Jane	193
George	62	Mary B.	65
Jabez B.	152	Medora A.	65
James	62	Nancy Armida	28
"	138	Nellie	69
Mary	66	Thomas	193
Mattie	21	W.M.	69
Sutton, Aaron	177	William	52
Cornelia	177	Teaby, W.H.	65
Suttrell, Hattie M.	204	Teague, Sarah Ann	169
Swain, R.M.	29	Teixeira, J.C.	3
"	37	Temple, C.	75

Name	Page	Name	Page
Temple C. cont.	165	Tighe, Kelly	83
Jackson	60	"	99
R.G.	180	"	143
Templeman, Linda	23	Mary	129
Tennent, Archibald	14	Tilton, Amanda	22
Terrell, Earla	29	Timm, Walter C.	200
Edna	29	Tirrell, Anna M.	191
Tevlin, James F.	127	Tivnen, John	182
Therkelsen, C.	161	Todd, Bemjamin F.	148
Thomas, A.	61	Mrs. Cal	4
"	163	George W.	148
"	178	James M.	148
"	194	John W.	150
Alonzo	212	Judith A.	163
Helen	134	Minerva	150
Isiah	89	Nancy Carolina	148
J.R.	205	Rodney A.	148
Luch H.	131	Violella L.	148
Mary Ann	127	Tomasini, Julieta	43
W.P.	21	Lila	43
Thompkins, Emilie	173	Valdo	43
Thompson, A.W.	186	Tounsend, Gen.	148
"	208	Tower, Richard	61
Amelia	11	Towey, Peter	93
Arthur L.	34	Towne, Lester	15
C.H.	114	Tracy, Ezra B.	210
George M.	11	Martin	192
H.C.	54	Trefrin, J.L.	92
Jane	45	Tremblay, Rosin	63
John	187	"	66
Nettie	67	Trimble, Patrick	109
R.A.	163	Susan	109
Robert	160	William H.	99
Thomas L.	161	Tripp, H.L.	139
W.P.	22	"	204
"	159	Trivnen, John	210
W.R.	25	True, C.N.	163
Thomson, A.M.	27	Thomas Jenness	163
Addie	200	Truitt, R.K.	172
Sarah Addie	108	Tucker, William	10
Thoroughgood, Lizzie	9	Tufts, Evaine N.	24
Minnie	9	Tull, Kate	207
Willie	9	Tupper, G.A.	40
Thourigood, Lissie	139	"	84
Minnie	139	"	147
Willy	139	George A.	35
Thurman, Matilda Ann	119	"	36
Richard	119	"	40
Thurston, M.	20	Harriet	35
Tibbitts, A.L.	52	Harriet R.	36
"	165	"	118
Gilman B.	74	Turner, Mary Ellen	158

Name	Page	Name	Page
Turner, Mary Emma	165	Vernon, Mary Ann	205
Tustin, Columbus	30	Ruth	205
"	32	William	205
May	30	Vesser, Leymiza	166
Tutt, Thos. R.	11	Vestal, Emily	37
Tuttle, B.F.	174	Lewis	37
Benjamin F.	34	Thomas	37
Twombly, Mary M.	21	Viets, J.M.	91
Tyler, Eliz.	58	Villain, Fanny	89
Ida	36	Jean Baptiste	89
Joseph Leander	58	Voss, August	76
Josephine	58	"	94
Serena	58	Mrs. C.	179
Viola	58		
		Wade, Henry P.	72
Underhill. W.H.	119	Wainwright, Hellen M.	203
Ungewitte, H.W.	175	Walden, Catherine	148
Upham, Anna Mary	51	Waldo, Wm.	14
Annie	51	Walk, Katarina	69
F.F.	51	Walker, Alexander L.	209
Upman, Lizzie	144	Elenor	132
Urbais, Eliz.	190	Elizabeth	150
		"	209
Vallejo, Mariano		Francis Whitmore	193
Guadalupe	39	J.M.	118
"	154	John	35
"	173	"	45
VanAlen, Egbert	165	"	46
Harriet	165	"	98
John	165	"	132
John J.	165	Lizzie	35
Sarah	165	Mary Ann	205
William	165	Mary Josaphene	132
Vance, E.H.	57	Maud	35
Vanderleith, John	81	O.V.	15
Vandernooth(?), Joseph	110	Wallace, Alzira	128
Vandervort, J.	173	William W.	38
VanEvery, A.J.	182	Walliser, Carl	203
VanGeldern, Charles	131	Walls, Arthur C.	95
"	184	David	126
"	210	Walsh, M.	146
VanHensen, Theo. V.	165	Maud E.	70
VanValkenburg, Noah	141	Michael	96
VanWinkle, Thomas	116	Walter, Alzera	12
Vaughan, Louisa F.	45	Walters, Mrs. J.M.	184
Vaughn, E.K.	24	Ward, Abram	186
"	57	Albert T.	114
Marvin T.	24	Charles D.	37
Veale, Emma Harriet	12	Ellen F.	37
W.R.	41	Estilla M.	37
"	160	F.B.	34
Vernon, Ira	205	John	194
Isabel	205	Martha K.	37

Name	Page	Name	Page
Ward, Rachel	114	Wertz, G.W.	65
Robert	154	Wescoatt, Alice	67
Robert H.	37	Effie Florilla	67
William H.	186	Nelson Glenn	67
Wardell, Nina Plaskett	94	Wescott, Jonas	202
Ware, A.B.	37	Wessenberg, D.W.	192
"	42	Daniel W.	192
"	64	Mervin	192
"	75	West, Alice	158
"	92	Guadelupe	154
"	145	Mary	18
"	169	Westbay, J.C.	37
"	188	Weston, Carie	126
Martha Ann	98	Mrs. H.L.	174
Warfield, Mrs. K.F.	48	Westover, Chas. H.	35
Warham, Easley	193	Weyle, Henry	146
Warn, A.B.	96	Whallon, Adelia A.	80
"	131	Murray	26
Warner, G.	39	"	41
Philamon	38	"	80
Warren, Emma	1	"	123
Watson, G.	128	"	131
George	80	"	149
"	178	Wheaton, John	100
Margaret	32	John Thomas	100
Maria	173	Wheeler, Mrs. E.A.	19
Wattles, S.L.	152	Ira A.	15
Weaver, C.W.	47	"	19
"	106	Wheelock, A.G.	188
"	152	Whitcomb, Annie C.	29
"	166	White, Ann Eliza	164
"	179	H.G.	98
Mary E.	95	Harrisin	193
Webb, Mary Otis	101	Henry	179
Sidney	93	J.L.	21
Weber, O.O.	197	J.M.	189
Webley, Frederick D.	147	James A.	27
Weeks, Parker E.	6	John	193
"	38	Lora	15
Rosetta L.	208	Margi	150
Weidersheim, H.	53	Martha Ann	148
Weightma, Elizabeth	77	Mary Alice	42
Weir, Robert	96	Mary Motherwell	164
Welch, Mrs.	167	T.A.	164
Weller, Silas	130	W.A.	15
"	180	Whitney, A.P.	9
Wells, Abigail J.	69	Harriet M.	86
Clark	141	Mary A.	148
James L.	196	William B.	73
William G.	3	Whiting, S.P.	66
Welshald, Theodor	131	Whitney, A.P.	191
Welton, Byron D.	17	Whitson, Margaret	50
Werneke, W.A.	73	Whittaker, Jas.	167

Name	Page	Name	Page
Wick, L.A.	51	Willson, H.M.	19
"	171	"	67
Wickersham, F.P.	153	"	114
Fred A.	179	Rebecca E.	152
I.G.	20	William	23
"	29	Wilson, Benjamin	127
"	31	Emma C.	134
"	39	James	181
"	79	John R.	139
"	112	John W.	98
"	128	John Wallace	47
"	137	Lovina	159
"	144	Maria L.	48
"	146	Rebecca	127
"	150	Thomas B.	35
"	153	W.W.	57
"	173	William	159
"	191	William Y.	161
Jesse C.	29	Wilton, Thos. G.	147
"	143	Winans, Lewis	95
Wieberts, Katie	144	Windsor, Uretta J.	28
Wiedersheim, H.	53	Winkler, Henry Jr.	52
Wiers, Margaret	119	Winter, Mrs.	17
Wiggin, Marcus P.	3	Winters, Maggie	129
Wightman, C.	43	Thomas	129
Wigmann, Martin	140	Wisdom, Annabel	18
Wilcox, M.C.	90	John	18
Wiley, Alexander	43	Sam'l B.	18
"	46	Sarah	18
"	100	Wise, Henry	93
Dean	92	Katie	71
Mary	92	Wisecarver, Elizabeth	65
Wilhite, T.C.	211	"	113
Wilkie, Henry C.	48	Mary Ada	113
Wilkins, Chas. P.	161	Wiseman, Maude	182
Hepburn	129	Wiswell, J.A.	207
James H.	129	Wissell, Albert	88
Wilkinson, Mattie V.	8	Withington, Hannah B.	150
Thomas	8	James	150
Williams, Abbie	144	Withrow, Wm.	58
F.R.	41	Witt, Charlot	210
George B.	134	Wilhelm	210
George R.	79	Wohlers, Otto	204
"	86	Wolcott, Frank	10
"	122	Guy W.	10
John	144	Horace	10
Joseph A.	52	Luella	10
Lucinda	152	Wood, Ben S.	54
W. Maurice	46	"	84
Williamson, Mary L.	41	"	86
Sarah E.	76	Ben S. Jr.	177
Sarah Ellen	131	Caroline	77
Willis, Henry M.	20	Frances Isabella	68
Wills, R.P.	205	J.J.	162

Name	Page	Name	Page
Wood, Mary	155	Zartman, W.H.	74
Z.Z.	53	William	60
Wooden, Ann Amelia	64	Zelhart, Martha A.	115
Woods, Leah I.	136	William	115
Zarilda	199	Zeller, John	106
Woodworth, J.P.	26	Zilhart, W.W.	142
Jenette E.	79	Zimmerman, F.	121
R.L.	89	Zophy, Fred	18
Woolridge, John H.	31	Zumpel, Margareth	74
Louisa Francis	31		
Wooly, Sarah Frances	118		
Worth, Mrs. C.	188		
Clarborne	142		
Louisianna	142		
Worthington, Ellen J.	33		
Wratten, G.L.	80		
"	123		
G.S.	198		
George L.	111		
Wreden, Claus	78		
Wright, A.	150		
Albert	109		
Chester F.	114		
Elizabeth Ann	149		
Lutitia J.	121		
Paxton	149		
S.B.	8		
Sheldon S.	149		
Sophie	83		
Winfield S.M.	131		
Wynant, Bettie	67		
Yale, Frank W.	160		
Yarbrough, Jemima A.	84		
R. Lee	84		
Yarkam, Henry	197		
Yates, Rhonda E.	134		
Yeagley, Mrs. Sidney	155		
Yercie, Frances	90		
Yerger, Theodore O.	188		
Yoho, S.R.	210		
York, Mark	78		
Walda M.	164		
Young, Geo. C.	16		
J.S.	142		
John	71		
Laura Ella	29		
Rebecca S.	71		
Sarah B.	70		
Younglove, Kate E.	7